A Diagram for Fire

THE ANTHROPOLOGY OF CHRISTIANITY

Joel Robbins, Series Editor

A Diagram for Fire

*Miracles and Variation in an
American Charismatic Movement*

JON BIALECKI

University of California Press

University of California Press, one of the most distinguished university presses in the United States, enriches lives around the world by advancing scholarship in the humanities, social sciences, and natural sciences. Its activities are supported by the UC Press Foundation and by philanthropic contributions from individuals and institutions. For more information, visit www.ucpress.edu.

University of California Press
Oakland, California

© 2017 by Jon Bialecki

Library of Congress Cataloging-in-Publication Data

Names: Bialecki, Jon, 1969– author.
Title: A diagram for fire : miracles and variation in an American charismatic movement / Jon Bialecki.
Description: Oakland : University of California Press, California [2017] | Includes bibliographical references and index.
Identifiers: LCCN 2016040710 (print) | LCCN 2016042081 (ebook) | ISBN 9780520294202 (cloth : alk. paper) | ISBN 9780520294219 (pbk. : alk. paper) | ISBN 9780520967410 (ePub)
Subjects: LCSH: Pentecostalism—United States. | Spirituality—Pentecostalism.
Classification: LCC BR1644.5.U6 B53 2017 (print) | LCC BR1644.5.U6 (ebook) | DDC 270.8/20973—dc23
LC record available at https://lccn.loc.gov/2016040710

Manufactured in the United States of America

25 24 23 22 21 20 19 18 17
10 9 8 7 6 5 4 3 2 1

For Clio, my muse

How monotonously alike all the great tyrants and conquerors have been; how gloriously different are the saints.

C.S. LEWIS, *Mere Christianity*

Contents

Acknowledgments	ix
Prologue	xiii
INTRODUCTION: CLEARLY WRITTEN ON HIS FACE	1
1. VINEYARD TIME	22
2. INSTITUTIONS AND GOD'S AGENTS	48
3. A DIAGRAM FOR FIRE	60
4. *TOLLE, LEGE:* TALKING, READING, AND HEARING	83
5. THE LIVING ROOM SEMINARS: PEDAGOGIES OF THE SPIRIT, TYPIFICATION, AND ELABORATION	102
6. THE BODY, TONGUES, HEALING, AND DELIVERANCE	135
7. COLLAPSES, TRAVERSALS, AND INTENSIFICATIONS OF THE PART-CULTURE	166
CONCLUSION: ON THE PROBLEM OF RELIGION AND ON RELIGION AS A PROBLEM	198
Notes	219
Works Cited	237
Index	257
Complete Series List	264

Acknowledgments

First, acknowledgments must go to the Vineyard Christians who shared with me, as well as with the numerous Christians from outside the Vineyard, who were equally generous with their thoughts, energy, and time. This includes the members of the Society of Vineyard Scholars; there can be no better gift for an ethnographer than a group of sharp-minded (and sharp-eyed) intellectuals who belong to the movement being studied!

Professor Roy Brooks at the USD School of Law was the first to suggest to me that I might have a career in academics—though I suspect he thought it would be in a different discipline.

During my protracted association with it, the University of California, San Diego, anthropology department has provided numerous mentors and colleagues. As for mentors, I am in debt to Suzanne Brenner, Tom Csordas, Jonathan Freedman, Michael Meeker, Steve Parish, David Pedersen, Melford Spiro, and Kathryn Woolard. Colleagues to whom I am indebted include Yoav Arbel, Chris Augsbuger, Sowparnika Balaswaminathan, Waqas Butts, Andrew Cased, Julia Cassaniti, Julien Clement, Jason Danely, William Dawley, John Dulin, Eli Elinoff, Ted Gideonse, Timothy McCajor Hall, Candler Hallman, Jordan Haug, Eric Hoenes del Pineal, Nofit Itzhak, Julia Klimova, Leslie Lewis, Katherine Miller, Marc Moskowitz, Joshua Nordic, Marisa Petersen, Ryan Schram, Greg Simon, Heather Spector Hillman, Allen Tran, Brendon Thornton, Deana Weibel-Swanson, and Leanne Williams. There are others I have shamefully overlooked; forgive me.

I finished my dissertation while serving as a wide-eyed, inexperienced visiting assistant professor at Reed College. I don't want to contribute to the legend of "Olde Reed," but it was certainly an interesting experience trying to think through the anthropology of Christianity at a school whose unofficial motto is "Atheism, Communism, and Free Love." I'd like to thank

Doctor Robert Brightman, Rebecca Gordon, Jiang Jing, Anne Lorimer, Tahir Naqvi, Sonia Sabnis, Paul Silverstein, Nina Sylvanus, and Emma Wasserman. Reed was also where I became acquainted with Rupert Stash, who was also with me when I returned to teach at UCSD for four years.

My time at the University of Edinburgh's Department of Social Anthropology was one of the intellectually happiest, and most productive, times of my life; almost the entirety of this book was written while I was there. I regret, daily, that family circumstances have kept me from staying there in my capacity as lecturer. Some of the colleagues and students at Edinburgh were old friends and some were new, but they all did their share in making that atmosphere, and hence this book, possible. I'd like to thank Richard Baxstrom, Francesca Bay, Tom Boylston, Janet Carsten, Jacob Copeman, Jamie Cross, Magnus Course, Alexander Edmonds, Stephan Ecks, Jamie Furniss, Ian Harper, John Harries, Naomi Haynes, Luke Heslop, Casey Hines, Lotte Hoek, Laura Jeffrey, Tobias Kelly, Lucy Lowe, Siobhan Magee, Diego Malara, Rebecca Marsland, Adam Marshall, Maya Mayblin, Alex Nading, Alice Nagel, Yi Qiao, Jeevan Sharma, Jonathan Spencer, Alice Street, Dimitri Tsintjilonis. While he was not at the University of Edinburgh, Adam Reed was a frequent and fascinating interlocutor while I was at Auld Reekie. Of those at University of Edinburgh, Tom Boylston, Magnus Course, Naomi Haynes, and Maya Mayblin bore a particularly heavy burden of conversation and hospitality. Additionally, Tom Boylston and Naomi Haynes also read substantial sections of a much more raw iteration of this manuscript, something that was even further beyond the call of duty.

Numerous others have contributed to this book. Some I have known for significant periods of time. Some have been kind enough to invite me to work out in public some of the initial thoughts that became this book. Some were kind enough to accept my invitations! Some made small gestures but with the right spirit and at the right times. Finally, some I have never met in person but have still been kind enough to help me. I imagine many of the people listed may not be aware of their labors, and certainly none of them should be blamed for any imperfections in this project's fruition. With that in mind, I would like to thank Razvan Amironesei, Andreas Bandak, Daniel Barber, James Bielo, Joshua Brahinksy, Fenella Cannell, Liana Chua, Simon Coleman, Vincent Crapanzano, Kathy Creely, Girish Daswani, Omri Elisha, Matthew Engelke, Annelin Eriksen, Doug Erickson, John Evans, James Faubion, Brian Goldston, Courtney Handman, Elisa Heinämaki, Jacob Hickman, Martin Holbraad, Jessica Johnson, Angie Heo, Marcel Henaff, Rebekka King, Brian Howell, Derrick Lemons, Ian Lowrey, Ruth Marshall, Caleb Maskell, Charles Matthews, Megan McCready, Keith McNeal, Mark Mosco, Minna Opus,

Gretchen Pfeil, John Rasmussen, Bruno Reinhardt, Bambi B. Schieffelin, Michael Scott, Rupert Stash, Michael Stevenson, Anna Strhan, Matthew Tomlinson, Todne Thomas, and Joseph Webster. Near the very last days of this manuscript's preparation, I was fortunate enough to attend the "Problems in the Study of Religion" 2016 National Endowment for the Humanities Summer Institute, which had Charles Matthews and Kurtis Schaeffer as directors. The *vigorous* interdisciplinary discussions there helped me develop a better sense for what I was trying to say in my conclusion, so I would like to thank Charles and Kurtis, as well as the other participants (David Anderson, Torang Asadi, Lilian Calles Barger, Neilesh Bose, Candi K. Cann, Natalie Carnes, Andrew Crislip, Rebecca Draughon, Diana Galaretta, Gregory Price Grieve, Ravi Gupta, Jean Heroit, Benjamin Hertzberg, Samuel Kessler, Sean Larsen, Catherine Osborne, Jeffrey Perry, Bharat Ranganathan, Sarah Rollens, Mary Ruth Sanders, Peter Schadler, Ben Schewel, Randall Stephens, Ashley Tate, Victor Thasiah, and Matthew Whelan). I also wish to acknowledge my debt to the editorial team at the University of California Press (especially Reed Malcolm and Kate Hoffman). From submission to publication they saw this book through with an exquisite degree of professionalism.

With the exception of a few snippets, this book is made up almost entirely of new material, though ethnographic depictions herein are also part of my "Disjuncture, Continental Philosophy's New 'Political Paul,' and the Question of Progressive Christianity in a Southern Californian Third Wave Church," *American Ethnologist* 36, no. 1 (2009): 110–23; "The Bones Restored to Life: Dialogue and Dissemination in the Vineyard's Dialectic of Text and Presence," in *The Social Life of Scriptures: Cross-Cultural Perspectives on Biblicism*, edited by James Bielo, 136–56 (New Brunswick: Rutgers University Press, 2009); and "No Caller I.D. for the Soul—Demonization, Charisms, and the Unstable Subject of Protestant Language Ideology," *Anthropological Quarterly* 84, no. 3 (2011): 679–703. I would like to thank these journals and presses for their generosity. Although the theoretical language used has changed considerably in an effort to create a series of relays between the other arguments in this book, the sections that use these ethnographic sketches are in essence making the same claims as those found in the original articles and book chapter. The same goes for spoken presentations. Elements of this book (often in larval or mutated form) have been presented in talks and at events at the University of Edinburgh, the London School of Economics, Rice University, the University of Toronto, William & Mary College, University of Copenhagen Center for African Studies, Reed College, the University of California San Diego, and Midway Contemporary Art.

Tanya Luhrmann has intersected my academic life in many different ways, at many times; and yet, our almost simultaneously deciding to take up the Vineyard as an object of ethnographic interest was done with each entirely unaware of the other. Given her rightful stature and influence, she could have starved my career of oxygen, and extinguished the diagram for fire. Instead, she has been supportive without fail, which is strikingly kind considering how different our ethnographies have ended up.

If memory serves, I first met Joel Robbins when I found him in my graduate student office, perusing my bookshelf; he had wandered in from an office almost literally directly across the hall. He was a friend long before he was a mentor and editor, and I like to imagine there is a primacy to that first capacity even today. He has done so much for me, but most of all, he has given me perhaps one of the most vital of academic gifts: *problems*.

I have endless debts that go beyond the academy: friends and relatives, who I will keep anonymous primarily as a favor to them. I will acknowledge that I have parents—Herman and Dolores—and that they have been tirelessly supportive. Judy, my wife, also has sacrificed and supported me in ways impossible to fully rehearse. She of course has parents, and they have also been indefatigable with their time and enthusiasm, and so thanks go Jim and Masako's way, too. But beyond anything and anyone else, there is my daughter, Clio. She was named after the muse of history (for some odd reason, the then nonexisting field of social science was not awarded a distinct muse by Hesiod). She has lived up to her name. Clio, this book is for you.

Prologue

I came to this project—or rather, this project came to me—in an unexpected way. I was an anthropology graduate student in the first moments of my career. I was so early in my career, in fact, that I was still doing the prerequisite work for being released into "the field" (starting fieldwork is a rite of passage in my discipline). In my case, preparation for the field took the form of presenting to my advisors a series of papers on my intended research topic: Islam in Malaysia. This project was on the ambivalent relations between Malaysia's opposition Islamic party, the Pan-Malaysia Islamic Party, and ritual healers, known as "bomohs," who were working in a tradition with pre-Islamic roots but who still understood themselves as Islamic. This project would track this tension as it was being played out in Kelantan, a northeastern Malay province. Kelantan is a place where during the day one would have to stand in sex-segregated lines at the local supermarket, thanks to "Islamic" regulation, but at night one could truck with all sorts of wild spirits and jinn as they came into and out of people's bodies and minds. While this framing is incredibly crude, this was to be a project about the differences between, on the one hand, a vision of religiosity that was centered on texts and their strict interpretation, and, on the other, an oral, incredibly participatory mode of religiously inflected subjectivity. Law to the right, spirits to the left, and an open contestation as to which is in control.

The sorts of presentations that anthropology graduate students have to make before they are released into the field may be rites of passage, the very kind of initiation ritual that anthropology itself has made so much hay out of, but they are also serious scholastic affairs, with important stakes for one's career. And so, in early September, after coming back from an intensive summer language study program, my future wife and I decided to go camping in the central Oregon coast sand dunes, where I would write up

xiii

my proposal in longhand, when we were not hiking, spying on the Roosevelt elks, or gathering wood for our weak little fires. It was a picturesque place, where the wind would shift the terrain of the dunes overnight (I later learned that, when watching these very same dunes, Frank Herbert conceived of his most famous science fiction novel). We set up our tent, and I got to work.

Our plan was to camp for about a week, starting around September 8, 2001. September 11 passed without our even knowing it had happened.

It may be a cliché to talk about the world changing on September 11, but at the very least it was definitely on another footing. Driving back down to our home in Southern California a few days later, we decided not to take the main highway, a gash that runs straight down the middle of the agriculturally intense Central Valley, but instead go south by the small roads that thread through the coastal mountains running from Southern Oregon almost all the way down to San Francisco Bay. These mountains have been a haven for those who wished to leave behind what they felt was an ailing society; anarchists, libertarians, socialists, hippies, and fundamentalists have all settled there, hoping the mountains would insulate them from the perceived corruption of civilization. Many of these runaways have set up small-wattage radio stations (of varying degrees of legality) to broadcast their critiques, and in the immediate shadow of 9/11, they all felt that they had a great deal to share. As we wove through the mountains, our antennae wove through the radio signals, and the radio stations being played would switch all on their own; without any marked interruption, we would jump from a station operated by a people's autonomous collective to a station consecrated to announcing God's impending judgment on the world. On one turn, we would hear that what had happened was the result of American imperialism or of American capitalism or of a toxic American alienation from nature, while on another, we would hear that it was a product of American unfaithfulness to God. As the roads wavered, these various voices bled into one another until it was hard to tell which station one was on, which voice was promulgating which position.

These switchback transformations were dizzying, vertiginous; by the time my fiancé and I arrived back in Southern California, the United States had been made strange in a way that rivaled anything I had seen in Southeast Asia. Two questions simultaneously rose up, blending into one another like those mountain radio stations had blended their voices. The first was my original anthropological question, now disembedded from its Kelantan framing: What was the relationship between the seemingly fixed insistence of law and scripture and the strange experiential becomings associated with spirits? The second question arose from listening to the blurred radio transmissions on the backcountry Northern California roads: Were the progressive left and the religious right diametrically opposed or was there some point where these voices joined, pointing a way to something new? I could not answer these questions by going to Malaysia, and so my anthropological attention slowly shifted its center of gravity to Southern California, the part of the country where I was going to graduate school, the part of the nation where I had grown up. The research in this book came directly from these two questions.

But what group I would be researching, and where I should research it, was not clear. After some looking around, I decided to study an association of like-minded churches called the Vineyard.[1] The Vineyard was an interesting mix of the nationally politically powerful Evangelical movement and the demographically diverse and globally powerful Pentecostal movement. My initial goal was to find a particular Vineyard church and follow it; the idea was that this church would "represent" this form of religion as a whole. To facilitate that research, I found myself talking to Vineyard pastors and attending Vineyard churches all over the Southern California region. I eventually found a church: a mixed fellowship of middle-aged Vineyard veterans, college students, and young professionals located by the coast in one of the most well-off regions of the country. But I also found something else: While in one way this church was representative of the Vineyard, in another way there was no church that was representative of the Vineyard. Churches ranged in size, from megachurches with multiple services and choked parking lots to small, fifty-member affairs that could only rent a hall by sharing the burden and space with unlikely partners (such as, in one case, a Korean-language Methodist church!). Churches pulled from a range of populations and reflected the character of the regions that they were located in, from working-class rural churches to urban churches that catered to the so-called creative class. Churches varied in the kind of politics they espoused. One church, for instance, celebrated the second Iraq war and hailed a church member from a Chaldean Christian background who volunteered to go to Iraq as a military translator, blessing her onstage. At another Church, the response to the war was more subdued; the pastor focused his prayers on requesting that God give succor to civilians who had died or been displaced and privately worried that neither America's nor Israel's then-conservative political leaderships understood the true meaning of Matthew 26:52 ("'Put your sword back in its place,' Jesus said to him, 'for all who draw the sword will die by the sword'"). Some churches were almost (but never entirely) free of the kind of affectively intense spiritual practices associated with Pentecostalism, and other churches reveled in them.

So my fieldwork with the Vineyard had two phases. One phase was directed at the Southern California church I spent the most time with; for a period of over two years, I attended all the church's services, lectures, and retreats that I was allowed to (some functions and meetings related to training for various leadership positions were closed to me). I attended some "small groups," the name for weekly weekday evening meetings held outside the church, where people would talk, study the Bible, and pray together. I interviewed the pastor and small group leadership numerous times, both formally and informally, and likewise interviewed other church members so often that I literally lost count. And finally, I did everything they did: I listened to the same sermons and read the same books, and I studied the Bible with them. I even did something that not many other nonreligious anthropologists of religion do: I prayed as they prayed, for healing and prophecy and visions, which included praying for other people in the in-person, and literally hands-on, style that is common to the Vineyard.

But the other phase of my fieldwork involved looking out to the Vineyard at large. During the time I was in the field, and even after my fieldwork was completed and my dissertation was submitted and approved, I continued to go to other Vineyard churches, including churches in other American geographical regions (the South and the Pacific Northwest) and other countries (the United Kingdom), whenever I could. I continued to talk to other Vineyard pastors, seminary students, and seminary instructors who had an association with the Vineyard, to Vineyard students of theology and Vineyard theologians, and to Pentecostal and evangelical academics who had thoughts on the Vineyard. I attended regional and national Vineyard gatherings. I even (briefly) talked to the then national director of the Vineyard. I paged through sections of an archive of papers, letters, documents, books, and objects that belonged to John Wimber, a man who had an important role in the founding of the Vineyard. I also talked to people who were at Fuller Theological Seminary, including people who were at the Fuller School of World Missions when John Wimber was associated with that influential evangelical institution; this was the period when he was also starting his Vineyard church.

The first phase of the field project gave me the sense of the dynamics of how a particular church operates, while the other phase gave me a sense of the wide range of churches and believers who identify as Vineyard. Together these two phases showed me how all these Vineyard churches and believers differed from other churches, movements, and people associated with even more intense versions of ecstatic Pentecostal gifts, as well as how all these Vineyard churches and believers differed from some of the evangelical and fundamentalist churches that eschew Pentecostal supernaturalism.

It would be easy to see all these differences, within and without the Vineyard, simply as ways they are separate from and independent of one another. That sort of nominalist thinking, after all, is very powerful in contemporary anthropology. But recent work in the anthropology of Christianity suggests otherwise. Ethnographic depictions suggest that between discrete Christianities, and particularly between discrete Pentecostal and evangelical Christianities, there are both differences and a great number of recognizable similarities.

The anthropology of Christianity has grown too fast for me to give a through recounting of it in this book. That might itself be a book-length project. Besides, there are other sources, which while shorter have still managed to do a good job of encapsulating this field.[2] But there is one thing that we can say about this literature. While the discussions they are having are comparatively recent when set against similar conversations in the discipline, authors in the anthropology of Christianity have strongly suggested that there are recurrent patterns in exchange, semiotics and speech, temporalities, and subjectivities for Christian groups.[3] This body of literature has focused primarily, and some would say inordinately, on Protestant and post-Protestant movements, such as Pentecostalism, though Catholicism, Orthodoxy, and other forms of religion are beginning to get the attention they are due as well.[4] Even with these limitations in mind, though, this literature has still made a case for striking regularities in Christian praxis as it is found in some quite different nations, societies, and languages. But at the same time it has also done what anthropology often excels in: identifying a myriad of particularities and exceptions that question any claim to an overarching unity.

In short, I experienced with the Vineyard the same resistance anthropologists have encountered when they have attempted to sum up Christianity. In the Vineyard, I had a nagging sense of some insisting commonality, and yet there was a wealth of difference that denied any easy totalization. In the anthropology of Christianity, multiple authors have suggested that no anthropological definition of Christianity is either useful or possible; and yet we have the frequent, but not omnipresent, commonalities that give the field shape, suggesting that however much we might be dealing with forces of decohesion, there are forces of cohesion operating as well.[5] And in a way it was also the problem that I encountered in my pilot trips to Malaysia, as well as when I threaded my way through the Northern

California coastal mountains, where the voices melted together, even as they militated for seemingly irreconcilable propositions.

In this book, I argue for a kind of commonality to the Vineyard. Specifically, I put forward a type of recurrent event that constitutes a set of relations and brings subjects into being (as opposed to proposing a more agentive reading that would see subjects as the active authors of this species of event). I gesture toward a similar, larger commonality in Christianity on the basis of recurrent patterns from my ethnography and the arguments that support it.[6] In the conclusion, I even take the argument so far as to suggest, in a moment of Peircian abduction, that a speculative commonality to religion exists; this commonality presupposes rather than denies the historicist complaint that religious variation exceeds any theoretical reduction to any shared feature, such as "belief" or "practice." None of these arguments is meant to insist that different Vineyard churches, different Protestant and post-Protestant forms, or even different religiosities are either identical to one another or are not in motion. Nor is it to say that the commonalities here necessarily always point to the most salient aspects of any phenomenon, whether salience is measured by the standards of the people involved in a form of religiosity or by the standards of the academics who study them. All of this is merely to suggest that just as the shifting dunes at the Oregon coast never repeat themselves, even though they bear similar patterns arising from the conceptually simple yet complexly emergent play of wind, water, and sand, different forms of religiosity are historically particular and are the result of different causal forces. Yet they also still contain elements that express a common problem. This work can also be seen as a contribution to other recent anthropological concerns, such as affect, ontology, and ethics.[7] It can even be considered to be a part of an incipient anthropology of the will and of volition, as well as part of a much more established anthropological interest in Gilles Deleuze; both are important planks in this book's argument.[8] However, it is this play of differentiation, this problem, that is the thread that runs throughout the book,

And in the Vineyard, one name that is used for the expressions that come from that problem is "miracle."[9]

Introduction

Clearly Written on His Face

For this first story, we need to go back just a little in time and space. We are in the air, perhaps thirty-two to thirty-eight thousand feet above the ground, a relatively short-haul flight that will not leave the lower forty-eight states. Sometimes when this story is told we are given a bit more detail: we are on a flight from New York to Chicago. We can imagine that we have a view out the plane's window. It is night (most likely, though this is not always part of the narrative); we can also imagine below us dim sulfur-yellow lights arrayed in a faltering checker pattern that stretches out to the horizon. We're in the upper deck of the 747; it's a lounge/wet bar, this being the late seventies (or perhaps the early eighties), when things like this were common. Seated next to us at the bar, two men are talking. One could be any married man, but perhaps he is middle aged, a bit jaded and worldly, someone with a great number of commitments that he does not always meet. The other is a bit older with silver grey hair and a matching beard; he is heavyset but animated, and his voice is at once impulsive and laid back with a twang that suggests decades of a Southern California veneer have yet to completely cover over a Missouri undercoat. He is one of those people who seems to naturally attract attention, even though his at-ease nature suggests he is not purposefully seeking it.

The two men are talking in the in-flight lounge because, after they had first sat down in adjoining seats on boarding the airplane, the heavyset man had been staring (or as he himself described it later on "gaping") at the first man. The first man had naturally asked, "What do you want?" The heavyset man had responded by asking if a specific female name meant anything to the man. This had shaken the first man up, and after a very brief conversation they had retired to the airplane bar to talk privately. During that conversation, the heavyset man passes along a message. He says that God told him that the first man had better turn away from his adulterous affair "or I'm going to take him." It is clear from the context that the pronoun "I" was spoken on behalf of God and that "take him" means death.¹ The first man "melts" on the spot, and the heavyset man leads him through "a prayer of repentance," at the end of which the adulterous man "accepts Christ." Two other passengers and a stewardess look on while all this occurs; according to the story, those onlookers also find themselves crying as they watch. Afterward, the first man walks back to the spiral staircase leading to the main passenger section, so he can tell his wife about what just transpired. When we are told this story, we are also told that shortly after being led to Christ himself the man leads his wife to Christ. We also learn exactly what it was that had first caused the heavyset man to gape at the self-admitted and now converted philanderer. When the heavyset man first set eyes on the man, he had seen the word *adultery*, as well as the name of a women, literally written in plainly visible characters all over the man's face.²

For the second story, we are far from the first in time and place. It is almost a decade later, and instead of being in the cocktail lounge of a 747, we are in the basement of a small Evangelical Covenant Church deep in the northern Midwest. Maybe the wall is wood paneled, maybe the room is full of folding chairs. The church has been struggling for about a decade now, ever since a particularly well-liked pastor moved on. On this day the church members are trying to do something about this long-running problem; they are interviewing candidates for senior pastor. When they come to the candidate they are presently interviewing, there is one issue the committee of church members is particularly concerned with. Some references had mentioned that at his last church posting this pastor had been a polarizing figure, an angry fellow who had sowed division. Naturally, the interview committee asks the candidate about this. He acknowledges he had encountered some problems when he was in his last position; he admits with a slight chuckle that there were members who had even insisted that he had a demon.

One of the members of the interview committee is a young man; he is the nephew of the Evangelical Covenant Church's original pastor, the pastor who had moved on all that while ago. When the candidate admits to the problem, the young man is suddenly more attentive. This is perhaps natural as this is not the sort of information one would expect a candidate to volunteer in a job interview. Maybe because of the subtle cue the young man gives off, the job candidate for the pastoral position attempts what linguistic anthropologists sometimes call "a conversational repair," an attempt to undo the damage caused by breaching implicit conversational norms: He tries joking with the committee by adding, "Now, I assure you,

I'm not demonized." Almost immediately after those words are uttered, the young man quickly gathers his things and heads out the door. He looks anxious (or as he would describe it years later "freaked out"). There is a reason for his panic: When he told me the story years later, he said he had seen the word *liar* appear on the candidate's forehead at the moment when the candidate denied he had a demon.

Many years later, the young man who fled the wood-paneled church basement learned about the heavyset evangelist on the 747. The name of the heavyset man on the airplane, the one who spied the word *adultery* on his interlocutor's head, was John Wimber. He was an experienced Jazz musician and a onetime sessions player for the American blue-eyed soul duo the Righteous Brothers. He was a raconteur, someone who knew how to thread together a good story. He was also a pastor, a specialist in the technical field of "church growth," and an adjunct professor at Fuller Theological Seminary, an institution that arguably was the center of influence for American evangelicalism in the second half of the twentieth century. While at that institution, he taught what has been called the most famous seminary class of that century: a course on miracles with an emphasis on miracles as an applied practice. That class was memorable for having a lab component, in which miracles were demonstrated to and practiced by the students. He fostered a network of churches called "the Vineyard," taking over the leadership of the seven original Southern California fellowships and seeing to their growth; they would eventually become a network of more than fifteen hundred churches worldwide. He claimed to heal people, and people claimed to be healed by him. He gave prophetic messages, and he cast out demons. Some people called him a prophet and some people called him an apostle, though he refused to adopt either term. A few people called him the *antichrist*, a term he also did not accept. He referred to himself simply as "just a fat man, trying to get to heaven."

CHRISTIAN PLASTICITY

At the time the young man from the Midwest saw the word *liar* emblazoned on the face of the candidate for senior pastor, he had never heard of anyone who saw words scrawled on people's faces, of the Vineyard, or of John Wimber. It was only years later after he joined the Vineyard that he was able to make sense of what he had experienced during that interview. But we should also note the original temporality of that strange moment in the interview. Before he made sense of it, that moment was still inchoate. It had a certain slippery irresolution, a kind of openness that only stabilized after John Wimber and the Vineyard helped give that experience a shape. Beforehand, it could have been anything: a mental lapse, a physical symptom, a trick of memory, a supernatural abnormality; the man who experienced it had trouble speaking of it for years because it was so "out there." It was only later that he would see this as a sign of God acting in the world.

Giving a name to this surprising experience was not merely a closing down of a sort of indeterminate openness. It was also a retrenchment of the experience, a grounding of it that made it no less weird but easier to keep alive, both for himself and for others (at least for those who shared the same understandings of how God or the Holy Spirit might operate). There was a loss of possibility, but as those alternatives receded, there was also a gain in clarity and the seeding of a new space of potential. There was also an opening up not just of time as memory (or of the time of the actual miraculous event) but also of cosmological time; there was a new eschatological horizon that ensured not just the past but also the present moment had potentials in ways that had not existed beforehand. That moment in the church basement became at once a bit of time akin to the Gospels or the Acts of the Apostles and an intimation of a future moment, in which God would act fully and freely, openly and continually, in the world again. It was simultaneously originary and apocalyptic.

Note though that it was not just this moment that was given shape, that is, retroactively given a specific intelligibility. For this event to become intelligible to that young man as a specifically Christian experience, Christianity as he understood it had to shift. As Christian believers did in previous ages when the miraculous was a possibility, or as members of other contemporary Christian traditions that the young man was not familiar with at the time do, he had to make room for a sensible articulation of heretofore novel experiences, in which the Holy Spirit and God's prophetic message are contained not only in books or institutions but also in peak moments that occur for individuals and collectivities.

At the same time, the Christianity he practiced could not distend so much that it would allow any odd experience in and become unrecognizable *as* Christianity. If that happened, it would rapidly drift away from ever-differing instantiations of concepts understandable as Christian, and the proliferation of new concepts would cause it to mutate into something else as so many of the new religious movements that started during the 1960s, 1970s, and 1980s did. Which is to say that it would have to be immanently self-organized in such a way that rather than being something other than Christianity it would merely become a different mode of Christianity.

The term *mode* is used here because we are not talking about denominations, or large cladistic typologies, such as "Protestantism" or "Pentecostalism." Those institutions and classifications help locate and sustain modes, but modes of Christianity are not reducible to them. Rather, modes are distinct ways of organizing and expressing the same material and concerns.³ And as a mode of Christianity, the Vineyard faces a particular challenge: how to remain a form of Christianity even if being a form of religiosity organized around a miraculous *recognizable novelty* seems to teeter on the edge of being an oxymoron.

This brings us to another important point. There is in these narratives more than a recalibration of emphasis and more than a bending but not a breaking. For the narrativized moments to be pliable, and for the Vineyard's understanding of what Christianity is to also be plastic, the constituent elements that make up Christianity, the set of concepts, practices, and entities (fictive or otherwise), had to have a certain preexisting plasticity as well. This holds not just for specific elements but also for the relationship between the various elements that make up Christianity. This plasticity is made apparent not just when different realizations of Christianity are compared, but also when features *within* a particular realization of Christianity are compared. Take, for instance, how the Holy Spirit works in the mode of Christianity that John Wimber helped to midwife. As we will see, for these Christians the Holy Spirit waxes and wanes, but it is never divisible. It is everywhere, yet it moves like a fire, searing some places for a while only to burn out, while bypassing other spaces completely. It is at once an all-pervading and a vanishing presence, sometimes palpable, sometimes intangible. Even worse, it can vanish in those moments when the Holy Spirit no longer makes sense, when it is undone by doubt even for those who say they know how to intuit its presence.

The Holy Spirit is not the only unfixed element. At least in some of its modes, Christianity can be seen to be about an absent God; this is a God who is transcendent to the point of vanishing and yet is still traceable through texts. It is these texts that act as stabilizing agents giving aspirant Christians wide-ranging access to him. But these texts only work if the protocols for accessing them, the hermeneutic processes and exercises that properly open up the Bible, are themselves invariant. Alternately, rather than a universalizing message that serves as proof through decoding, there is the possibility of finding God not in texts but through the body (individual or collective). In that case, the message would take the form of a particularizing, sensory presence: a voice, a vision, a feeling, a coincidence, an event. This route involves a ratification and instantiation of divine presence through the sensorium instead of the textual. This path seems to offer a different kind of certainty than that granted by texts, giving the surety of experience rather than the faithfulness of scripture, but that is not the only work it does. By bringing the divine down to a level where it can be sensed with the flesh, the transcendent becomes laminated with the immanent. It also entangles God in place, presence, and subjectivity in a way that threatens to solipsistically constrict the divine message.

This instability, this question of whether to think of God as distant or near, of the Holy Spirit as waxing or waning, of God as something grasped through texts or intuited directly has been called the "problem of presence" in the anthropology of religion.[4] These two solutions, a God inscribed in text and a God who discloses himself through the senses, are not the only solutions, and they are not even necessarily mutually exclusive. For many of the Christians who constitute the Vineyard, texts *about* the divine and experiences *of* the divine are interwoven, sometimes by alternating between these two modes and sometimes by threading them together so tightly that they appear as one. There are degrees of play between the two, and different groups of Vineyard and Vineyard-like believers will lean toward one or the other, sometimes for moments and sometimes for years, only to reorient themselves to some other balance between the textual and experiential when circumstances change.

As we will see, this flexibility between the textual and experiential can also be found in the way that time is structured; even temporality can be stretched, folded, cut, and broken. For many anthropologists who study self-described Christian populations, Christianity is a religion of rupture, something that (at times) works through the instantiation of sharp breaks that give time a direction.[5] In the Christian temporal imagination, there is the guarantee of a culmination to history, or at least a culmination can be read into it in some Christian forms. But even being on the far side of these ruptures, even after the Incarnation, after the Crucifixion, after being "born again," Christians are not guaranteed the kind of stability and sureness that some nonbelievers imagine to be the primary lure of the religion. At the same time, that does not mean there is not another strain in the way that time is imagined, a Christian cosmic time that is not about Jesus breaking into history but about God founding and sustaining history, in which time is about long-running continuities in the way that nature (including human nature) is imagined. This then is not about a God who changes history but about a God who never changes.[6] Again, these different senses of time, time's flow, and time's import are not necessarily in opposition. As we will see, one of the most common ways of figuring temporality in the Vineyard is to simultaneously take up both rupture, the idea of a new and redeemed moment in human, and the sense of being continually ensnarled in a fallen world; there is a perception of religious time as "already/not-yet," where God's grace is present in the world but has yet to complete its inevitable triumph over the Devil and his damaged earth.

This polyvalence in figures and temporalities is associated with a wobble in the scope and form of the religion itself. Christianity is a universal creed that is at the same time territorially delineated, at once everywhere and yet found only in certain locales, for all believers and yet expressed only in local forms for the faithful remnant.[7] Even its borders are uncertain; it has been argued convincingly that the question of the borders of Christianity, of figuring out, both in the abstract and with specific persons, what "counts" as Christianity is one of the greatest challenges of this religious form.[8] Needless to say, this determination is rarely carried out in the same manner by all the Christian groups that exist.

NOMINALISM, PARTICULARISM, AND ACTUALLY EXISTING CHRISTIANITY

If Christians themselves cannot determine or agree on who counts as a Christian, then what are we to make of all these different claimant forms of Christianity? Do we not count the Vineyard as Christian if some would argue against it (and some do argue against it) by saying that the type of odd miracles they truck in is sensationalism and not faith? This is not a question that applies to the Vineyard alone, of course; there are other forms of Christianity that bring up similar challenges. Do we not count the extreme cases of mainline Protestantism, Christians so liberal that they question the very existence of a Christian God—or of any god at all?[9] Do we not count Catholics, Seventh-day Adventists, Jehovah's Witnesses, the Church of Jesus Christ of Latter Day Saints, the followers of Sun Myung Moon?

The best way to think of this challenge is not to ask which of these claimants is truly Christian and which is not, or to ask whether they share any specific, definable trait or set of traits. That is to mistake one of a whole raft of possible immanent choices made by a small group of particular believers for a transcendent and transcendental definition. It would be in short to choose sides, serving as an anthropological police officer who is self-authorized to pronounce what is authentic and what is a counterfeit. Nor is it productive to ask which churches are paradigmatically Christian and thus should serve as pure exemplars to which all others can be compared; this would be to cast any variation from these exemplars as a fallen form or simulacra, a manqué, damaged, or diseased copy. If we were to choose that option, we would not be police officers but art critics and commercial-goods quality inspectors. Finally, the worst option would be to throw up our hands in a nominalist gesture and say that characterizing Christianity as having any determinate characteristics, qualities, or modes is impossible. Refusing to play the game by rejecting its rules may seem canny, a way of adopting the splendid indifference of the sage. But our vision would become so clear that we would be blinded by the light; through this hyperparticularism, we would lose the possibility of speaking comparatively about phenomena because the basis of any comparison would be erased. Or even worse, we could still make judgments—perhaps about other "real" forces, such as economy or politics—even after pleading nominalism. That would mean playing the game halfway, anointing ourselves as the true visionaries, who are able to judge what are and what are not valid and meaningful categories in the world, even if we can offer no grounds for the validity of these categories. Rather than police officers, inspectors, or aesthetes, we would become demiurges, embedded in the real world and yet convinced we are above it, usurping only a fraction of the possibilities in the world and congratulating ourselves on having found—or perhaps authored—what is the truly real. Even if we were not to fall into the trap of taking our nominalism, our particularism, only halfway, if we saw it all the way through to the end, we would still be in a bad way; having completely forsworn any kind of comparative move, we would find ourselves unable to comment about our particular objects in any way at all. Without a broader horizon to hold the object against, we would become unable to say anything meaningful (which is to say, anything that has any effects) about what it is that we are holding up for a shared gaze. Unable to talk about it in relation to anything specific because we are capable of talking about it only in relation to everything in total, we would be unable to say what is particularly striking about our object. We would be like mystics, undone by the wonder of everything and therefore incapable of saying anything.

How then should we think of Christianity, and of these diverse claimant forms of Christianity? Here, we will be considering them as "actually existing Christianities."[10] This is in part a reference to the phrase "actually existing Communism," a concept used by Soviet-affiliated socialist countries in the waning days of the Cold War to distinguish existing forms of state socialism that for pragmatic reasons often existed in ways not reducible to an abstract Marxist logic; the implicit contrast was with an ideal socialism that arguably was never made real in its pure form, or (as the argument went) was only made real through particular forms. If we were to think of these as actually existing Christianities, they would be copies without an original, an iteration of a pure Christianity that could never be realized in itself because *it has no one particularized form*. If we make this move, the plurality of Christianities is not a problem but, rather, an important object of knowledge. The various actualized Christianities could potentially be organized in an array governed by the way some aspects of the religion changed over time; alternatively, these Christianities could be organized not by the historical processes that shaped them but by their current characteristics, the ways they each uniquely fold and stretch "Christianity in the abstract" to make their own variations on a schema of pure potentiality instead of a definite shape and contour. These Christianities would be like species, each one an expression of the form found in the genera but none being the pure image of that genera's form. Furthermore, their expression would neither be *closer* to that abstract form nor a *better realized* version of it than any other expression; it would be analogous to the way both tigers and house cats are members of the taxonomic family *Felidae*, even though there is no form of *Felidae* that is not expressed through a particular and specific species.

RELIGIOUS PROBLEMS

The schisms between this moment and eternity, between presence and absence, between the textually collective-objective and the sensorially individuated-subjective, in short between and among the imaginary spaces created by the juxtaposition of a variety of actually existing Christianities, may seem like the kinds of opposition that would capture the heart of an abstract philosopher. It is easy to imagine that we are speaking in a way too rarified to have any traction in forms of practice; that is, to think that we are stuck in intellectual deformations that are engendered by specific historical disciplinary practices, such as philosophy and theology, and not moving in the empirical tumult of anthropology.

When couched in this way, the problem does seem to be one for philosophers. One of the core arguments in this ethnography, though, is that this is also a problem for Christians in the here and now. Furthermore, for believers this is a problem that is more acute than it is for academics, in that it is not worked through at the level of self-reflexively articulated and alienated intellectual systems but through the ethical practices and ontological and epistemic structures that shape the contours of their lives. It is common in anthropology to refer to an issue, a topic, or a situation as "problematic." It is rare, though, to see the problem not only as generative but also as a problem for all—participants and observers alike. Just as anthropologists are interested in the concerns of their informants, they are also troubled by the same problems as their informants—the problems appear to be simply academic when these life issues are inscribed in an academic register and expressed through an academic medium.

Definition may make this clearer. The word *problem* is not meant here in the sense found in a riddle or an arithmetic test, for which there is only one answer. The multiplicity of Christianities shows that any search for a way of producing singular answers must fail. *Problem* here is used in two senses, neither of which is suitable for thinking about answers that come solely in quantitative form. In the first sense, problem is meant as a challenge, something that suggests multiple ways forward after it has been given careful and sometimes well-tutored attention.[11] This makes sense. There have been too many answers to the problem of time and presence in Christianity to suggest that there is only *one* solution, as if other offerings were the result of sloppy thinkers. There have been far too many different, and even seemingly irreconcilable, answers to the challenge of Christianity to continence the idea that a singular solution exists. Rather, this is a problem in the sense of an equation that is made up not of fixed sums but multiple, enchained, and differentially related variables.[12] By *variables*, we are speaking here about elements in religion that are themselves without determinate content but can be given content from specific instantiations and set in relationship to one another, producing radically different results. Again each different result, each particular answer, is still a proper instantiation of the original formula. And when all the potential answers to a problem are set alongside one another, they together form a *possibility space*, a concept that will be explored in greater depth in this book's conclusion.

If we think of this as something along the lines of a qualitative variant of an algebra problem, or as a function for which the variables are given identifiable values so that the two sides of the equal sign mirror each other even as they initially appear to be vastly different, then the proliferation of different forms of Christianity becomes explicable. Different forms of Christianity (the "outputs" of the function) are the result of the same set of variables being given different content (the "arguments" of the function), even as the variables and their relationship to each other remain the same (the function's formula or algorithm). Particular Christianities are expressions of the immanent, but abstract conflux of forces descended from a moment when the shape and character of those already structured forces were still yet to be determined. When these undetermined, not-yet-individualized elements are invoked in different places, what is produced may look different and not only because it appears in different iterations; in an odd way, it may at times even look different from itself.

If this is the case, why is it so hard to identify the problems/equations that subsist under these Christianities? I would argue that the specific realizations in the form of particular Christianities overwrite the phantasmic unfixed elements of the undetermined form, making them hard to see. When variables are given content and then concretized, they become obscured; a fixed form covers up the product of the underlying relations between certain always-open, not-ever-specified variables. "Solving" the problem with specific exemplars seemingly erases the underlying relations that summoned it forth.

This obscuring work brings us to the second sense of the word *problem*, by which the word is not understood as a conscious challenge but as the insistent relation between aspects of things that are indifferent to whether they are too familiar or are too far from our consciousness or senses for us to see. We should also note that this second sense of the word *problem* is slightly oblique from the first sense, in which we were speaking of it as an issue that after it becomes visible demands a response. In the second sense, the shape of things can shift as their constituent elements wax or wane without any notice being taken of them. In a way, the first sense of problem (problem as difficulty or challenge) is just a special case of the second sense of problem (problem as a play of forces), that is, the first set of problems is merely a specific and subsidiary partial set of the second set of problems. For problems in the second sense, we would have juxtapositions always occurring but only when one of the elements either is given reflexive attention, or has reflexive attention as one of its constituent elements does it become a problem in the first sense.[13] Of course, the reverse argument could be made as well—that the first sense of problem as a conscious challenge is the prior one, that over time "thinking" problems become unconscious through processes ranging from inattention to repression, slinking away from neglect or thrust into darkness to curtail anxiety. Either way, what has to be remembered is that seemingly fixed practices are problems as well, albeit ones temporarily frozen in one solution; in proper circumstances these problems can open up again, generating new solutions that are a function of novel shifting values for the variables that are expressed by way of the problem. We have already seen the contours of one problem—the problem of presence—as expressed in different textual and sensorial responses, but this is only one such Christian problem, one structured set of variables.

PENTECOSTAL AND CHARISMATIC ACCELERATIONS AND INTENSIFICATIONS

When it comes to the history of Christianities, we could ask whether the "equation(s)" have changed. This is an open question: Are we dealing with the same open problems as those of other historically prior Christianities? And, if so, which other Christianities and when? Regardless of how that question is answered, it is certain that the value given to the variables that make up this open equation have shifted dramatically in the past 125 years; they now have accelerated velocities and heightened degrees of intensity.[14] This is in large part attributable to a rapid expansion of Christianity in what is sometimes called "the Global South." There has been a Christianization of large portions of Africa and Southeast Asia, often in the form of new strains of conversion-prizing species of evangelicalism; it has also become rather common for new forms of Christianity, such as the African Independent churches, to be invented locally. The conjunction of the imported and the invented has also fueled Roman Catholic attempts to maximize gains, where the Catholic Church has experienced growth, and to renew attempts to decelerate losses, where it has been hemorrhaging followers.

The specter of demographic loss means we have to acknowledge growth has not been tout court globally. Christianity and various Christianities have withered in Europe, even though the tangent of growth has not been continuously negative and there is some reason to suspect that it might even be ready to start gaining adherents again. Even the United States, which has been going through a tremendous expansion of religion—some would say a revival—since the seventies, has seen various forms of atheism, agnosticism, and idiosyncratic, consumerist improvised religiosities ("Sheilaisms," to use the unforgettable phrase from *Habits of the Heart*) claim some of the space that was ceded to more recognizable forms of religion during the height of the revival. Even with this numerical whittling away, though, Christianity has grown tremendously worldwide, and this has had an effect even in places, such as the United States, where the numbers have dropped off.[15]

The type of new Christianities that did best involved democratic access to experiential, and often ecstatic, forms of divine authority. This is not to say that ecstatic religion with democratic (or at least a decentralized) potential is unprecedented. Since the Cathars and Franciscans, and possibly since the initial moments of the originary Christianities, there have been modes of Christianity that have emphasized aspects we could call "spiritual" or even "charismatic." While opinions differ as to whether its authority is historical or paradigmatic, the New Testament's book of Acts narrates the sober drunkenness of the first night of Pentecost, when members of the early church were supposed to have spoken in tongues as the Holy Spirit descended on them ("Amazed and astonished, they asked, 'Are not all these who are speaking Galileans? And how is it that we hear, each of us, in our own native language?' But others sneered and said, 'They are filled with new wine.'").[16] In an epistolic intervention in the fractious first-century church in Corinth, the Apostle Paul mentions gifts, such as prophecy—"distinguishing among spirits"—healing, and speaking in tongues, all of which were supposed to have been done "in the Spirit" (even if the purpose of his writing was seemingly to warn against prioritizing any of these practices in collective worship).[17] Even during the eighteenth and nineteenth centuries, it was common to find ecstatic Methodists and other spiritual athletes roaming the "burnt over" districts of the American East Coast, where religious revival had come so many times there was a sense that there was no more kindling for spiritual fires; likewise, many of the early Mormons spoke in tongues during the religion's tumultuous first century.[18]

But it was during the late nineteenth and early twentieth centuries that spiritual longings emerging from places as diverse as Wales; Topeka, Kansas; Los Angeles, California; and Portland, Oregon, all found ways to catalyze each other. This resulted in enthusiasms, admonitions, and techniques circulating with such speed and thickness that a new mode of Christianity appeared, complementing, informing, and sometimes surpassing other Christian modes, such as Protestantism, Roman Catholicism, and Eastern Orthodoxy, in the speed and intensity of its transmission. While this mode took several forms, the movement is known collectively as Pentecostalism, named after Pentecost, that first night in the book of Acts when the Holy Spirit supposedly poured down on members of the fledgling church.

Pentecostalism, built around New Testament texts and long-running religious enthusiasms, may not have been entirely novel, but it came across as new—at least new enough to be resisted by some of the Christianities that it emerged from. At first, Pentecostalism may have seemed to be merely a distillation of a mode of Holiness Methodism that stressed *extasis* to a slightly more rarified degree than other cognate forms of Wesleyanism. And indeed, many Holiness Methodists took up their practices, folding themselves into Pentecostalism. But many more did not. There were numerous reasons for this rejection. There was an inability to accept Pentecostal truth claims, such as *initial evidence*, the name given to the belief that speaking in tongues—the original central practice in Pentecostalism—was the only guaranteed evidence of receiving the Holy Spirit, which was in turn understood as the only reliable index of salvation. Other factors, like early Pentecostalism's indifference to both the racial boundary lines and gendered pastoral roles that informed so much of US society, probably did little to help. But distasteful or not, Pentecostalism, with its tendency to make ministers through relatively quick spiritual inspiration, instead of years of seminary education, had a powerful capacity to reproduce; and the religious obligation to spread this news around the world, combined with the common early Pentecostal belief that speaking in tongues was actually an instance of xenoglossia, the instantaneous command over foreign languages through fiat of the Holy Spirit, ensured that this capacity to reproduce was widely distributed.[19] Eventually, Pentecostalism would differentiate and solidify, with loose associations of churches desiring to collectively turn themselves into denominations; denominational authority frequently came hand in hand with centralization of prophetic authority in a few key figures or select offices. Increasingly, only a select circle of individuals were becoming authorized to serve as intermediaries with God when it came to issues that spoke to the church as a collectivity. But this institutionalization, and the relative deceleration in the production of both novel authority and the ease with which believers could self-authorize as pastors, helped create the cohesion necessary to form a network of missionaries, pastors, authors, speakers, and radio performers; in turn this helped this fast-moving offshoot of Protestantism to quickly become its own identifiable mode of religiosity, with its own set of recognizable practices and discourses.[20]

Identifiable, that is, but not *distinct*. Pentecostalism may have begun by calving off from more sober forms of Protestantism, but that does not mean that Pentecostalism did not in some ways transform the terrain of these other Protestantisms. Even as the differences between Pentecostalism and other forms of Christianity promoted a separatist aesthetic that encouraged the Pentecostals to draw away from other forms of Christianity, the supernatural capacities claimed by followers of Pentecostalism encouraged other Christianities to take the risk and seek them out. In the first moments of the twentieth century, to receive the gifts of the spirit associated with Baptism of the Holy Spirit, and most particularly to receive the gift of speaking in tongues, was to leave (or be cast out of) one's previous religious affiliations and join a Pentecostal church or denomination. During the middle of the previous century, however, individuals (and sometimes even entire churches) would often opt not to leave their previous affiliations when the Holy Spirit alighted on them. Instead, they would attempt to combine charismatic expressions with the ecclesiology, rites, and theology that they already identified with. At first, these enclaves were often contained, either by institutional limitations or by a certain disquiet in the body of the larger church. But as we will see, the spread of the practice accelerated within a larger Evangelical church in a way not dissimilar to the way that the original form of Pentecostalism itself spread.

Even modes of Christianity for which the cladogenetic moment with Protestantism occurred as long ago as the Reformation were caught up in this wider moment of Pentecostalization: in the late 1960s, select vanguard Catholic groups began to speak in tongues in the United States.[21] Alongside this proliferation, these practices also took on a middle-class aesthetics that would be hard to associate with that first generation of Pentecostal activists.[22] Eventually, these Pentecostal recesses in Evangelical and Roman Catholic bodies began to be christened as charismatic. Within decades of the name charismatic being coined, though, it was used not only to designate glossolaliac enclaves within existing denominations but to refer to gift-practicing movements and churches, which were not affiliated with any particular denomination and which chose not to refer to themselves as Pentecostal.

The reasons for this charismatic denial of a Pentecostal identity is debatable. As we will see, those churches that often saw themselves as charismatic refused the label Pentecostal for reasons having to do with historical fidelity (they wished to emphasize a wider Protestant heritage), contemporary stylistics (they viewed particular modes of public Pentecostal speech as contrived), theological exigencies (they refused the initial evidence doctrine), or future ambitions (they imagined charismatic Christianity was a "new movement" of the Holy Spirit on earth, marking not so much an expansion of Pentecostalism in the form of charismatic Christianity but, rather, Charismatic Christianity as complementing, or perhaps superseding, Pentecostalism). More archly, it sometimes seemed that the charismatic problem had more to do with the disfavored regional, class, and racial associations that Pentecostalism had in the United States: too Southern, too working class, too rural, and often too black. Regardless of the motive or motives for this decision regarding classification and self-identification, to these charismatics, Pentecostalism was something other.

The Vineyard was one such "charismatic" movement, a later and somewhat displaced child of a Pentecostalism that had wide-reaching roots. Its origin lay in the Fuller School of World Mission, a subdivision of Fuller Theological Seminary, the Southern California academy that played a central role in the mid-twentieth-century creation of contemporary evangelicalism.[23] The Fuller School of World Mission was imagined by its founders as a clearinghouse for best practices among evangelical missionaries.[24] However, in the period after World War 2, it was increasingly clear that best practices were not evangelical practices; in the developing world, and particularly in Africa and Latin America, it was clear that the efforts of American evangelicals could not compete with those of local Pentecostals. Missiologists at Fuller began to believe that Pentecostal church organization, Pentecostal class status, and particularly Pentecostal promulgation of the miraculous gave these local churches an advantage that they lacked. They eventually began searching for an evangelical figure capable of reproducing these Pentecostal miraculous effects. They found such a figure in John Wimber, who not only had a knack for engaging in charismatic-style miraculous activity but who was also already associated with the Fuller School of World Mission as a "church growth consultant." Prominent missiological scholars at the Fuller School of World Mission gave their official imprimatur to his efforts to promulgate global Pentecostal-style miraculous practices throughout the United States and encouraged him to start a church in his home of Orange county. This church would eventually join forces with a small, but already-established network of Jesus people–type Christians, forming the "Vineyard" association of churches.[25]

What resulted was an amalgam of the disparate landscape of late 1970s conservative Southern California Christianity: an odd mix of hippy-like Jesus people, middle-class evangelicals, and seminary-based Christian intellectuals. Under John Wimber's tutelage, this assemblage would undergo striking expansion in a decade and would repeatedly also be at the heart of some of the most controversial moments that occurred in American charismatic Christianity during the 1980s and 1990s.

The disparate nature of this assemblage was consciously acknowledged by the Vineyard. As the movement developed, many members began referring to the Vineyard as a stapling together of evangelical theology and Pentecostal/charismatic experiential religious practice that together constituted a "radical middle."[26] Indeed, in their narration of events, it was the mix of Pentecostalism and evangelicalism—an experimental attitude toward the supernatural combined with reverence for Protestant creed—that was the source of both the growth and the difficulties that they experienced under Wimber's guidance. In the minds of the membership, this tension-filled, and to some degree self-contradicting, opposition was challenging and sometimes heartbreaking to maintain; but if it were successfully upheld, it would open up a way of life that they felt was one of the most authentic forms of Christianity that was possible at the time.

This self-consciousness about the tensions in this form of religiosity echoes both senses of the word *"problem"*—as an ethical challenge and as the focal point of a set of disparate combinatory forces—which were discussed earlier. As might be expected, the ethical challenge was taxing and the contesting forces created instability. The problem was also Promethean. This tension gave those who chose to take it up a set of capacities that, if not unique in Protestant, Pentecostal, and charismatic Christianity, resulted in a mode of religiosity that could be taken in several disparate directions at once.

RELIGION, TRANSFORMATION, AND THE DIAGRAM FOR FIRE

The stories of the Vineyard, which involve the contemporary shape of both Vineyard practice and that of later movements having their origins in the Vineyard, are all important for grasping not only religious change in America but also the complex reverberations among networked world Christianities. But a study of the Vineyard gives us more than that. It also gives us a vision of the human capacity for change in the abstract.

This may seem to be a bold claim, but it is credible if one considers that Christianity is not the only thing that was changing. Remember when the word *liar* appeared on the face of the pastoral candidate. That young man changed because something about Christianity had changed for him; but we should not think of these as necessarily *causal* in the crudest sense as a specific experience in one place having specific effects in another. Rather, the potentiality of the experience—a potentiality that had outlived the moment itself—was open ended, as was the sort of Protestant Christianity available to the young man.

In fact, there were multiple parallel transformations because the man himself was transformed, becoming a different kind of individual as he himself was *individuated*. This individuation was not just a shift of allegiances or a sharpening of cognition. Not only were his beliefs and practices different but his orientation to the world was as well; it is not merely that he acceded to a different set of beliefs about what might be in the world but that his world was now constituted by different relations and agents with the set of more-than-human entities that a fully charismaticized Christianity provides: not just a God in heaven but devils and the Holy Spirit here on earth.

We should pause to notice that the nonce structure of a moment—a memory, a person, and an idea of religion—was not the only thing in flux. There were also mediatic and technical changes facilitating the formation and circulation of the form of religiosity that the young man was participating in; for instance, the internal structures of denominations and the organization of Christian publishing and radio all transformed during this period. Finally, there were changes in the overarching social and cultural make up of America that contributed to the conditions of possibility for this change in religiosity; arguably, these changes in America and religion were inseparable, even if they can be analytically situated as occurring on different scales or ontic substrates with respect to words and thoughts, practices and bodies.

But to return to our main point, this mode of religiosity and the people who realized themselves through it unfolded together.[27] To many, this change in the mode of religiosity is the very promise of this form of Christianity, that is, the opportunity through what is often the cauldron of a very experiential (and sometimes very therapeutic) Christianity to "become a new Creation in Christ."[28] Now, while these kinds of changes, this pliability and the capacity to continually become a new sort of individual, or, rather, to continually engage in becoming a new sort of individual, may be valued by some strains of Christianity, they are not characteristic solely of these kinds of Christianity or of Christianity alone. Whether this production of the new is a fruit of a Protestant or Christian inheritance, or is instead completely orthogonal to Christianity, it can easily be argued that the shared promises of modernity, postmodernity, and the Enlightenment open up the possibility of creating almost de novo entirely new forms of thought and being in the world.[29]

But that is at the level of value and ideology. These forms of charismatic religiosity may be animated by ideational imperatives to endorse or desire change (or at least certain kinds of change), as opposed to attempting to retard or arrest change; but they do not speak to a fundamental *capacity* for change, the underlying ability that is being given value. This capacity for change is of a different order. A certain kind of pliability, a range of unfixed *potentia*, an abstract map of different possible forms and configurations, is universal—or at least effectively universal—for anything that may fall under anthropological scrutiny. It certainly does seem to be a characteristic of social life, which can be described as a continuous "Heraclitean" chain of creative action.[30] What is of interest is not an ontological prioritization of change—the endorsement of change or specific changes—as a good in itself. What is worth attending to is the play of play—the moments of contraction and dilation, of acceleration or deceleration—and how this may be working at different but enchained strata: social organization, ethical subjectivity, discourses, the human sensorium, and the physiological mechanisms of both the brain and the body. What is vital is not just that we attend to the changes that are being effectuated in each strata but also that we take care to note how these changes are simultaneously realized in different ways within and across multiple strata; and just as important is for us to maintain a concern with the manner in which change is constrained as well. Change that occurs too fast, or cuts across too many interlocking social, political, ethical, cultural, cognitive, psychological, and physiological strata, may mean more opportunities for creating new modes, but it also threatens the differing capacities for reproduction that all these systems depend on; the autopoietic nature of social life, which has been given too little attention in recent anthropology, is vital.³¹ A retrenchment, or even the production of capacities to harshly or violently fight back the undertow of change, is just as likely to be the product of change as is revolution.

That brings us to how this book works and to what this book intends to do. This book asks a series of linked questions. The first is about the *range* and *variation* in Vineyard modes of religiosity and in those people and groups that engage in them: How is it that the Vineyard produces novel experiences, and how is it that these novel experiences are not corrosive of the necessary regularity and recognizability that are required for them to stand at the heart of the Vineyard? Or to put it differently, what if anything is insistent in the different forms of novelty continually produced? This book will suggest that the miracle is both the mechanism through which novelty is produced and the sieve used to strain and order novelty. It will make this argument, however, only after elaborating on the way that various other forms of differentiation unfold in different registers, identifying where it is that constituent Vineyard events are socially and ontologically situated, and ruling out competing explanations for the Vineyard's particularities in terms of aesthetics and institutional social organization.

A second question arises from the first. Vineyard religiosity is not a stable thing; it arose from other modes of religion, includes a wide range of variations, and changes over time. It has also already given rise to other forms of Christian religiosity. Further, what is particular about Vineyard Christianity is often only visible if it is contrasted with other forms of Christian religiosity, and to contrast is always to acknowledge both relevant difference and equally controlling similitude between the counterpoised social forms and practices.³² Therefore, our second question is implicit in the first: What is the wider range of variation in Christian forms and is there any hidden continuity or ongoing set of relations that can be found subsisting in seemingly quite different Christian religious modes?

Just as the second question is implicit in the first question, the third question arises from the second, but it is so large that it can only be gestured at in the conclusion of this book. To speak of different forms of Christianity is also to raise the question of Christianity's place in relation to the larger category of religion. The third question, therefore, is what (if anything) do all forms of religiosity share. Discussions of religion qua religion have not been very popular in recent social science; the general consensus is that such conversations are essentializing in that they occlude the range of variation that has been displayed by phenomena that are currently classified as "religion." There is a great deal of sense in this as religion has been different things at different times, and there have been places where and eras when religion was not thought of as religion or did not exist at all. However, what the ban on discussing religiosity and religion as broader categories in turn prevents is thinking of variation, differentiation, and transformation as the work of religion. If religion is intimately related to difference, then this wealth of difference actually points to what it is that modes of religiosity share. This is not to say that religion has always entailed change or difference; religions can work to conserve as much as they work to transform. Nor is it to say that change occurs only through religion or in religion. Rather, it is to say that specific features of the semiotics and ontology of religion, through production, control, redirection, acceleration, and deceleration, control the expression of difference and do so in a way that suggests commonality. But this is a commonality in difference and not a commonality despite difference.

One figure in the book stands metaphorically for the concerns encapsulated by these three questions. In Pentecostal and charismatic Christianity, the Holy Spirit is spoken of in several ways, among them wind, breath, and bird; all of these take the physical and sensual aspects of the various phenomena and make use of them to iconically reference the quicksilver-like nature of the Holy Spirit and Pentecostal-charismatic *extasis*. Similarly, another common metaphor for the Holy Spirit is fire. Fire, because of the way its plasma dances, is often put forward as the essence of mercurial change. But fire still has its immanent causal forces, and the relation between them and the way that fire unfolds from them are still recognizable.

The philosopher Gilles Deleuze had a term for the relations between social forces that can be actualized in different modes, and for how the relation between these social forces can be transposed to new spaces and can further play out to different effects: he called this a *diagram*.[33] We could possibly speak of there being a wider Pentecostal/charismatic diagram; we certainly could speak of there being a Vineyard diagram, actualized in coffee shops and conference halls, in living rooms and warehouses that have been turned into churches. This book is another realization and transposition of that diagram, a sketching out of its potential, but this time as it is realized through the medium of a secular anthropology. There will be infelicities because of the peculiar manner of its actualization in this instance; but there is hope that the immanent pattern that subsists in this actualization will still be graspable, that this book can convey—with the word *convey* used as much in the sense of *carry over* or *transmit* as *make comprehensible*—a diagram for fire.

Chapter 1 focuses on the Vineyard's practice of collective musical worship; through a discussion of worship, it sketches some of the institutional features of the Vineyard and more importantly the Vineyard's manifold, distinctive time. Chapter two starts the search for a set or series of relationships that can be used to understand both what is particular to the Vineyard as a movement, as well as for what might be shared with larger Pentecostal and Charismatic forms of Christianity, interrogating institutional governance, the larger political-economic milieu, and aesthetics.

Chapter 3 proposes that both the particularities of the Vineyard and its resonances with the greater Pentecostal-charismatic world might be charted through thinking about the diagrammatic generative structure of the miraculous. Chapter 4 uses the diagrammatic miraculous to chart quotidian practices, such as private prayer and biblical reading, as well as reports of singular life-changing events by those who were spontaneously hailed by God to convert, rededicate themselves, or shift vocations. Chapter 5 expands this discussion to examine the seeming contradiction implicit in the intentional cultivation of spontaneous communication from God. It describes training for prophetic visions and discusses how these visions go through processes of typification and elaboration.

Chapter 6 takes the arguments of the last three chapters to work through the register of embodiment in processes, such as speaking in tongues, healing (including raising the dead), and deliverance from demons. Relying on the anthropologist Simon Coleman's concept of Evangelical and Pentecostal "part-cultures," chapter 7 shows how the diagrammatic miracle concatenates with and expresses itself though the religious-life trajectories of individual believers, as well as of larger Pentecostal/Charismatic movements; it also discusses how this diagram can make an appearance in economic and political spaces. This book concludes by taking the concepts and approaches produced to help think through the Vineyard and speculates about how they might be expanded to a general theory of religion. Relying on ideas such as relative degrees of freedom and probability spaces, it argues that one of the basic semiotic and material challenges inherent in religion—the sensible absence of a more-than-human interlocutor—might actually also be the engine of religion's central capacity, the ability to conceive and control in the abstract both change and change's antonym, eternity.

1. Vineyard Time

The first time I walked into a Vineyard church, I was worried I was late. I needn't have worried. Even on my way to that church, there was a sense of time being out of joint. This particular church was located in the kind of Southern California inland industrial park that you find on the trailing edge of some suburbs. This part of town was built to a vehicular rather than human scale. A thin low line of chaparral-clad mountains was along the immediate horizon, trapping the air and ensuring the sky was an exhaust-fed shade of beige. The few cars on the roadways (who would go to an industrial park on a weekend?) made it feel as if time had stopped.

It was the overall stillness that made the action of the parking lot all the more striking. The vehicles were mostly small economy cars, some of which were the worse for wear, and midsized family SUVs. The latter were almost always adorned with various stickers. One common motif was representations of the family members as stick figures.[1] There were also stickers with the initialism "NOTW" (standing for "Not of This World," a Christian apparel company). The letters were stylized, with the *T* fashioned to look like a cross and the *O* to look like a halo floating over the *T*. (This logo was not just for cars; more than once while working with Southern California evangelicals, I saw people who had it tattooed it on their bodies).

As I walked to the open doors of the warehouse, I could hear the music play: uplifting, midtempo, catchy. It was Christian pop, though it is more commonly referred to as "praise music," at least when it is deployed in worship sessions. There were a couple of people working the door; like most Vineyard churches, this one had a small set of volunteers referred to alternately as the *welcome ministry* or the *welcome team*. These positions were more than just names. Enthusiastic handshakes and sometimes hugs were offered to familiar worshippers as they passed through the door. The members of the welcome ministry were handing out that weekend's announcement bulletin, which invariably included the following information: the name of the pastor, a list of home groups one could attend, and the nominal starting times of *meetings* (the term usually used for church services). Often these flyers also had information about the "word" or "message" for the day, what other churches would call the sermon or homily. Other information might include upcoming workshops; church community–building activities, such as picnics or barbecues; and news about various other ministries, or teams orientated around concerns, such as the homeless, food donation, or the short-term mission trips, which are basically vacation-length jaunts to assist churches in other nations.

As I crossed over the threshold, I was greeted by a large, heavy man with a shaved head and a goatee, who was wearing denim and a t-shirt. He looked like a cuddly biker. The biker held out a copy of the circular to me. While he was obviously friendly and happy to be greeting people, I was put on the back foot by having to engage in conversation after arriving late (on this initial visit, I had intended to sit in the back as an observer). I murmured an apology for being late. He immediately said that I wasn't late at all. "We're on Vineyard time," he stated, laughing.

WHAT IS VINEYARD TIME?

And they *were* on Vineyard time. Vineyard time was not a commonly used phrase; in fact, I don't think I heard it uttered again for years, though I would eventually hear it often enough at different Vineyard churches and meetings to know that Vineyard time is a very real phenomenon. Time was loosely kept at almost every church service and Vineyard event I ever intended, whether they were open to all or just a select few. As this chapter will show, Vineyard time is a complex, heterogeneous entity, a direct expression of a series of institutional, embodied, and cognitive practices made up of numerous different pneumatological and practical strands that work as much in conjunction as separately.

In its marked form, Vineyard time serves a specific purpose: When people say Vineyard time, or otherwise refer to the movement's flexibility regarding punctuality, they are invoking a sense of belonging that presumes shared traits. Notably, they are usually speaking tongue in cheek. This is both a way of casting playful aspersion on the Vineyard as a totality and a performative expression of the group's cohesion. It is no accident this is the same formula sometimes heard in ethnic jokes, particularly among those ethnic groups that enjoy telling jokes about themselves—for example, about "Spanish time," "Italian time," or the like. While suggesting an equivalency between ethnicity and a denomination-like movement may seem odd, I saw similarities between the two in the Vineyard. Vineyard believers often refer to the Vineyard as "their tribe," and the Vineyard pastor at the church where I spent the most amount of time often addressed the congregation with the phrase "let us be a people that." This would be followed by, for example, "aspires to" (some ethical or spiritual trait) or "will accomplish" (some ambitious collective project). Expressing a tribal-like identity is not unique to the Vineyard, but it is a recurring theme among other Christian movements. Recall the "Not of This World" bumper stickers that suggest unity and otherworldliness among the people whose cars or bodies bear this logo, at the same time distinguishing these believers from nonbelievers and notional Christians, who presumably *are* of this world. This framing had a historical pedigree; it was not uncommon for the early church fathers to refer to Christianity as constituting an *ēthnos*.[2] The work of an ethnic joke (when it is not meant as a form of sublimated aggression) is to articulate some trait that might be ascribed to a particular group, thereby making that group distinct from outsiders. Vineyard time works in a similar way. Vineyard time works as a joke because each time it is told, it makes one of the particular traits that define the Vineyard seem more real.

But Vineyard time is not just a joke; for several reasons it is a substantive phenomenon. First, Vineyard churches are often staffed by volunteers. The ratio of volunteers to paid church staff is a function of the size and age of the church. Smaller and younger churches are more likely to rely on staff, who receive only notional or no pay; sometimes this includes even the pastors, who may be what evangelical Christians refer to as "bivocational," that is, either by desire or necessity they work outside the church to support themselves and their families (almost all Vineyard pastors are men with families). Even when pastors are running a church full time, they are not well heeled: a pastor at a fair-sized church, which might draw two-to-five hundred regular members, might make about as much as a public school teacher in the area. The vision of the megachurch pastor who drives over to his Lear jet in the back of his limousine may hold true in other movements and in other parts of the world, but it does not capture the circumstances of the majority of Vineyard pastors.

The use of volunteers, though, is informed as much by sensibility as fiscal constraints. There is a Vineyard expression going back to John Wimber that says "everybody gets to play." This is usually understood to mean that everybody gets to personally engage in the miraculous signs and wonders associated with the Vineyard. But that is not its only meaning. Playing also means participating in the running and management of the church. In churches that have elders—a small set of select members who have agreed to advise on pastoral and management decisions—"everybody gets to play" may mean that some get an opportunity to engage in hands-on church governance.

Vineyard churches are organized in this way in part because of their egalitarian tendencies, derived to a certain extent from the fiction of equality found in much of middle-class America. But it is also because of the Vineyard's Pentecostal- and charismatic-influenced ideas about the Holy Spirit. The egalitarian aspect can be seen in the Vineyard's unofficial dress code, which is weekend casual. This is part of the group's rejection of "religion"; in the Vineyard, as in much of evangelical Christianity, *religion* means the presence of a highly coded vocabulary, marked sartorial expectations (such as black suits on Sunday), and formal rituals. The Vineyard's egalitarianism is not just about not being religious, though, but also about having a democratic sensibility; it is harder to convey status when almost everyone is wearing jeans and a t-shirt. Money counts in the Vineyard, of course, particularly at the pastoral level; a small church can really feel the effects if a relatively well-off or generous family that tithes on a regular basis leaves the church, and this is a particular worry in Vineyards that depend on mobile populations like the military. And most pastors are very aware of who is tithing regularly and in large amounts. But at the interactional level, all members are at least ostensibly equal,[3] and this equality is not necessarily fictive. Many Vineyards tend to be somewhat homogenous, drawing their populations from specific segments of the cities where they are located: students, young adults, people who are starting families, baby boomers, and so on.

This general American tendency toward a fictive or actual egalitarianism works in conjunction with Vineyard pneumatology. In the Vineyard, everyone has access in some way to the Holy Spirit, though given the unpredictable nature of the Holy Spirit, it might be more accurate to reverse the agency and say that the Holy Spirit has access to all Vineyard believers. And one way the Vineyard is different from some forms of classic Pentecostalism is that everyone is presumed, at least in theory, to be able to invoke any of the charismata associated with the Holy Spirit at any time (in many forms of Pentecostalism, there is a tendency for charisma to be centralized in particular leading figures). That being said, there is also a sense that some people are granted greater capacity to invoke a specific charism, such as healing; those with an extraordinary capacity or perceived heightened levels of success when invoking a particular mode of charism are considered "gifted."

This means that in theory everyone can do everything, but people also have gifts particular to them. Despite this, some are unable at a practical level to speak in tongues, have no special capacity for healing, have no prophetic gifts, and cannot have the kinds of sensory experiences during prayer that constitute what is understood as hearing from God. This can be a source of frustration and self-questioning; one way to deal with this lack is to consider positive personality traits or talents, such as being empathetic, encouraging, or well organized, as gifts that are equivalent to those that are more overtly supernatural. And these gifts are often expressed through volunteering. Also, people who understand themselves as being capable of hearing from God sometimes believe they should be more active in the church, which leads them to volunteer.

What this means for the Vineyard is that there is a sense almost any Vineyard member could conceivably have any talent. At the same time, there is also an acknowledgment that people may have more enthusiasm than ability; sometimes it's thought that people might at times imagine they have a talent for narcissistic instead of spiritual reasons. This is particularly the case for those in highly visible or leadership positions, such as heading a bible study group, preaching, or perhaps most compelling participating in the "worship" or "praise" ministry, that is, performing worship songs in front of the whole church. Not every church is large enough to have a choice about who performs in what capacity; new churches, or older Vineyard churches that are fading away, may not have enough active members to discriminate when it comes to who does what. But a sufficiently large church can slowly open up possibilities for members who wish to be more active; they may play guitar for a home group, and if that goes well, they may be asked to play at a night meeting of the whole church (typically affairs with much lower turnout unless the meeting really captures the imagination). Substituting for someone who cannot make it to the worship service on a particular Sunday morning might be the next stop, perhaps followed by regular participation in the worship ministry. Similarly someone might progress incrementally from running a Bible study group to being an assistant pastor. Leaders training leaders can be a successful vetting system and a way of encouraging greater participation, but even in the most well-oiled churches, it can also encourage a pattern of unpaid people taking over many of the church's functions.

Therefore, while there are all sorts of forces, from aesthetics to how they understand the Holy Spirit, voluntarism is the functional reason for the Vineyard's noted informality. Though it may seem counterintuitive, informality makes employing so many untrained people easier. But it also contributes to the lack of punctuality known as Vineyard time.

The temporal choppiness that comes from voluntarism is not unchecked by other imperatives. As we shall see later on, the culture of voluntarism is counterpoised by both an organizational imperative and a secondary aesthetic sensibility that demand commodity-centered perfectionism. This aesthetic sensibility stems from the way that the commodity functions as the measure of quality; the replicability and seamlessness of that form and of "branding" as well is held up as a certain standard in much of the Vineyard. This relates chiefly to the Vineyard's material culture, but it is present in other aspects as well.

Commodity-oriented perfectionism has its own temporal effects. While it would be ridiculous to say that Vineyard churches aim for absolute uniformity, I was told by one pastor that "uneven experiences" between meetings at different churches can be a problem. At some level, novelty is attractive to Vineyard believers, but many believers want to know roughly what to expect at a church service. This is especially the case when evangelizing is a concern; if you are bringing a colleague, friend, or family member who has expressed an interest in Christianity in general or the Vineyard in particular to a service, you don't want to be surprised at what happens after you have walked through the front door. Quality control means evenness, and evenness means having some sort of schedule.

Voluntarism's effect on punctuality and consistency is also partially checked by the Vineyard's historical ties to the church growth movement. During John Wimber's long association with the Fuller School of World Mission, one of his chief responsibilities was to train evangelical church leaders in social-scientific–derived techniques for growing churches. This movement in applied missiology aimed at identifying and circulating numerically quantifiable and replicable practices that would allow churches to bring in greater numbers. The Vineyard has never quite lost its connection to the movement, though it has to some degrees been diluted by both the imaginative shifts that have occurred with charisma and a lack of connection to the original stringency that founding church growth figures like Donald McGavran brought to the movement. But it still persists in the Vineyard's weakness for the genre of business-improvement literature, often centered around celebrating efficiencies. The literature itself of course is as much about innovation and change as it is about ratcheting things just ever so slightly tighter; especially during the period from the 1980s to the present, there has been a celebration of the deterritorializing creative distraction, or "disruptive innovation," in the sort of business efficiency literature that keeps popping up in the Vineyard. Using a business model casts a shadow on the organization, which is perhaps most evident in the variations in internal Vineyard nomenclature. Many Vineyard churches hesitate to acknowledge that they often switch between the term *ministries* and the more business-oriented term *teams* when speaking about groups working with the homeless, children, or missions; in fact, though, ministry and team are often used synonymously.

WORSHIP TIMES

Commodity and business imperatives can push back against the softening of schedules that comes with voluntarism, but they are no match for the temporal forces that arise from the experiential side of charismatic worship. This has its own temporal self-organization, with overlapping timescales operating at different levels of magnitude and resolution. And this time does not work to one end, but to several, producing a disjunctive synthesis that gives rise to independent and crosscutting axes of Vineyard time, temporalities that run orthogonal to all the other colors of time discussed so far. An example will help clarify how these various modes of time operate.[4] Charismatic time as an experiential force can be seen operating through worship music.

In the Vineyard, to worship almost always means to listen to or participate in performing worship music. Worship as a collaborative, participatory musical performance is experiential because when it works it performs a series of operations on those present, including the musicians. It reconfigures their sensory attunements and their affective states. It reframes and reorients the believers, allowing them to open up to a different set of sense memories and bodily dispositions; in essence this allows a set of latent capacities to come to the fore. While most listeners/participants are not fully aware of how worship music's specific mechanisms work, they are definitely aware that something is transpiring. People who come to church preoccupied with quotidian concerns, such as the low-level intrafamilial strife associated with getting small children and sleepy spouses to Sunday morning services, find that worship distracts them so that these issues seem less pressing. At its best, worship creates psychic space and a sense of freedom. At the same time, though, worship always has the potential to act not as a mode of training the body or allowing believers to escape their cares but as an event in which something—such as God—reconstitutes the subject through an immanent encounter with *évènementiel* signs. In short, worship is a place where small miracles can occur.

Given that all this is implicit in worship music, it should be no surprise that this process takes time; the first challenge is knowing when that time begins. When I walked into church that first morning, I was not aware that very few people had arrived before the worship band played its first note. Church services begin softly and slowly, sometimes an hour or even more before the stated start time, yet they don't begin in earnest until well past the scheduled start time. Volunteers come early to prepare the empty space; in churches that rent locations like a school gym or auditorium, this may mean setting up the half-circle rows of folding chairs that are common in midsized congregations. Coffee and donuts are placed on a back table and recommended books for sale on another. All this happens as the band tunes up and perhaps does a rough dry run over a song or two. A few minutes before the church service is scheduled to start, the skeleton crew setting up chairs might come together with the band; the pastor will then lead off with a brief, semispontaneous prayer asking God to help them present "a powerful message," "reach people where they are," or "give a sense of God's goodness," to give a few examples.

The band then begins to play the worship songs, as attendees straggle in, slowly filling the room. The songs are often not hymns but covers of commercially crafted Christian music made for general consumption and written with worship in mind. The choice of music is not incidental, though. In fact, music labels often facilitate use of their music by distributing chord charts and music sheets to encourage churches to adopt their songs.[5] The economy this give rise to is simple. Believers become exposed to songs as they are used in worship, creating a familiarity and an emotional cathexis with these tunes that primes them to purchase the music or pay to the see the song's authors perform the music live.

The songs' dual purposes—as commodities and as part of worship—encourage certain features: songs have to be catchy enough lyrically and musically to be identified and remembered. The capacity of these songs to become "earworms" seems to surpass that of most other forms of pop music by several orders of magnitude. The practice of projecting the song's lyrics on screen during worship also serves to imprint them on the minds of the listeners. Only one or two new songs are introduced each month in order to maintain the fine line between familiarity and novelty. There are fine differences between familiarity and routine, novelty and chaos; inhabiting the productive spaces between these extremes can be difficult.

Inhabiting these spaces is in large part facilitated by the internal organizational features of these songs. They are structured (verse, chorus, and bridge) to allow their performance to go on indefinitely (worship music hardly ever has its length contracted). Likewise, inhabitation of productive spaces is facilitated by the sequence of songs. A typical worship period covering anywhere from half an hour to an hour and a half will have about four-to-seven separate songs. Songs are put together thematically so that they share the same motif, such as God's love, sacrifice, or forgiveness. Songs are also arranged by key—there is a marked tendency (sometimes communicated as a rule of thumb by people in worship teams) to have one song followed by another that is either in the same key or the relative minor key. Songs are also organized by a perceived sense of their energy, oftentimes expressed in terms of beats per minute or rhythm. The idea is that the songs in a worship set should have a "curve," a sequence, in which the songs shift speed and are different in length. There are several possible curves, but the classic Vineyard curve starts out with a series of songs that have an accelerated number of beats per minute (on the upside of a hundred), proceeds to a succession of songs that slowly decelerates to a low point of roughly fifty-to-seventy beats per minute, and concludes with a run of songs that once again accelerate to a higher number of beats per minute. Sketched out schematically, it looks a bit like a roller coaster: plunging from a height just to coast after the dip before rising again.

The reason for this organization, as well as the concern that the music be familiar and the lyrics accessible, is that this is a participatory exercise and participation is important mechanically in the experiential edge of worship. As people walk into church, their attention turns from greeting friends (often with a hug) and the free coffee and donuts to the music itself. People listen, tap their feet to the music, and sing along (though some sing more loudly than others; the volume they sing at is often an expression of their confidence in their voices as the degree of enthusiasm they have for the moment). Hands are raised in variations of the classic charismatic gesture: some worshipers raise just one hand and others two, while others raise both hands over their heads in what looks like a receptive gesture directed toward the sky. I have heard the latter pose self-described by some of its practitioners as cupping grace as it descends and channeling it to their heads and hearts. Hands can be raised this way for the length of a song or songs, making it more a position than a gesture. Eyes are often closed and faces emote more as they sing. A few worshippers might turn around and kneel in front of their seats, clasping their hands and looking like children praying at the side of their beds. A smattering of people might go off to some area set aside for dancing, their movements becoming larger and more dramatic as they become increasingly lost in the experience. One or two people might lie down on their stomachs or backs.

Tears are sometimes shed. Tears are not constant nor guaranteed and when there is crying, it is not always the same people who cry every time.

It is difficult to articulate the affective state indexed by these tears. Sometimes it is sorrow or regret—more properly couched in the context as repentance—triggered either by the lyrical content of the songs (about which more will be said later) or recent events in the person's life. A slight lowering of the person's emotional guard during worship may allow for a cathartic response. Sometimes the tears are tears of joy or exuberance, often they are just the tears of people overwhelmed by worship. But often they are just *tears*, a reaction to a *too muchness* of worship, an excess, that is neither quite pleasurable nor unpleasurable but rather has elements of both at the same time.

Changes in affect are more likely to occur later in the worship, after the shift from songs with a relatively high number of beats per minute to ones with slower tempos. Sometimes the affective transformation of few people acts like kindling, sparking a response in those around them. It is not quite enough at the level of proximity and automaticity that the word contagion should be used, but it is not too far from it either. When worship reaches these emotional plateaus, it is not uncommon for the worship team leader or pastor to take to the microphone to reference the "presence" of the Holy Spirit, either retroactively or contemporaneously. In the latter case, one of them might say something like "I can really feel the presence of the Holy Spirit here this morning" or "Come Holy Spirit!" In contrast, worship is sometimes discussed as not interacting with the Holy Spirit, who is often imagined as an impersonal force, omnipresent but not always experienced at the same level of intensity. Rather, there are moments in which worship is described as an interaction with God in his mode as an individual—expressed either as feeling "closer to God" or "closer to Jesus."

These are people who have been primed to tears, having learned (or, rather, having taught themselves) that crying is acceptable and has value; most importantly, they have learned the hardest lesson and become comfortable crying in public. Just because members are primed to cry does not mean they are being "artificial" or "phony," any more than an athlete, who has through practice become better at lifting weights, is.[6]

More to the point, affected worshippers do not lurch into tears at a moment's notice. Nor do they instantly become lost in song. In other words, no one walks into church, finishes off a glazed donut, and then falls to his or her knees wearing an ecstatic facial expression like Bernini's "Ecstasy of Saint Teresa." And such rapture is not guaranteed in the first place. Sometimes despite the intent of the band and the receptivity of the worshippers nothing happens and there is no excess. Worship then is a pleasant musical exercise, a chance to chat or perhaps withdraw a bit from the world through song. There is a bit of solemnity but not much more. But even failure is unstable. Occasionally a worship session will seem as though it is not coming together, but then suddenly for unclear reasons the session will lurch into exuberance and repentance; when this happens, the subjective sense of time shifts as well. It may feel as though minutes are passing in an instant or alternately that time itself seems to have slowed down and congealed. Worshipers glancing at their cell phones may be surprised to discover that hours have passed or equally surprised to find that hardly any time has passed.

This emotional state or affective plane does not exist in many places outside religious services, though it shares things in common with the sense of *communitas* found in comparable social forms. Worship does not necessarily have the same triumphal edge as something like a rock concert (though that sometimes can be found), and the introspective aspects seem to be much more foregrounded. It strikes many people as strange, at least at first; converts often joke that they wonder "what in the hell are these people doing" when they first see worship. Nonbelievers with a passing familiarity with the practice sometimes describe it as weird or even wrong, which is not to say that its relative outlandishness does not have pleasures for outsiders as well. There are Vineyard narratives—effectively urban myths—about passersby, who hear the music while on their way someplace else and become so curious that they are lured into entering the church and captivated by the strangeness of it all. In some of these tales, the music alone is enough to make them convert, even though it is important to note that these narratives often wryly suggest that these accidental catechumens are initially openly uncertain or confused about exactly what they are joining. In some tellings, the converts didn't not even know they had walked into a church.

Several authors have suggested that the play of time and emotions associated with worship results from a global but temporary shift in subjectivity, something along the lines of a trance or positive mode of dissociation called absorption.[7] That reading seems to fit with this part of life in the Vineyard and will not be contested here. The point made here is more of a primitive observation, with primitive used not as a polite synonym for savage but in the sense of something that is foundational or basic. That observation is that time itself is fundamental to worship as a process at several different levels.

The first level is that worship is parasitic on the worships that came before: that is, past worships are still present in the sense that those experiences have conditioned the bodies, senses, sensibilities, thoughts, and nerves of the members in such a way that they can re-express their earlier experiences in the current moment. The template for worship is carried over from the past, as are the increasingly honed bodily capacities that the enactment of worship presumes. In a way, the past is a force in and therefore a part of the present.

Carrying these practices from the past to the present is only one aspect of time's importance to the Vineyard; worship also points to a future, though not in the sense of an afterlife. As far as I know, I have never met anyone in the Vineyard who does not believe in some form of life after death or in a paradise of some sort where he or she will be in the presence of God. Not all members endorse the idea of "heaven"—some believe in bodily resurrection on a perfected eternal earth instead; I have even heard people invoke both eschatological visions at different times without expressing a great deal of concern about reconciling these two framings. Believers' lack of uniformity when it comes to the existence of an afterlife tells us something important, as does the fact that some members' conceptions of life after death are not fixed or are underdeveloped. This lack of clarity is important because it accords with the Vineyard's understanding of the miraculous: that is, interest in the miraculous is not about escaping this life but is rather about living this life in a more fulfilled manner.

Not all Vineyard members have a heavy investment in the Vineyard as a life project, but those who do desire an ethical and effective life in the here and now—or rather, in their own futures. This futurial aspect is important in that worship can be considered not only expressive (or even cathartic) but, as we will see, part of a project of the self—one of many techniques for transforming the believer into a certain ideal type of person. Despite the fact that this is to a large degree about overcoming resistances and is hence reflexive, the focus on transforming the self should not be thought of as narcissistic; rather, the shift away from focusing exclusively on the self's relationship to God implies the development of relationships with those with whom one consociates (and even at the most abstract with one's predecessors and successors as well).[8] Viewed this way, worship is a moment in a long (and sometimes speculative) trajectory, whose goal is to overcome the self and slowly inaugurate a stronger relationship with God, so that one can become the person one desires to be.

This vision of worship as having a transformative effect on one's future self is not to diminish the short-term temporal aspects of worship; worship over a lifetime has a shape but so does an individual Sunday morning worship session. Rather than seeking to have a transformative effect on a believer's future self, an individual worship session foregrounds an *extasis* in the present moment. This shape of worship, found in both the experiential sense of time and in the "curve," the technical diagram that gives rise to it, is more than instrumental. *Extasis* has a value not as a single desideratum, a state to be achieved as quickly as possible, but as a part of a slowly unfolding process that takes place during particularly charged worship sessions. It is a familiar temporal form, and the constitutive transformations are important to that familiarity.

The emphasis on smooth transformations over the middle term of a life or the shorter term of a worship session is not to say that temporal immediacy in the sense of instantaneous transformations is not a part of the Vineyard's imagination. There are stories of people falling over onto their backs, being slain in the spirit, or falling instantly into divine laughter. These stories are usually about peak moments that took place in a special time. Among older believers, these are usually stories involving the early days of the Vineyard and John Wimber at his best or about the various revivals that periodically spring up in the wider charismatic world. Language expressing the instantaneousness of shifts in states is meant to index the relative rarity of these peak moments and their perceived power and capacity to transform lives (though sometimes only temporarily). In short, these stories of instantaneous transformation are only legible against worship as a process of unfolding.

Part of this emphasis on immediacy is to stress a kinship with New Testament miracles, particularly those done by Jesus, which (perhaps because of the telegraph-like sensibilities of Biblical Koine Greek) are rather punctual, happening in an instant as the result of a single command. When discussing these occurrences in the Vineyard, stressing their instantaneous miraculous temporality is to limit any possibility of naturalistic double coding, that is, attempts to attribute the miracle to something other than an expression of the supernatural agency of God. As we will see, naturalistic double coding of supernatural phenomena is a common framing in the Vineyard. Like a shady legal operation that has two different sets of books, parallel naturalistic and supernaturalistic accounts are often produced concurrently about the same phenomenon.

The real proof that discussions of instantaneousness do not vitiate the importance of process in the Vineyard is that stories of instant transformations are often embedded within larger processual accounts. A description of being slain in the spirit, for example, may be folded into a story about someone who attends a revival, is skeptical, is prayed over, realizes that being slain in the spirit right there is a possibility, tries fighting it as he or she feels a softening of the body, and—BOOM!—falls backward with such speed that his or her body has to be caught by someone before it crashes to the floor. Depending on how the story is told—for example, whether it is presented as a testimonial or in conversation—it may be elaborated on in detail or abbreviated to focus on the instant the person collapses.

The important point is not that there are narrative exceptions and variations to worship as duration. The point is that a sense of the processual unfolding of worship and other charismata are so readily available that they form the unarticulated presumption against which any specific narrative of worship is thought; the instantaneous nature of these particular and storied miraculous events require the grounding of other processual events (like worship, which is itself a sort of miracle) in order to be made visible. One could not markedly claim instantaneousness if instantaneousness were not shocking. Worship, even miraculous worship, is made from extended plateaus of time, even when some tales of worship presented it as something that can be contracted to a single instance.

In short, just because worship makes other miracles readable does not mean that we should forget the heterogeneous times that constitute worship. All these transformations take place in relation to another temporality, one that exceeds both the ethical telos of the memory of prior moments and the excitations of a specific punctuated moment of ecstatic worship. There are numerous other moments that are also present and are in fact *implicit in* (but not *subsumed by*) worship. Hearts race or decelerate, breathing slows down or quickens and becomes deeper or more shallow, individual muscles contract and relax, the capillaries in the face vasodilate, the rate at which governing hormones and neurotransmitters are released varies, collections of neurons cycle through their chemical and electrical discharges. These changes, which take place in seconds or milliseconds, go unnoticed by the observational ethnographers. And when they are perceived by worshippers or participating ethnographers, they are only perceived in the most visceral ways.

It is easy to conceive of these biological processes as the subsidiary building blocks of larger processes. These biological moments would be the substrate that forms the "base" on which everything else is built, the "real" upon which everything is dependent. What this understanding elides is that these heartbeats, breaths, and tremors are synthetic and in mutual relationships with events occurring at other timescales and on different orders of magnitude; just as these cycles are what allow for bodies and brains that worship or enable people to engage in the ethical process articulated as a "desire for God," it is the thoughts, perceptions, and sensations at these other levels, at greater physical registers and slower scales of time, that have "downward" causation, shifting the manner in which heart, lungs, muscle tissue, and brains engage in their cycles.

This fact needs to be remembered, though not because worship is a more embodied activity than some other human endeavors or has physiological and anatomical aspects that other activities and events do not have. All human activities involve shifts in bodily and neurological processes; and while the various minima and maxima of them may vary and the sequence and degree of shifts do not all follow the same path, there is *in the abstract* nothing that distinguishes worship from these other endeavors. This is important not because bodily processes are involved but because in worship these various systems are pushed to their limits in ways that other practices are not. This is the reason behind the seemingly contradictory copresence of intensely pleasurable and simultaneously heartbreaking excess that is experienced during worship; cycles and systems are operating at states far removed from those of most of life. (This is only a contradiction for outsiders; for evangelicals with a concern for their "brokenness," this pairing is natural.)

Given the way that worship pushes some bodily and affective systems to the limit, it is no accident that the shape of these experiences is that of a crescendo, that is, of something that is pushed to its limit and then (sometimes precipitously) falls back, often after lingering at a plateau.[9] Consider the roller coaster–like "shape" of worship. This is an arrangement of excitations and transformations that would be familiar to the Freud who wrote *Project for a Scientific Psychology*; and while it is easy to make too much of this by viewing worship as merely a displacement of or substitution for some other biological process, a certain kinship in bodily response to other human activities should be kept in the back of the reader's mind.

This kinship brings us to another issue. These systems, following their own emergent trajectories, do not always go in the direction that conscious minds might desire or anticipate. Variations in initial conditions at the levels of cognition, affect, or physiology or in the state in which one is presently with respect to a wider biographical arc could cause worship not to kindle at all or, alternately, to rush ahead with a surprising velocity. This will affect the speed of the contagion. People respond to the energy of those around them—sometimes at the level of consciousness, where they are spurred to greater efforts by the sight of someone completely enraptured during worship. But they also respond to shifts in pitch and volume or to the degree and speed of bodily movement that affect others and savvy worship bands can work with. These are the moments when the Holy Spirit is really present, when an intimacy with God is truly felt. The converse can happen as well—in a seemingly identical situation, nothing may occur at all and greater efforts by worshippers individually or collectively can do nothing to make something come to pass, presuming the desire to do so is truly present.

Worship leaders know that as well, though they need to continually remind themselves; books, magazines, and websites for worship leaders are full of suggested techniques, including when to vary songs and sets, to catalyze states in the audience. They are also full of stark reminders that the Holy Spirit will come when the Holy Spirit wills and sometimes there is nothing that can be done if the Holy Spirit doesn't will a palpable presence. It is this variability, with things coming quickly, slowly, or not at all, that produces the charismatic side of the temporal elasticity and lags that constitute "Vineyard time," and it is the fact that the Holy Spirit can always surprise one with his appearance that makes it miraculous.

ALREADY/NOT-YET

We have spent so much time on worship because it is an exemplar (though again, not a prototype or an archetype) of charismatic religious practices. As will be argued in later chapters, there is an underlying set of relations that can be found both in worship and in charismata; and indeed for many Vineyard believers worship is a charismata like tongues or healing because it indexes the presence of the Holy Spirit. Like worship, charismatic practices are dynamic, and as is evident particularly in the tendency for things sometimes to take and sometimes not to take, they have striking effects. This dynamism and the tendency for things to falter have been thought through in the Vineyard; further, the Vineyard's account of this indeterminacy has actually been so important that it has been elevated to the level of a pneumatological theorem; at the level of practical theological discourse, it may be the Vineyard's greatest contribution.

In the Vineyard, pastors and other "religiously musical" members have a name for the patterning they discern in the intermixed successes and failures of moments of charismatic practice. The multifarious precariousness of charisma is called *the already/not-yet*. The already/not-yet, however, is more than a way of referring to how charismatic acts sometimes do not go as desired. It also refers to an indeterminacy in eschatological time that Vineyard believers identify in the biblical narrative, especially its Pauline aspects. The various charismatic hesitancies and triumphs in the here and now have become laminated with a wider stretch of cosmological time; and these moments have also become part of what they see as the war that God is undertaking to redeem history.

According to the logic of the already/not-yet, because Jesus has been crucified and raised again, Jesus's soteriological work is already accomplished; death has been triumphed over. Hence, the "already." However, this triumph has not been fully consummated and will not be until Jesus returns to this world: therefore, the trailing "not-yet" part of the equation. This bifurcated concept is part of what people in the Vineyard call *kingdom theology*, an account of the kind of order they believe Christ inaugurated in the world and of how it contrasts with and supervenes Satan's kingdom.

In many ways, discussions about the Kingdom of God are nothing new in Christianity. References to the Kingdom of God and the Kingdom of Heaven, which the Vineyard treat as synonyms, abound in the New Testament, particularly in the three synoptic gospels. Because of the biblical use of this term, the various elaborations of it as an organizing trope over the last two thousand years of Christianities exceed any possible enumeration here. It is enough to observe that it had a particular salience during the nineteenth and twentieth centuries; especially during the nineteenth century it was turned to by Christian thinkers pulling away from Christian nationalism, millennial triumphalism, and personal conversion.[10] One of the chief twentieth-century American deployments of the term has been carried out by mainline Protestants. Mainline Protestants are the liberal denominations that represented "respectable" Christianity for most of the twentieth century and the ones that may be most antithetical to the Vineyard; to some degree there is something almost schismogenetic in the way that mainline Protestants have taken up naturalism and modernism to the same degree that the Pentecostals and charismatics have embraced an antimodernist charismatic supernaturalism. Unsurprisingly, their articulations of the Kingdom of God appear to be quite different, at least at first blush. One of the central planks of mainline Protestantism is the social gospel, an early twentieth-century movement that militated for social, political, and economic reforms for the benefit of the impoverished. This idea was seen as another articulation of the Kingdom of God; in the social gospel's effective charter, Walter Rauschenbusch's 1917 text *A Theology of the Social Gospel*, we are told that the Kingdom of Heaven "is itself the social gospel" and if believers wish to practice the social gospel, they "must not only make room for the doctrine of the Kingdom of God, but give it a central place and revise all other doctrines so that they will articulate organically with it."[11] This makes the Kingdom of God central to both the social gospel and the Vineyard. Considering the animus directed toward mainline Protestantism and the social gospel by that first generation of Vineyard believers, it is well worth keeping this small irony in mind.

Given this hostility to mainline Protestantism, it is no surprise that the direct inspirations for the idea of a kingdom theology and an "already/not-yet" comes from a different source. Variants of the concept of already/not-yet and the Kingdom of God that are more along the lines of the Vineyard's sense of the terms can be found in the writings of theologians, such as Oscar Cullmann and Geerhardus Vos.[12] Given the Vineyard's history, it is probably no great surprise that this source runs yet again through Fuller Theological Seminary, the institution that in its earlier years had employed Wimber and given C. Peter Wagner an academic home. This time, though, the locus was not in the School of World Mission but rather the seminary itself, the institutional nucleus around which the rest of Fuller formed. And the seminary figure responsible for the already/not-yet is George Eldon Ladd.

Ladd was part of the first wave of hires made when the seminary was set up in Pasadena after the Second World War; Ladd was lured out West from Gordon College of Theology and Missions (now known as Gordon–Conwell Theological Seminary), a respectable East Coast Baptist institution. Harvard educated, Ladd was attracted to the idea of Fuller as a place where first-rate theological conservative scholarship could be fostered and conservative theological thinkers could become respected interlocutors with liberal Christian scholars and academics working in the German tradition of historical-critical biblical scholarship.[13] His goal, in short, was not for conservative evangelical theologians to become more liberal but rather for conservative evangelical thought to become so rigorous that liberal Christian intellectuals would have to engage with it in order to be credible scholars themselves.

One of the largest barriers to this, at least at the conceptual level, was the adherence of fundamentalists to dispensational millennialism. Dispensational millennialism or dispensationalism as it is sometimes called is a cosmological vision of biblical and church history with a particular emphasis on the end times. Dispensationalism makes use of two rough intellectual apparatuses. The first is an undifferentiated mix of allegorical and literalist readings of the book of Revelation and other Christian apocalyptic biblical texts. This technique creates a series of striking and often conspiratorial readings that relate the Bible to the current technologies, societal tensions, and political climate (dispensationalism always keeps one eye on the extant social-political forces). These readings are then ordered by a second conceptual apparatus, the presumption of a dizzying array of "dispensations." Dispensations are clearly bounded ages, and in each of these ages God chooses one chief modality over all others as his form of interacting with the world. During these ages, he privileges certain parties; for instance, the current era, which is on the cusp of the apocalypse, is often referred to as the "Church Age," in contrast to the early "Prophetic" or "Patriarchal" ages. The lynchpin of this thought is that the current age is one doomed to fail as wickedness increases and the era of the antichrist grows ever closer. It is for this reason that the anthropologist Susan Harding has called dispensationalism a "willfully mad rhetoric." Dispensationalism holds that the world is inherently turned toward evil, incapable of being salvaged by any human effort and in need of destruction and judgment by God. This challenges all the progressive teleologies, ranging from liberalism to communism to evolution, associated with Modernist thought.[14]

Because of both of these literalist claims and the challenges to the modernist narrative, dispensationalism became popular in fundamentalist circles during the late nineteenth and twentieth centuries. One reason for its popularity was that because it viewed biblical texts as containing veridical allegories and predictions about what was to come dispensationalism was able to claim that it was reading the Bible "literally." That strength was also part of the problem, though. The difficulty was that as a mode of biblical scholarship (as opposed to a popular theology), its quilt of allegorical and literalist claims from seemingly unconnected parts of the New Testament seemed indefensible to scholars, who were interested primarily in framing the Bible as a historical document that should be understood in terms of the Greek-speaking Roman Mediterranean culture in which it was created. The gap between conservative evangelical eschatology and historically informed practices of biblical hermeneutics was a problem for midcentury evangelists like Ladd, who wished to purge theologically conservative Christianity from what they perceived of as fundamentalist anti-intellectualism. Ladd in particular saw his academic project as creating a new evangelical eschatology. The first desideratum of this new eschatology was that this new reading should not be naturalist or modernist in the way that mainline Protestant thought was; at the same time, this new account had to grow out of a theologically defensible conservative reading of biblical texts that still kept an eye on the meaning of the texts as they were presumably understood in the original milieu in which they were produced. Finally, this reading also had to not come across as fevered in the ways that dispensationalism often does to theologically moderate or secular eyes; the liberal biblical scholars that Ladd wished to engage were individuals who had little time for accounts full of seeming anachronisms, in which ancient metaphors like stinging insects are imagined as heralding contemporary technological innovations, such as military aircraft.

Ladd's solution was to shift the eschatological emphasis from the book of Revelation to the Gospels and center attention on the paradoxical ways that the Kingdom of God is described: already present but yet to arrive, concerned with the spiritual but also focused on the political and governmental. The following passage from Ladd gives a sense of both the biblical sources he relies on and the way these sources can be seen as contradictory:

> The Kingdom is a present reality (Matt. 12:28), and yet it is a future blessing (1 Cor. 15:50). It is an inner spiritual redemptive blessing (Rom. 14:17) which can be experienced only by way of a new birth (John 3:3), and yet it will have to do with the government of nations of the world (Rev. 11:15). The Kingdom is a realm into which men enter now (Matt. 21:31), and yet it is a realm into which they will enter tomorrow (Matt. 8:11). It is at the same time a gift of God which will be bestowed by God in the future (Luke 12:32) and yet which must be received in the present (Mark 10:15). Obviously no simple explanation can do justice to such a rich but disperse variety of teaching.[15]

It is exactly such contradictions that are fodder for historical-critical biblical scholars, who would see this seemingly contradictory welter of contradictions as a sign of the multiple sources and numerous waves of redaction that those scholars postulated.

Ladd argues that this seeming confusion is actually an effect of a historically uninformed understanding of the term *kingdom* as a particular political body or form of governance. Working in a philological mode, Ladd corrects this by attending to the original language of these texts: "The *primary* meaning of both the Hebrew work *malkuth* in the Old Testament and of the Greek word *basileia* in the New Testament is the rank, authority and sovereignty exercised by a king ... When the word [Kingdom] refers to God's kingdom, it always refers to His rule, His sovereignty, and not to the realm in which it is exercised."[16]

This leaves Ladd with the position that the "Kingdom of God" should best be understood in contemporary language as the *authority* of God or at least can be understood at times to be speaking metonymically about encounters with and submission to that authority. The eschatological aspect of this argument comes from the understanding of this authority as being alive in the present day, even though it will be exercised to its fullest (in both the intensive and extensive senses) after the *parousia* (the Second Coming of Christ) and the resurrection of the dead. After that, the kingdom will be fully present, but until then, as would be expected in an era when God's authority is held back, it would be a fallen age, ruled by Satan and dominated by "evil, wickedness, and rebellion against the rule of God."[17]

But this current era, though it is under the sway of the devil, is not entirely subservient to the power of the devil: "The Kingdom of God is future, but it is not only future. Like the powers of the Age to Come, the Kingdom of God has invaded this evil age that men may know something of its blessings even while the evil Age goes on." The wicked quality of this age is waning, since Jesus's triumph over death promises a similar triumph for believers to come. As Ladd says, "We are living on the heavenward side of the stage of the resurrection."[18]

Satan is in effect bound, but that does not mean that his sting is absent. For Ladd, it is important to stress that the taste of the kingdom in the present day is only a partial taste. While the future has invaded the past, it has not eradicated it, and the character of the fallen age remains as an effective limit on the capacity of the future age to realize itself now: "While we may taste the powers of a coming Age, it is the Biblical teaching that we shall never experience the full blessings of God's Kingdom in this Age."[19]

Ladd's hope was that this reading would be acknowledged by mainline and secular scholars, but he never experienced the kind of reception he aspired to; furthermore, his rejection of dispensationalism caused him to be the target of critiques from fundamentalists, who understood their apocalyptic vision of things to be an integral part of any true Christianity. In his later years, he grew caustic, and in ever-increasing levels found solace in alcohol.[20]

Ironically, despite his sense of failure, Ladd had an influence the scale of which he might not have been able to imagine, albeit on a different population from the one he originally aspired to reach. Ladd was neither a charismatic nor a Pentecostal; at the historic moment when Ladd was most intellectually active, the tensions between evangelicalism and Pentecostalism were too high. Further, the presumed social gap between Pentecostalism and evangelicalism was also too wide for someone like Ladd to dabble in Pentecostalism—even if he hypothetically had an interest in engaging with a more charismatic form of Christianity. Despite that fact, much of the evangelical wing of charismatic Christianity eventually embraced him.

This was because Ladd saw the Holy Spirit as "first fruits" of the time to come—a "promise" of the coming age, but at the same time "more than promise"; it is "not the harvest, but it is the beginning of the harvest. It is more than promise; it is experience. It is reality. It is possession."[21] Ladd seemed to have in mind a certain quality of life, through which it was possible to intimate the way in which the Holy Spirit would "come to indwell us and to transform our characters and personalities."[22] While the exact theological language may not be the same, and though it is given an entirely different emotional charge, it is a vision of transformation closer to that imagined by Jonathan Edwards than by John Wesley. But despite this difference, this was an evangelical account of the Holy Spirit that could be used to frame a Pentecostal-oriented understanding as well.

The ease with which Ladd's point would later be repurposed was also the unintended result of another of Ladd's arguments, this time regarding the purpose behind miracles. For Ladd, the various New Testament miracles were intimately connected to the concept of the kingdom; rather than being goods in and of themselves or acts that directly expressed a messianic function, miracles, especially miracles of healing, were speech acts or as Ladd put it they served as "pledges of the life of the eschatological Kingdom which will finally mean immortality for the body."[23] Miracles were signs of the kingdom, proclamations of the Good News. It was a thoroughly evangelical vision of salvation that viewed the effects of the Holy Spirit neither as an additional unnatural capacity nor as a necessary sign of salvation but as a foreshadowing. What is more, given that this is just an intimation, there is no particular reason following this logic to believe that it would always be presenting the same mode.

This was the lure of kingdom theology for Wimber, who made it a cornerstone of Vineyard understanding. First, for Wimber the usefulness of something like kingdom theology and the already/not-yet is that it gave him a way to dismiss the Pentecostal idea of initial evidence; further, he could do so by way of referencing a known evangelical theologian at an institution to which he not only had a great number of ties but which was also one that had tremendous evangelical social capital. Under Wimber's presentation, though, this meant that miracles also have evangelical value in the sense that they serve as tools to bring nonbelievers into the fold. At least as presented in Wimber's writings and preaching, it was this evangelical aspect of the kingdom that was seen as the chief warrant for the existence of the miraculous.

The kingdom does something else for Wimber. It disarticulates the miraculous from the church, thereby placing in question the value of churches and denominations that would dismiss Wimber's message out of hand. As Wimber puts it, "The Kingdom of God created the Church at Pentecost through the outpouring of the Holy Spirit. The Church is the primary (though not the exclusive) residence of God's dynamic rule. This means the Church witnesses to the King and His Kingdom, but it does not have authority in itself to build the kingdom. Only God has that authority."[24]

This framing does particular work. It suggests that churches are not per se implements of grace; it is possible that in some circumstances other manifestations might have a better claim to the attention of believers. Accordingly if there is ever a moment in which someone is forced to choose between the miraculous and the church governing structure, the choice should always be with the miracle, since miracles are always on the side of the kingdom. And the Vineyard was the church headed by the man who taught a course on miracles. This argument eased the way for individuals and sometimes entire churches to loosen their previous denominational ties and join the Vineyard. It was also a way of articulating the importance of miracles that would haunt Wimber near the end of his life as other figures, both inside and outside the Vineyard, claimed a capacity for the miraculous that exceeded Wimber's comfort levels.

The "miracle-as-Evangelism," as well as the "miracle-as-disembedding-the-kingdom-from-the-church," were important elements of the kingdom theology that even had effects in a generational shift on some aspects of how the Vineyard imagined the potential implicit in the political. However, vital as these turns were, they were not the chief work done by these concepts. The most powerful aspect of the already/not-yet was that it gave Wimber an argument as to why this foretaste of the future found in the miraculous was not always available. It was an explanation of why sometimes prayer fails, the spirit does not come, and people are not healed.

The answer was that believers were in a state of war. And in war, there are casualties. As Wimber put it,

> the Kingdom of Satan was and is Christ's real enemy, and there is a war going on. Jesus is about His Father's business, which is releasing those held captive by Satan. The final outcome of the battle has been assured through Christ's death, resurrection and ascension to the place of all authority, the right hand of the Father (1 Cor. 15:20–28). But Satan is not yet cast out, and he will not be until Christ returns to establish His kingdom forever. So we are caught between two ages. The fight continues, and we are in it.[25]

This fight is a bitter one, and all the more so because the outcome is already determined. One of Wimber's favorite ways to illustrate this was taken from Oscar Cullmann, who was himself an influence on Ladd. Wimber presented the argument in this manner: "Our situation is similar to that of an underground army living in a land still occupied by a defeated enemy. Such was the French underground's role after D-Day during the Second World War. Though their eventual defeat was certain, the Germans were still capable of committing atrocities on French civilians."[26]

This was a much more elaborated version of the illustration that Cullmann operated with. Cullmann merely presented the argument more pithily: "The decisive battle in a war may already have occurred in a relatively early stage of the war, and yet the war still continues."[27] True, Cullmann's observation, made immediately after the close of the Second World War, carries a sting in its unspoken invocation of a still-traumatic memory; but Wimber's more elaborated version not only recasts his audience as French partisans but even invokes the specter of Klaus Barbie, whose trial for crimes against humanity was occurring during roughly the same period that Wimber was first expounding on the already/not-yet.

Of course, Cullmann, a theologian, had a different charge than the one that Wimber had. Cullmann only had to clarify a particular theory of time through analogy; Wimber by contrast had to *make it real for Vineyard believers*. This is because for Vineyard believers what this analogy was supposed to address and order was already real and in fact doubly real. There was the pain of failure, the puzzle of the moments when prophecy is wrong and intervention through prayer makes no difference. This alone could be frustrating, but it never came alone because it was always accompanied by the underlying misery that these prayers were supposed to cure. However, the already/not-yet takes this problem by the horns and converts an absence of meaning into meaning and suffering that challenges God's goodness into a faith in God's goodness that is all the more stronger.

TIME'S DISJUNCTIVE SYNTHESES

How does Wimber work this conversion? The already/not-yet works as another sort of time, at once independent of and working in conjunction with the numerous other times; the already/not-yet runs orthogonal to the rolling cycles of the body and unfolding (and often nested) transformations that arise from conscious projects, such as a worship session, a prayer group, or even the totality of a Christian life. These other times also give content to the already/not-yet; it is their variations and vicissitudes that cause things to fall on the "not-yet" that is Satan's kingdom or the "already" that is God's. When things work, it is a sign that God is on the move; when things do not, it is a reminder of the pernicious nature of Satan's rule. As we will see later on, there is more to this as well: a certain attitude toward novelty lies at the center of this formulation, and furthermore there is a lure for those who might struggle against making their religion primarily a moral code or legalism. But the chief work done by the already/not-yet is to provide a lens for and be a regulator of projects and events that exist at other evangelical timescales.

But despite its relation with different timescales, it would be a mistake to see the already/not-yet as another instance of any of these other times. In fact, none of these times are interchangeable with each another. The cycles of the body are always repeating in a now—another heartbeat, another inhalation, another synapse fire. Each instance may have more or less speed, strength, charge, and so on, but this bodily time is always striking again and again, like a tom-tom. By contrast, the time of biographical growth and conscious projects is different in that it is not simply a repetition but an unfolding; this is the reason why this time can have the same shapes that worship does or contain a telos in as much as this time is working *toward* something. But these processes are *experienced* as already being under way, since they cannot be experienced before their inception; for the same reason, they are always experienced as somewhere in the middle even if not necessarily in the dead center—one has started to worship or is having worship, is in the middle of praying, is still learning to hear from and obey God. And when these processes are finished, they are done—gone except for how they affect the current unfolding of the believer's training or memory, which means in some ways even though the processes are in the past, they are still constituent elements in the present insofar as they are being reimagined or repurposed by other unfoldings.

The already/not-yet is different. The already/not-yet is a time split in twain through the event, a cleaving of the present moment into past and future. This dual citizenship of the present moment as a sign of the future or as a remnant of the past makes the already/not-yet an operative aporia, a kink or joint in time resulting from its actually being two times as once; as the philosopher Gorgio Agamben characterized this, speaking about the Pauline messianic time that the already-not/yet is a partial derivative of, this time works as "a kind of border zone, or even a transitional time between two periods . . . the first which determines the beginning of the new eon, and the second the end of the antique eon, and as such, makes it belong to both eons."[28] In a way, none of the possible coded states is read as an expression of the present; rather, the current state is either actually past or future. When the opposition is between already and not-yet, "now" is not one of the options. When this time is what is foregrounded, things are either redeemed or are in need of redemption. The present is just the disjunct that these two times shoot out from.

We should not think, though, that the "already/not-yet," that is, this timeframe that reckons its position with an eye on cosmology and eschatology, is always relevant for Vineyard believers any more than the other times are always relevant. Nor should we forget that the substantive (as opposed to the formal) way that these times operate is filled by the contingencies of the social technologies they invoke. Much like the church growth techniques they inherited stress a certain professionalism, the disruptive and decelerating effects of a participatory ethos of voluntarism affect the flavors of these abstract categories as well. Which brings us to this point:

the gap between the formal order of time and the substantive elements that give this formal order specific shape is not only small but in a way is only a perspectival gap. These projects, these excitations, and these eschatological horizons come out of a plurality of actions—of worship, but also of prayer, witnessing, healing, deliverance, or miraculous providence. And not only are these all different processes but each iteration or instance of one of these processes has its own particularity as well, deriving not only from the effect of whatever milieu it is embedded in but also from the elasticity inherent in these practices. It is the question of how this play occurs, and what relations these practice have to one another, that we turn to for the rest of this book.

2. Institutions and God's Agents

In chapter 1, I discussed Vineyard time, the heterogeneous and composite phenomenon that is specific to the Vineyard. Is it too much to talk also of sets of relations that have enough integrity to be considered central; are flexible enough to occur in numerous, seemingly diverse practices; are mutable enough to account for the other religious movements that spring from the Vineyard; and are open enough to allow the Vineyard to be plugged into numerous other networks, technologies, economies and topographies? If these conditions pertain, can we articulate these sets of relations in a way that allows us to think of a movement that makes space for a series of different capacities—from personal healing to prophetic visions, to moral and political projects—across the vast and variegated canvas of fifteen hundred Vineyard churches within the United States alone?

These questions are necessary because for many the Vineyard has a sufficient number of recognizable characteristics that people who have to move away and leave one Vineyard church will often look for another Vineyard or similar church once they have relocated. Further, there is a sense for many of *belonging to* (as opposed to merely *preferring*) the Vineyard, something that is unusual in an age of denominational decline. As mentioned in the previous chapter, people often express their sense of belonging as though they were part of the same ethnic group, sometimes even referring to the Vineyard as their tribe. This might be a function of careful Vineyard branding (discussed below) or an effect of the series of regular movement-wide, Durkheimian-Corroboree-like conferences that the Vineyard holds.[1] Therefore, even if practices vary by institution, we should still be able to identify a set of relations portable enough to be found throughout the Vineyard. And we should be able to do so without overwriting the local particularities of Vineyards situated in quite different milieus. At the same time, though, the Vineyard is just one instance of a larger movement. While it is overtly evangelical in its aesthetics and theology, it is also recognizably part of the Pentecostal and charismatic Christianities found worldwide. Even if we say that this is just a genetic continuity, given the Vineyard's (Fuller-mediated) global roots we should be able to say what the set of relations common to all these groups is; this is the same problem as identifying "what is particularly Vineyard," albeit on a different scale. We are left having to speak neither of a universalism that would deny difference nor of a particularism that is only readable against a universality. Rather, there is a shared specificity in different places, in different scales, and at different levels of temporal resolution.

There are certainly numerous candidates for this set of relations or approach; it is easy to identify different modes of organizing in the Vineyard that might arguably be seen as characteristic or determinative. There are what we might call, for lack of better words, "theological" processes apparently modeled on, or derivative of, theology as a specific academic exercise; these are typological and technical modes of thought, however, abstract or discursive conceptions of the divine that do not necessarily directly affect people's intuitions about (or interactions with) God. There is also a plurality of social and economic processes imported into and integrated with the Vineyard and Vineyard believers; late capitalism and neoliberalism, among other forces, are considered by some to be central to charismatic and Pentecostal churches elsewhere in the world. It would be difficult to argue that all these phenomena do not affect the Vineyard or that they can be discounted in our discussion.[2]

However, if we are to argue that there is anything about the Vineyard that is recognizably Pentecostal or charismatic, let alone specific to the Vineyard, it would be reductive to characterize the Vineyard only in terms of late capitalism or neoliberalism. While late capitalism or neoliberalism may be important parts of the Vineyard's milieu, the Vineyard (or Pentecostal and charismatic Christianities, for that matter) can be seen as being something other than *only* a direct product of its environment or milieu. Further, we must consider the Vineyard's (and even more so Pentecostal and charismatic Christianities') capacity to start new churches in numerous cities and countries; while not all Vineyard churches thrive to the same degree, it tells us something that Vineyard churches are located not only in Santa Monica and Hollywood but also in Bakersfield and Redding, not only in Edinburgh and London but also in Rome and Nepal. It is unlikely that these forces play out in the same way, with the same effects, in all of these different locales. The Vineyard does have a relationship with broader social forces, but these broader forces are not the *sole variables* here. Finally, to see these religiosities as a function of some other economic or social force would be sidestep the embarrassing question of how to account for the neoliberals and late capitalists, who do quite well without Vineyard religiosity, or for that matter religiosity of any sort.

GOVERNANCE

If we choose not to see the Vineyard as either epiphenomenal or superstructural relative to some other force, then how can we view it? One kind of classical social anthropology or sociology would approach this as a problem of institutions that needs to be examined in terms of the Vineyard's various modes of governance starting at the level of the denominational. As we will see, the organizational material is important, but it should be viewed more as an expression of the Vineyard and wider charismatic sensibilities than as a central and determinate cybernetic system or command structure that gives the Vineyard its texture.

I have seen the Vineyard's headquarters, which are across the street from the Vineyard Church of Sugar Land, Texas (actually located in Stafford), about twenty-three minutes from downtown Houston. In this case, it is off US 89, a few turns off the main road on a street with other churches, gated apartment complexes, and fields of green, well-cut grass. When you drive to Vineyard headquarters, you see a large, well-kept tannish-brown two-story building with a portico, surrounded by a sizable parking lot. While the church is not quite as large as the Assemblies of God church down the road, it is a close competitor; both are recognizable as small megachurches.

That brown two-story building, though, is *not* the headquarters of the Vineyard. It's the Vineyard Church of Sugarland Texas, currently pastored by Reagan Waggoner, the son of the original pastor of the church, Bert Waggoner. The *headquarters* of the Vineyard is a small building tucked away across the street, a one-story structure just slightly larger than a modest suburban home with a parking lot just a hair's bit larger than might be found in front of a dentist's office. The only marker here is an understated wooden sign saying "VINEYARDUSA a community of churches," followed by the street address. Next to the larger church, the Vineyard USA building looks a bit like a granny flat.

This small building is here because Bert Waggoner, the former pastor of the church across the street, was for while also the head of the Vineyard; after he was appointed to the position of national director of the Vineyard in 2000, he continued to serve as head pastor of the Sugar Land Vineyard until 2009, only stepping down from the national director position in 2012 (the same year that Phil Strout, who as of this writing is the current national director, stepped up to fill this position).

That someone could serve as senior pastor of a respectably sized church while overseeing an organization composed of 1,500 churches suggests something about the movement, as does the rather unprepossessing building that houses the "headquarters." The Vineyard is by design a decentralized operation; indeed, it is not even a denomination in the technical sense of the term. The lack of denominational status is a fixture of sorts. By 1988, the Vineyard had grown to a respectable 233 churches, and John Wimber thought that it was time to institute some sort of formal governance structure. To that end, he convened a Vineyard pastors' conference for the express purpose of forming the Vineyard into a denomination. This was a contentious issue. Cavalry Chapel, which had been the original affiliation of many of the early Vineyard churches, operated under the guidance of Chuck Smith in an organizational form called the "Moses model" of church leadership. There was no board of elders to answer to and in fact the closest thing to formal oversight was each pastor's personal, albeit autocratic, relationship with Chuck Smith. Further, one of the original though implicit planks of the Vineyard was that it would never move toward denominational status; hence the preference for members of the Vineyard to refer to themselves as a "movement." None of these sentiments seemed conducive to an organizational shift to denominational status.

The real pushback, however, came in the form of a dream that John Wimber's wife, Carol, had during the conference. As Wimber wrote later, "In the dream Carol was in a house with a back porch. She came out through the back porch into the backyard. The house was a comfortable home, and the back porch was substantial, built of stones and mortar. From the backyard she noticed Evan, one of our grandsons, following her. She called Evan out onto the porch to come and see Grandma, and when he came the porch collapsed. Then she woke up."[3]

According to Wimber's interpretation of this dream, the porch represents the new denominational form and the house the already-existing structure of the Vineyard. The dream occurred at the same time as a prophecy from a board member "admonishing John not to be afraid to make hard decisions and act on them even if they were unpopular or caused temporary confusion."[4] At the end of a conference that was dedicated to making the Vineyard a denomination, it was suddenly announced that the Vineyard would remain a movement.

The Vineyard's status as a movement has meant a great deal of decision-making power, along with a concomitant lack of any meaningful institutional or financial support, has devolved to individual churches. As pointed out by Todd Hunter, the man who filled Wimber's leadership position after

Wimber's death, "the Association of Vineyard Churches does not ordain (this is done at a local level); it doesn't own property (the individual churches do); it doesn't have paid bishops (just area pastoral coordinators, who themselves are pastors); it doesn't have a centralized pension plan (one better have a well-employed spouse!); and there is no centralized health insurance."[5]

Given all this, it is no surprise that the institution's headquarters is small enough to tuck into a granny flat.

SANS-SERIF FONTS AND THE COMMODITY FORM

The lack of proper denominational organs grants a certain freedom to individual churches, but this freedom is not unlike the kind Marx described when he observed that the worker is free either to sell his labor or perish. Churches have to take on a certain entrepreneurial dint if they are to grow or at least stay well. This entrepreneurialism brings us to one of the other candidates for a mode or template of structuration. In the last chapter, we saw that privileging voluntarism resulted in a certain slackness counterpoised with a business-efficiency sensibility that was a remnant of the church growth techniques Wimber had learned from Fuller School of World Mission associates, such as Wagner and McGavran. This business sensibility goes alongside another unmarked distinction in the Vineyard—one that is not consciously elaborated in public statements regarding the identity of the movement but that none the less gives a certain consistency to the Vineyard while serving as a functional ethos—sans-serif fonts.

The font for almost all printed matter produced by or made in conjunction with a Vineyard church is either Helvetica or a variant.[6] This includes the materials made by Vineyard USA, PowerPoint-style slides of worship music lyrics, and the church bulletins handed to people as they walk in the door. There are exceptions. Every so often, one sees a script in a postmodern Gothic font set against a background saturated with neon colors, gold, or black, often appearing as a purposeful palimpsest juxtaposed with other layers of script in different fonts. This suggests that Helvetica is just the design of the current dispensation. In the time before Helvetica dominated the Vineyard, there was a preference for the sort of melting serif font common in the 1970s, a slightly more modest version of the font used when surf t-shirts and "keep on truckin'" signs had their heyday (though fonts associated with the early twentieth century Arts and Crafts Movement were also popular Vineyard choices before Helvetica became dominant).

Focusing on fonts may seem wrongheaded and perhaps bizarre, but the purposefulness in choosing fonts among numerous local, regional, and national Vineyards speaks to a concern with design and aesthetics. Some churches are careful about sticking to a particular set of colors even for their folding chairs. Almost all churches have logos made either by graphic designers, who volunteer their services, or paid consultants. Many churches have Internet video feeds. While some videos are just raw footage of a Sunday message uploaded to the church's YouTube account, a substantial number are not only carefully edited but also use filters and effects. Some even have digitally added graininess and scratches associated with film, while others use jump cuts or have key words flashed on screen; this attention to detail punctuates the message and ensures that the presentation (which is often nothing more than one or two people talking) has visual interest. Finally, church websites are often objects of art, featuring arresting photos and elegant though perhaps slightly generic minimalist designs; unsurprisingly, this has created a market, and numerous specialty web design firms compete with one another to fill this niche.

Not all churches excel to the same degree in the area of design, and while there is a certain level of consistency the Vineyard does not have a uniform stylebook. The point here is there is not only a care for presentation but also a concern for quality, consistency, and aesthetics in branding across different media that is associated with the brand, logo, and modern commodity.

It would be easy to take this concern with aesthetics as a sign of inauthenticity in the Vineyard churches and churches like them; it would be just as easy to read it not just as the triumph of a late capitalist-derived aesthetic but also as a capitulation to capitalism itself. For many churches, this is undoubtedly the case, but even when this explanation holds, it is not the whole story; interpreting the Vineyard's concern with branding as the triumph of a capitalist logic is off. To understand why, one has to ask Vineyard pastors about how they imagine things were conducted in the past. Many speak about an age of church bulletins mimeographed by grandmothers, of inconsistency in self-presentation, and a general amateurism that was caused by an underlying lack of care.

As referenced earlier, consistency is a concern for many Vineyard pastors, probably because the Vineyard's charismatic orientation makes it vulnerable to disruption. Take, for example, how prophecy works. In many churches, if someone believes they have received a prophetic word that is intended to be shared with the congregation, it is not unusual for the person to be given a microphone. Pastors may take into account whether this person is a long-standing member of the church, the person's prior history of prophetic words, or the specific content of the word itself, but however much the risk of disruption is minimized in advance, there is no way complete control can be exerted once someone is in front of the church.

And the hazards are numerous. There is the danger that the person will perform badly, interrupt the momentum of the service because of awkwardness or nervousness, or spoil the emotional climate of the moment. The content of the message also carries risks. As will be discussed in greater depth, prophecy or words of knowledge usually come in the form of a vision of some sort. The recipient usually describes the image or experience to the congregation and then offers her or his interpretation of what God is trying to say. Different Vineyard churches place different emphases on what is put forward, and not every church or person follows this two-part structure exactly, but articulation of the vision followed by an interpretation is typical. The order of presentation has the benefit of allowing listeners to challenge the interpretation without questioning the veracity or origin of the vision. There is some risk that a listener will offer a negative response to the recipient's interpretation of what God is trying to say. It is also possible that the description of the vision will suggest other, disturbing readings.

A seemingly anodyne message approved in advance by the pastor can, therefore, go wrong, especially if the visionary aspect is elaborated in ways the pastor did not foresee. I was told about an infamous prophetic word that was given well before my time at a church I worked quite closely with. Details varied depending on who was telling the story, but most versions involved a fairly well-respected church member, who had given prophetic words at past church services without creating any problems; this time, he related a vision he received of a column of water thrusting out of the ocean. As he went on, it became increasingly hard for the listeners to avoid thinking about the phallic nature of a column thrusting upward, to the point where it became awkward. There was no uniform memory about the recipient's interpretation of the prophecy, but the relating of the vision was recalled by some of the leaders in the church as a bit of a debacle; I heard it referred to jokingly as the "penis prophecy."

The point is not that Vineyard churches are wracked by people wandering to the front of the church and giving poorly sublimated sexual visions; this story was remembered because it was exceptional. Rather, the point is that a charismatic church is always in danger of an awkward "divine" presentation taking place during worship when the church is vulnerable to outlandish and even bizarre behavior. While this is not the sort of thing that is policed by most churches, it can be off putting, especially for people who may be relatively new to either Vineyard-style Christianity in general or that church in particular. The risk is not limited to prophecy. One couple, transplants from the South, attended a Southern California Vineyard, where they found the people engaged in impromptu dancing in the church aisles "weird"; they stopped attending soon after.

And then there is the danger of someone being attacked by demons during a service and thrashing about while people gather around to cast the evil spirits out. This is not as common now as it once was. I was told by Vineyard veterans that in the 1980s and '90s, it was not usual for someone to fall to the floor while having fits and "take out a row of [folding] chairs." When this occurs now, there is usually an effort to get the person into another room where he or she can be prayed over away from everyone's gaze. Despite these relatively more recent containment techniques, these sorts of disruptions are always possible. Then there is the danger of the pastor, or other leadership figures, suddenly getting a sense that the service should change course because they have an intuition they attribute to the Holy Spirit. While many experienced pastors will sit with a feeling for a while to be sure what they are experiencing really is the Holy Spirit, following this lead can still tip things into chaos if a pastor suddenly begins a new topic midsermon or even just opens up the service to collective impromptu prayer.

The risk is compounded by the Vineyard's interpretation of the purpose of miracles. "Signs" are both indexes to and icons of the kingdom, simultaneously proclaiming it as a future certainty and as evidence of its realization in the here and now; thus these supernatural wonders serve to persuade as well, which was how they were assimilated by an evangelical Christianity that has conversion as its central desideratum. This means there is an implicit pressure to retell many of the miracles, in particular healings (whether physical or emotional), so their purpose can be fulfilled. Often the retellings are personal communications—stories told to extended family members over the phone or colleagues at work—but they are also considered appropriate for services. It is possible for the pastor to present them secondhand during a sermon, and many do, but this can come across as somewhat suspect because it interferes with the immediacy of hearing from the persons themselves. The desire of the audience to hear directly from the source and the Vineyard's desire to take a chance on church members' participating lead to people giving testimony from the pulpit, sometimes right before or in place of a sermon. There is also a danger of an awkward presentation if someone comes across as too flat, too mannered, or simply not credible. They may fluster the members, read poetry, go on too long, or be too perfunctory. And if the testimonials are scripted in advance to inoculate against these problems, then there is the danger they will come across as too mechanical, or too well rehearsed and thus interfere with the sense of immediacy that comes with hearing directly from the person who had the experience.

The challenges inherent in charismatic Christianity make it understandable that the Vineyard would seek some measure of control by enforcing consistency in its fonts and presentation. The commoditization of the Vineyard's brand/logo restrains the centrifugal, deterritorializing, and decelerating aspects of charismata. What is nice about this framing is that it captures the way these charismata are what the Vineyard is about at the same time that it highlights the reflexive anxieties that come with charismata: the danger of being too uneven, too unpredictable, too weird.

If this were the only set of forces in play, you would expect to see a set relationship between self-commoditization and charismata and some correlation between how charismatic a church is and how commodified it is. This would be the case whether the correlation were positive (the greater the charismata, the greater the need for commoditization) or negative (at times charismata is unconstrained by commodity and commodity is unconstrained by charisma). You would also expect that there might be a positive or negative relationship between the degree to which a church is concerned with commoditization and the degree to which it engages in voluntaristic experimentalism. But the degree of variation in different Vineyard churches suggests this is not the case. Midsized churches that very much rely on voluntarism and are careful to give volunteers exposure can have their material and mediatic expressions almost obsessively defined by the regularity and aesthetics of the late capitalist commodity. By way of contrast, other similarly sized and staffed churches can be relatively light on the degree of both commodification and charismata and resemble other staid services of other denominations.

This suggests that while, as some pastors say, it is important to create a sense of consistency and identity in a church, that goal is not the only operative factor in the commodity aesthetic. Another element is probably technological. Given that presentation and graphic design software and printing devices are made with businesses as the intended end users, it is no accident that much of church material culture looks like business material culture, down to the sort of clip art that is used to illustrate websites, PowerPoint–type presentations, and flyers. However, I would argue that there is an additional factor. The relations, concerns, aesthetics, and technologies that we have discussed here are intensified by a resonance between on the one hand the sort of agency found in the church and on the other the agency of the institution that gave rise to the idea of brand and of the commodity form, the contemporary corporation.

Matthew Engelke has written about the British and Foreign Bible Society as a group working to promulgate a sense of the Bible as both relevant and contemporary in an increasingly areligious Britain. In a bit of exegetical nomenclature, he refers to them as "God's agents," relying on a polysemy in how the term *agent* can be used. As people charged to promote a text commonly understood to be directly or indirectly authored by God, they are like literary agents for the divine. But in another sense, they are God's agents because they subscribe to kingdom theology. Influenced by a Vineyard-suffused reading of Ladd, they see themselves as charged with bringing about the kingdom in the here and now though not by any means through their efforts alone.[7]

In his depiction of the British and Foreign Bible Society, Engelke notes how the media campaigns, the office spaces, and even the language of the society all borrow from a business model. Engelke's finding is striking in its applicability to the Vineyard. This should not be surprising. All three entities (the corporation, the Bible Society, and the Vineyard) have a similar relationship to authority. The corporation works on a model of stewardship: that one is exercising agency and using resources on behalf of another, in this case the shareholders. The shareholders have a voice, but they don't always use it. Because they are a heterogeneous group, when a shareholder does express an opinion, it won't necessarily be consistent with that of other shareholders. Managers must infer what the shareholders want since they do not speak with one voice, and the presumption is they want to profit. But given the vagaries of the market, producing a profit is not guaranteed. From the managers' point of view, all the shareholders can actually expect is a level of care that is measured by the consistency and quality of the actions taken on their behalves. For the managers, the shareholders are an *abstraction*, whose only determinate trait is a pure, unalloyed, and insatiable interest in profit. Their abstract nature means that since they can never be pleased the quality of oversight exercised by their fiduciaries cannot be exhausted. The fiduciary standard is not acting "well enough" for oneself but, rather, "well enough" for a fictive other, who has been presumed to have a singular and sole desire. Even if the shareholders are not interested solely in profit, they are effectively incapable of communicating an alternative desire.[8]

The church is in a similar situation. The resources they have are not their own but, as the parable of the talents suggests, on loan from God; the church as the recipient of resources will ultimately be answerable for how it uses these resources. And like the owners of publicly traded corporations, God is a reluctant communicator. Vineyard church managers believe that

God speaks, but as we will see, God's language is either a language of already-known ethical obligation or punctual surprises. At times God is silent and because of the charismatic expectation that people can hear from God directly, God's silence is more deafening in the Vineyard than it is in other Christianities, which presume God's voice is either quiet or mediated through ancient texts. This means that, even though the possibility of hearing from God exists, in many cases God's desires must be inferred from first principles. In churches like the Vineyard, God's desire is presumed to be legible in the "great commission," the charge made by the postresurrection Jesus in the book of Matthew to "make disciples of all nations."[9] Converts are the church's version of a capitalist corporation's profit: the most necessary and easily quantifiable sign of success. Like the corporation, which can only infer the desires of the shareholders, members of the Vineyard must judge their success in gaining converts not by their own standards but, rather, by inferring whether they have done well enough for a transcendent other. In short, like the corporate agents who must carry out a pure desire for maximization of profits they presume is held by an abstract "shareholder" they will never meet in person, members in positions of responsibility in the Vineyard are beholden to an unalloyed desire, presumably held by a God, who may be similarly distant.

What is being argued here is that the commodified and capitalist edge of Christianity is not bad faith or the result of a desire to profit; at the least, profit does not seem to be the motive for the many Vineyard pastors I have met. Many live modestly, sometimes hand to mouth, while performing a job that demands they serve as orators, counselors, and chief executive officers, all while having to come across if not as perfect, then at least as continually striving toward virtue. Many pastors have to consciously carve out one day a week when they do not work, and even that day is vulnerable to an emergency involving a member of the fellowship as the pastor is always at the mercy of receiving an evening phone call about a spiritual or marital or health crisis. Burnout is something that many pastors worry about consistently and many others experience. The tendency to present church material in a visual argot resembling the business model is not about greed but is a sign of a sacrificial capitalism driven by a fiduciary logic of stewardship rather than immediate reward.

It is also a logic that is constantly being challenged by the people who follow it. Many pastors are aware of and troubled by the instrumental and affected nature of the desire to produce a controlled and regular object. I remember talking to a pastor in the early part of the first decade of the new millennium; his church had instituted a "seeker friendly" approach that was designed to maximize evangelical results by toning down some of the charismatic aspects of the Vineyard, in effect doubling down on the idea of cultural currency.[10] There was one regular meeting, however, that was labeled "believer-style." When I asked him about it, he made a pained faced and stated that every church service should be believer-style. Though it is difficult to know for certain, his discomfort seemed to be directed more toward himself and his choices than toward me.

The smoothness of the commodity form also seems to challenge the church's desire to present itself as separate from the world; recall the stickers on SUVs that bear an acronym for "not of this world." More than once, I heard pastors saying that Christianity or "the church" had to be more than "Microsoft with a Christian logo" or "Jesus with a Nike swoosh."

Finally, as will be discussed later, the Vineyard itself is saturated with narratives, in which, despite a human obsession with planning and quality control, God intervenes in what is often referred to as a "messy" way—acting at cross purposes with, indifferent to, or actively opposed to human will and intention. We have already seen this in the always-present capacity of charismatic church services becoming strange. John Wimber frequently recounted an experience, in which, during the height of his involvement with the technocratic church growth movement, God expressed his displeasure with the movement. As one Vineyard veteran recounted it, "In the middle of the night God woke him [John Wimber] up, and said, 'John, I've seen your ministry.' I've heard John say that the Lord's tone of voice expressed the attitude 'and I'm not very impressed.' Then the Lord said to him, 'and now I'm going to show you mine.'"[11] This quote points us toward an important caveat to all that was said above. Even though the Vineyard has relied on church growth techniques since its founding, it is still possible to read the Vineyard's charismatic interests and self-told origin stories as counter-reactions against technocratic regimes intent on managing and packaging the church.

This is an important tension, and it suggests something deeper is at work. But it is also a tension that appears in management, which is realized at the level of pastors and experienced by most believers only during those moments when they are in a Vineyard church. But the Vineyard cannot be reduced to what happens on Sunday. People read and pray, alone or together, and there are times when they either do more, or sense that they have been asked to do something more. If we are to identify something that is "Vineyard," we must find some pattern or effect that travels well beyond the church walls.

3. A Diagram for Fire

In the last chapter, I examined the problem of whether there is an arrangement that is both particular to the Vineyard and an expression of wider Pentecostal, neo-Pentecostal, and charismatic instantiations. The discussion of institutional forces along with the charting of the manifold temporalities that constitute Vineyard time in chapter 1 make such a possibility seem more cogent. There are enough regularities that one might rightfully suspect some shared commonality. At the same time, at least on the institutional level, none of the constellations of practices and conditions can be seen as solely responsible for the Vineyard, let alone a wider Pentecostal/charismatic Christianity.

This is not because the arrangement we charted in the last chapter is heterogeneous; heterogeneity seems to be an inescapable condition of this movement. The Vineyard is not a technocratic form oriented around control and planned growth. Nor is it a completely voluntaristic and egalitarian organization where the spirit can alight on anyone, at any time, in ways that have to be publicly attended to. The Vineyard is both of these things, though the ratios vary among churches and can even be different at different times within the same church. A church might go a year or even years with no one sharing a vision, and then one day someone is walking up to the front of the room with a microphone in his or her hands, talking about what God showed him or her. There may be periods lasting months, during which few people at worship pray for healing and even fewer talk about the results of such prayers, then healings start up again unexpectedly one day.

This problem is not unique to the Vineyard or specific to this moment of charismatic history. These tendencies rhyme, for lack of a better word, with tendencies found in earlier iterations of Protestantism; the idea of a messy and intimate God whose plans are always threatening to be at odds with those of any particular religious leader and who grants truths directly to the individual is broadly recognizable as a Pentecostal trope. As we will see, while these messages do not void other classical evangelical modes of authority, such as mentoring, biblical texts, or even evangelical tradition, they do often serve to short circuit these authoritative forms even as they leave them in place.

MAPS, WRITTEN IN RUBBER

Variation between and within Vineyards, which themselves echo larger variations found between and within Pentecostal and charismatic Christianities, suggest two different ways of thinking this phenomenon through. One way would be to frame this phenomenon as the expression of two forces working against each other.

The first force might be thought of roughly as desire for order. We could see this in the obligation to care for material held in trust for God. We could also see it in the degree of care given to issues of presentation and planning. This would be in the end about caution and a foregrounding of human responsibility to a divine authority outside the subject. This force would be an expression of a Vineyard religiosity that has paid close attention to the parable of the talents. Because of the way that it centers on fixed, agentive subjects, we could call the force centripetal.

The other force would be democratic about divine participation and unconcerned about relying merely on human knowledge and powers. It would be egalitarian, be disinterested in if not disdainful of planning, and have a desire for surprise and variation. It would be oriented toward a God in a way that would be more about immediate, pneumatic participation than about duty and the maintenance of scriptural and institutional mediation. This would be a religiosity centered on the miraculous and the "enthusiastic." Because this force would focus not on self-mastery but on being open to an outside that disrupts existing orders, we could call this force centrifugal. Under this model, any particular Vineyard church would be positioned with respect to the war between these two forces.[1]

This is just one possible articulation of the set of relations here. A second framing would mean shifting from a focus on the forces at play to a concern with the landscape these forces traverse and create. Here we would frame all the imaginable permutations of the Vineyard as a possibility space that stretches from an extreme of pure planning at one pole to a pure charismatic lack of structure at the other. Between these two poles we would find the varying topographies inhabited by particular Vineyard fellowships. At one pole would be churches peopled by stewards speaking about God in well-structured services and at the other would be churches where people show up for worship with no idea what the Holy Spirit intends for them that day. Churches could not only be situated in this possibility space but might also travel from a locale in one possibility space to one in an adjoining space, becoming more charismatic or more technocratic. And if we change the way we imagine the organization of our quasi-spatial framing and think of axes rather than poles, we could imagine a church at times simultaneously increasing or decreasing in both the technocratic and charismatic registers.

These models are both correct. We could see both centrifugal and centripetal forces as the dilation and constriction of particular churches or personages, and the possibility space as the field that can be traversed. They are valuable frames, and we'll return to them at the end of the book. In another way, though, both these heuristics are incomplete. The former Manichean model of opposing forces has the appearance of being causal, but that is just an appearance. Under that model, we have no way of thinking about what it is that gives rise to a church's orientation, or about the different forces that drive it. We also have no grasp of how and where the contestation of these forces is specifically located or particularly expressed. The latter model of an expanse of possibility spaces may serve as a rough way to situate and compare specific churches and talk about the wider range of variation within the Vineyard and similarly situated groups, but it does not provide a way of identifying what conditions, practices, and events might place a church at one point on the continuum rather than another, or of knowing how the continuum could be traversed. Forces and possibility spaces are real, but they do not point to the generative, immanent mechanisms of dilation, contraction, and movement. We need to talk about the specificities of how forces and counterforces act at particular junctures and to particular effects, as well as about the specific mechanisms by which possibility spaces are crossed. And we still need to map the specific "degrees of freedom" in the statistical or mechanical sense of the phrase, that is to say we still have to map the number and range of independent variables that define the Vineyard.

There is also another problem. Both of these models threaten to occlude scalar and fractal variations. Not only churches but also individuals may and do tend more toward one of these positions than another. In most churches, there are members who are wildly charismatic, living their lives as a running conversation with God, and others, who see religion as primarily an ethical exercise and use biblical texts and controlled exegesis as their primary manner of "engaging" with God. It would be easy to claim that this individual variation is epiphenomenal or temporary given how churches vary and churches as collectivities provide consistency of character through a normalizing effect. But how would churches/congregations and individuals interact? A normalizing effect could be achieved in two different ways. Churches could achieve a certain profile as an effect of self-selection, that is, individuals choose to attend churches whose styles are more resonant with their own. Alternately, a normalizing effect could be a result of what the sociological literature calls religious competition: churches and denominations shift in their attitudes to adapt to the changing sensibilities of older members and accommodate the differing sensibilities of new members.[2] This shift could of course go the other way, that is, rather than individual choices or preferences shaping the character of a church, the church shapes the character of the individual. An alternative to the competition model is one in which achieving a norm is a result of a transformation *of* believers *by* the church. This could occur through the direct action of church officials by means of rhetoric or education, depending on the framing. This could also be effected by the church becoming a space where individuals are encouraged to engage in work on their own selves, to engage in exercises of subjectification that have been such an important part of recent developments in the anthropology of ethics.[3]

Again, there is something to be said for all these approaches, each of which captures aspects of the process. In terms of forces or traversable fields of potentials, the effects of individuals on churches, or of churches on individuals, are all productive. But we would still have to have a way of accounting for the kind of religious Brownian motion that makes the continual imposition of a norm (be it by churches on members or by members on churches) necessary in the first place. This is because this Brownian motion seems to constantly occur. We could say it is the result of a greater Christian media sphere—a person might pick up a book in a Christian bookstore with a decidedly un-Vineyard stance or listen to a podcast or an a.m. Christian radio station with a different take from that of his or her pastor. Even then we would have to show where these ideas or practices came from and understand their shape and function in order to establish them as either the objects of or objects opposed to some kind of normalizing effort.

The other thing to remember is that not only are there limits to any imaginable normalizing process, but any particular Vineyard church is to some degree dependent on the idea of internal differentiation; a homogenous composition is a hindrance for two reasons. The first is that different positions in a church require people with different capabilities; an administrator may need a slightly more sober form of religiosity and be less open to interruption from the divine than someone who is leading a prayer ministry. Second, the idea of the church as a place where one endeavors to become a certain kind of person by engaging in ethical projects suggests there are people who are not where they wish to be as believers. Assuming that the activities that take place in a church do any work in this regard, this still means there might be people at different stages of ethical formation working on different aspects of themselves that are "willful" or "unwilling."[4] As we will see later, there is also the possibility that members will not become the sorts of people they foresaw themselves becoming when they initially took up these practices. There may be a telos for any one practice, but there are also mutations of practice and hazards that one can fall into along the way. If a member does not achieve his or her original goals, the result may be either a renewed engagement with Vineyard-style ethical practices or new goals that were unimaginable at the outset. If the traveler is changing during the journey, then there is no guarantee that the traveler's goal and the destination will remain the same.

Restricting our analysis to individuals would not be helpful. It would be easy to say we need only to account for the religious variation among individuals, but this would be to overcorrect. Churches are subjects as well: pastors address churches, people speak of the character of churches, churches can have specific legal statuses (especially when it comes to tax law), and churches can have specific relations with other churches and overseeing bodies, such as Vineyard USA. Churches have an overall character and are not just the sum of the people who make them up; not to take sociality and institutions into account is unanthropological.[5] Whether or not there is such a thing as society, there are at least collectivities. Therefore, it follows that we need to have a way of thinking through the Vineyard where the "subject" is scalar: at times an individual penitent, at times a clutch of people, at times a church, and at times the movement as a whole. Further, we need to do so in a way that acknowledges both formal similarities and the substantive differences between an individual embedded in a field of sociality and larger entities that subsume individuals.

None of these scales has such a level of autonomy that it can foreclose the importance of the environment. We have to remember when thinking through whatever engine drives the process of differentiation within the Vineyard that it has to be able to encompass a simple observation: there are many different Vineyard churches in many different places, just as there are many different Vineyard believers. From Southern California and Midwestern megachurches to fellowships in the United Kingdom, Rome,

South Africa, and Kathmandu, we are looking not only at something that is capable of being iterated but is also capable of being transplanted to numerous differing locales.[6] And different locales have different effects on how any particular church is expressed. Differing locale does not mean only another nation or continent. A locale may also mean the type of venue for a particular Vineyard church, whether it is a traditional church building (either owned or borrowed from another congregation), a school auditorium, an industrial space, or even a barn or coffee shop or private home. Stained glass and steel girders can both change the atmosphere. There are also regional variations. Vineyard churches occupy both urban centers and rural expanses, prosperous regions with a highly educated populace and places where education is lacking and employment is hard to find. Finally, the amount of ambient Christianity in the region and how much it is a part of day-to-day life make a difference. A Vineyard in a place, such as Alabama or Idaho, that is saturated with a certain stamp of Protestantism will be different from one in a place like Portland, OR, where Christianity is seen as odd and perhaps ethically and politically questionable.

The Vineyard's capacity to plug into different national and regional locales may be a result of commonalities among them. In other words, as in the parable of the sower, Vineyards may only crop up in places with enough shared features to be hospitable to Vineyard churches in the first place. Still, there has to be some kind of underlying resilience, or capacity for self-reproduction in the forms, if they are to persist (even with differing degrees of success) in different social and geographical areas. The language used here, of being "plugged into" a space or locale, should also be treated cautiously. There is every reason to believe that there is not a simple modular operation. Rather, not only are the external relations between a church/believer and other entities affected by their locations, but "internal" relations also bear the inscription of the larger milieus where they are situated. Finally, we need to remember that there are moments when something like a mode of religiosity may be found, or occur outside of, the territorialized space of church. Indeed, there are many scholars who would consider the spaces outside of the churches or denominations the real sites of religious action. Those places are where contact with other modes of being can occur and the division between "religion" or "spirituality" on the one hand and the local antipodes on the other is realized and renegotiated.[7] This observation makes considerable sense in our specific case. The idea of an immanent God who "makes a difference in the world" is one that is important to many Vineyard believers; this can be manufactured in interactions with nonbelievers or in prayer, whether it is reflective prayer or exigent prayer put out to deal with immediate circumstance. As is often said in the Vineyard, "God can happen anywhere."

In sum, we need to think through the different speeds, intensities, rhythms and relations both within and between Vineyards churches and Vineyard believers, as well as between the Vineyard as a whole and the various forms of the larger world that are imbricated with it. We need to think through something that is variable, which means not thinking of it solely as an extensive something "out there" that we could capture in a moment in time. We need also to be able to frame whatever we are working toward as something that is capable of unfolding in different ways as a process of creation rather than as a still set of social ties. And we need to think of something that is combinatory and concatenated. In short we need to think of something that is *topological* and capable of being realized as different *topographies*. In essence this is to say that we need to think of some set of relations as if they were drawn on a piece of rubber or fabric that is capable of being folded, twisted, stretched or compressed in numerous and possibly infinite ways (this flexibility, it should be stressed, is different from saying that it can be stretched or compressed into any shape whatsoever). And this rubber map has to be capable of being sown into a broader sheet (or tapestry?) in many different ways. And we need to do so in a way that says that this rubber sheet has no "natural" shape or tension that it desires to return to: this "theoretical" rubber is flexible, infinitely so, and is not prone to "snapping back" into any one shape in the same way that churches and believers seem not to snap back into any one form.

This is the only way to think about both the identity and the diversity of a distributed movement like the Vineyard without running into three dangers of representation:

- Privileging one instantiation over the others
- Stressing difference to the point that the idea of these different Vineyards being a return to, or repetition of, something is occluded
- Thinking of different instantiations as being different expressions of a presumed "same" so as to be blind to the specific texture of any one congregation, believer, or moment

Even this is in a sense not enough. We have to understand that we are dealing with a shard or swath of rubber or fabric that is stitched together out of numerous other sheets; we have to be equally careful to remember that these are sheets sown on top of and underneath other sheets: the orderings and limits of bodies and biology, or economies and politics, and the possibilities of an environment that may be thought of as extending to the level of geography, or even the planetary. And we must remember that these other strata have their own plasticity. For the most part, we can forget these laminations, because we can make certain assumptions when it comes to our case studies. Indeed, there are moments when their *occlusion* is their most important aspect. But there also may be moments when any one of these forgotten aspects may insist on reminding us of their existence. And we have to keep a way of folding these moments in if we want to think through not just what sometimes is in a moment but also horizons of latent potential that gave rise to that moment and the latent potential that moment gives rise to in turn.

Finally, we have to remember that while our other candidates for "models" (a play of centrifugal and centripetal forces or a terrain of possibility states) are not causal, the proposed alternative is also not a causal force but a map of the way that specific, particular, multiple, and autonomous causal forces *interact* with each another. The topological form presented here does not *force* anything to occur; rather, it charts the way the various constituent elements affect each other simultaneously. It is a history of the emergence and catalyzing, a "quasi cause."[8] This is important because when thinking with this map, there will be an unavoidable desire to temporalize these workings, to think of some elements as "coming first" or "acting on" other dependent or determined elements. And as these elements simultaneously work on one another, this simultaneous work also has a retroactive effect and works changes on the past.[9] Changes in current intensities reposition the present's relation to previous intensities in the way that, say, an uptick in affective energies means a retroactive, relative downgrading of prior levels of affective intensities; an ebbing means a retroactive heightening of the levels of intensity that were present before; or a repetition of intensity creates a rhythm or pattern out of what was before a single instance.[10] We must be open to thinking of time as something other than a series of independent, linear moments.[11]

EVENTS AND DIAGRAMS

To build an adequate framing device for the Vineyard, one must think in terms of both potential and specificity. To do this, embracing what might seem obvious is useful.

So let's start: The Vineyard values miracles. Miracles are things that happen. We can call these happenings events.

The most basic unit of possibility is an event; events, which do not have to be instantaneous to achieve that status, are necessary because it is only through change that time is made visible. An event by nature involves some kind of contact between two entities: either an actor who is working on another actor or two actors engaging each other simultaneously. There is also the event structured as a doubling up on or a folding that thereby creates a split subject. There is *never* a singular actor as even a moment of seemingly solipsistic effort involves the partitioning of the actor by the action and a response (either immediate or delayed) to an internal division or external event.

This is a framing simplified to the point of idiocy to make its features visible, but I am casting the net as wide as possible to capture the (miraculous) event at its most generic. This model could be elaborated on: Are some events more eventful than others? Is there a demand for novelty, either in the elements being combined or in the nature of the outcome, that is necessary for something to be called an event? These issues, though, are in the end a discussion of thresholds of *saliency*—of what events are worthy of more attention than others—and thus should be understood as identifying or creating a particular genus of event, rather than taking up what in general constitutes an event.

Putting aside the issue of which events are worthy of our attention, all events will have this doubled structure. But which things are acting on each other? One parsimonious framing would be to see the event as two *forces* acting on each other. These are not the forces—centrifugal and centripetal religious belonging—discussed earlier; the centrifugal and centripetal can at most be ways of talking about the tack that a force (or an entwined set of forces) takes. These forces may have a centrifugal or centripetal valence, but that is only apparent when they are held up against some other frame of reference. It says nothing about the forces themselves. These forces should be thought of instead as primitive qualities: particular gradations of color, sound, light, darkness, and affect, all of which have effects on other forces. Because these primitive forces tend more toward the qualitative than the quantitative, we can call them intensities.[12]

This is not to say that these forces will not concatenate in identifiable patterns. Clashing forces will have certain dynamics that we will learn to recognize over time; they will catalyze each other and contest or double back on themselves in ways that become familiar. That a recognizable pattern exists does not mean that every instantiation of the relations between lines of force will play out the same way each time. The proportion of two forces, their intensities, speed, or rates of change, can vary depending on the larger context, and this variation will result in the play of these forces being made actual in different ways.[13] This is also to say that the relations of force may be to some degree autonomous from the particular material in which these forces are expressed; a tornado, a waterspout, and a fire tornado are all expressions of the same relations of forces even if the particular constituting material varies in each case and waterspouts are notably different from fire tornados. This, of course, does not make the forces completely independent from the particularities of the constituting materials: tornados made of solid stone are rare. Nor is it to say that the same relations between forces work to different effects, depending on the forces set in relation to each other: a waterspout and a dust devil rarely give rise to the same consequences. But still, articulating this emergent ordering as a relation between forces is a framing that is independent of whether the ordering is situated on a social, linguistic, or cultural/ideational plane—or to be more exact a plane that is indifferent to jumps between these different registers, even as these jumps in registers still have their own effects.[14]

We can call these sets of relations *diagrams*, abstract maps of how forces play out that point as much toward the different potentials in outcome as they do toward a similarity in relations or constitution. We use diagram here in the sense it was used by Gilles Deleuze.[15] It is important to distinguish the use of the term here from other ways that it is understood. For instance, we do not mean diagram in the sense used by Charles Peirce; Peirce's diagrammatics, occasionally referred to by him as "existential graphs," or occasionally as "moving pictures in thought," were conceived of as iconic representations of formal logical operations; as such, they have the universality and also the abstraction of formal logic. Diagrams as spoken about here may have a certain sense to them, but it would be wrong to see them as expressions of a formal logic.[16] Nor is diagram meant here in the sense of anthropology's long-standing practice of presenting ethnographic material in a schematized two-dimensional form.[17] These anthropological schematics are the *re*-presentation of social facts, which usually maps discrete objects or kinds of objects as they relate to each other in an actual or metaphoric space. While they may do heuristic work, their primary purpose is illustrative.[18] Diagrams as used here should also not be taken to mean structures in either the mechanical or statistical sense of structure as laid out by Lévi-Strauss; while like structures' diagrams are made up of a series of relations, the qualitative intensities of the materials placed in relation have effects on how the diagram plays out.[19] The importance of the specific nature of intensities and qualitative characteristics is antithetical to the high-structuralist claim of sense being a function solely of reciprocal negative difference.[20]

Rather, the diagram is an abstract machine, a set of pure relations that fold in, interrupt each other, and, when given content, have a product or expression.[21] This abstraction means that these relations could be expressed in numerous different milieus, with different ratios in the relative strength of the forces. An example of the diagram is the regime of the visibilities and invisibilities that Foucault described as characteristic of the early modern period in his work *Discipline and Punish*.[22] When realized in prisons, this set of relations formed the Panopticon, but the same set of visibilities and invisibilities was also expressed in the school, the prison, the workshop, and the hospital. Note that despite an underlying diagrammatic unity, these instantiations are not only differently formulated but also produce different objects—students, prisoners, factory workers, and patients. But the diagram's abstraction also means that none of these specific forms exhausts it, or could be said to best represent it, in the sense that some earthly objects are better instantiations of the *edios* of a platonic form. There are not better or worse instantiations of the diagram, only different ones. Thus diagram sits somewhere between a pure virtuality of the question of how a concatenation of forces will play out and the various concrete forms that could result. The diagram is best thought of as a partial solution to a problem as long as we understand that problem and solution as used here are indifferent to whether we are considering them either in the sense of a self-posed query or alternately in the asubjective sense of a problem found in mathematics; thus a consciousness of the problem or of the contours of the diagrammatic solution is not a prerequisite to its operation.

Except for those moments when it is bordering on chaos, any instantiation of a diagram is always appurtenant to the instantiation of some other diagram that is constituted by different forces arrayed in another set of relations; this is similar to the way that one map can be put alongside another map to show how two different terrains align.[23] The difference here is that, because the diagram is an abstract sketch of potential instead of a representation of a swath of a broader, fixed topography, the other diagrams that it can be placed alongside and thereby interact with are not fixed. The diagram then is like a map but only if the underlying geographies of maps were capable of being shuffled anew every time they are put side by side. On one shuffle, a rubber map of Scotland is next to England; on the next shuffle, perhaps it is next to Belize or Mongolia.

A DIAGRAM FOR FIRE

The idea of the diagram is in the end an anodyne one.[24] The real question is whether we can go so far as to identify a diagram, one looking for a certain kind of relation with divine authority and with the divine capacity for immanent and imminent action that is specific to the enthusiastic forms of Christian religiosity. We start out with the observation that when people are operating within this mode of religiosity, they are at least in their own eyes not operating alone, or are at least operating at the limits of their capacity to act alone. What then is the diagram for speaking with God? And if diagrams have relations and products, what is the product of speaking with God?[25]

Because divine entities are not present in the easy way that other interlocutors are, numerous and often quite different communicative strategies have arisen to engage with them, from sacrifice to ritualized or liturgical speech and even to Western Protestant attempts at a fully sincere and transparent language that is adequate to a nonmaterial God who is indifferent to human conventions.[26] So communication is a problem, which is to say it is also a moment in which numerous varying and vying diagrammatic relations present themselves. For the kind of charismatic Christians we are concerned with, one diagram situates messages from God in parts of the quotidian; that is, locates it in the day-to-day material external to the person, as well as in aspects of what we might call the sensorium or the psychic landscape. However, the quotidian event that we are concerned with here is one having a surprising saliency that cannot be accounted for. This saliency is usually framed as the statistically improbable, the physically impossible, the aesthetically striking, or the uncanny. It often involves the crossing of bodily boundaries: divine messages inscribed on the body, divine thoughts injected into one's head. Regardless of which particular shade it takes, God's speech constitutes a sort of rupture, something that is untimely in an already/not-yet manner in that it points at once to biblical narratives and to a future-realized eschatology but not to a "conventional" model of how the world is supposed to be constituted; this is the reason why "surprise" has been cited as being constitutive of Pentecostal and Pentecostal-like religiosity.[27]

The centrality of surprise gives some hints as to the contours of the diagram; but then there is the question of when is this diagram realized. In one way God is always present, but in another way he comes and goes. Only in the limited case of mystics is God a continual actively sought partner in every encounter; typically believers turn to God only in moments when they feel that because of limitations in a person's capacity they cannot act alone: when they are at "the limits ... of analytic capacities, at the limits of the powers of endurance, and at the limits of ... moral insight."[28] Note that this crisis also suggests a doubling in the person, an element that wills an act and a different will internal to the person, which because of stubbornness or weakness either interrupts that first will with a "perverse" second one or

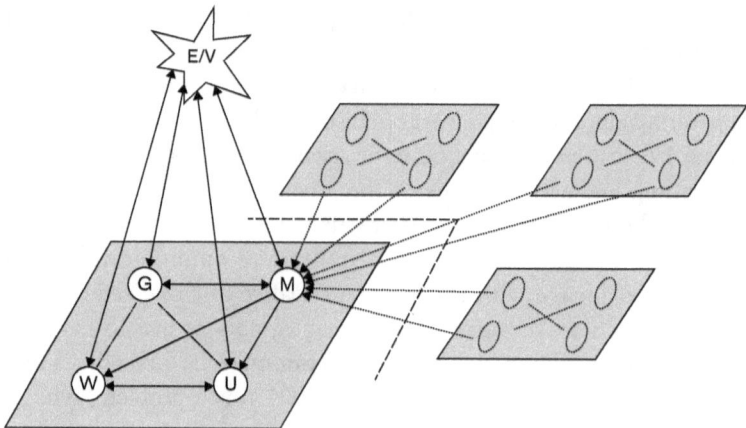

A schematic presentation of the diagram. E/V stands for the event in its most virtual or larval form; M stands for the miracle as *sign*, W for that which is willing, and U for the unwilling—the willful and unwilling aspects that contest against the will. Willing and unwilling aspects can be either different aspects of a single actor, or distributed among several actors or objects. G is the ground—meaning not foundation but the aspects of the situation that instantaneously recede with the appearance of the miracle (in essence, the *border* of the diagram). The further planes connected to M are the vying candidates for causal agent that are opened up by inquiry. These accounts of the genesis of the miracle that are potentially opened up by inquiry are mostly *naturalistic* but also include theistic accounts such as theology. Opening any account expands the number of players and *reconfigures* the diagram, vitiating some emergent effects while simultaneously creating others.

fails to fully expedite the will. We have then both the event as an external encounter and the diagrammatic event as a partition of the self.

This doubling has a long genetic history in Christianity—consider Romans 7, where Paul is also obsessed with the limitation on the will:

> I do not understand my own actions. For I do not do what I want, but I do the very thing I hate. Now if I do what I do not want, I agree that the law is good. But in fact it is no longer I that do it, but sin that dwells within me. For I know that nothing good dwells within me, that is, in my flesh. I can will what is right, but I cannot do it. For I do not do the good I want, but the evil I do not want is what I do. Now if I do what I do not want, it is no longer I that do it, but sin that dwells within me.
>
> So I find it to be a law that when I want to do what is good, evil lies close at hand. For I delight in the law of God in my inmost self, but I see

in my members another law at war with the law of my mind, making me captive to the law of sin that dwells in my members. Wretched man that I am! Who will rescue me from this body of death? (15–24, NRSV)

While there is reason to think that Paul's formulation is dependent on earlier theories of the constitution of the person that were particular to antiquity, this is a useful formulation for our problem.[29] The specifics of this Pauline split and the sort of different substances, such as spirit, soul or flesh that it presumes may matter for those interested in filling out a historical genealogy. For those who have an eye toward the array of possible relations of force, what is important is the idea that an act of turning to God is at the same time the production of a split in the petitioner.

POTENTIA AND THE TANGENT OF THE FUTURE

This scission either of the person or persons and other unwilling agents that are being contended with, *or* within individual or collective subjects (as in the Pauline case), may appear to be either overly structural or procrustean. However, if we remember the simultaneity of all aspects of the diagram, the mutability of the different relations between forces, and the way in which forces are themselves composed of differently constituted materials in different actualizations of the diagram, then the inherent plasticity of this diagram becomes graspable.

The key to the plasticity in the diagram is this: first come lines of force, followed by the various fields, such as the two aspects to the sensorium or the willing and willful aspects of the scenario. This is not about temporal or causal priorities, however. Rather, the relation between forces and fields is the same as that between a set of intensities—desires, affects, sensations, and qualities—that are lines of force and the fields that are their simultaneous extensive expressions. This is more along the lines of the two sides of the coin than it is of a sequence as the actualizations affect the intensities even as the intensities affect the actualizations. A fictive priority should be given to the lines of force, though, if our desire is to articulate the various ways this pattern can be actualized. This is because while forces and the actualizations of the forces are simultaneous in appearance forces tend to be *obscured* by the actualizations that they constitute, a phenomenon that directs our eyes not toward the intensities and affects but rather toward concretized objects that are expressions of the forces.

We should, therefore, avoid misapprehending the diagram as a *series of steps* in an unfolding, well-ordered, sequential causal chain (even if it might look that way from the viewpoint of the various actualizations themselves provided we ignore the forces that constitute them). As we will see in the next chapter, one influential discursive prototype for prayer and the miracle is *petitionary prayer*, a term for the sort of imploring speech acts that originate with a person voicing the prayer and result in an answer from God (we should note here that for these purposes, speech acts include thoughts, which are structured like speech and made with the presumption that the addressee is capable of hearing them). The adequacy of the diagram for this prototype is obvious: a willing aspect is orientated toward the sensorium, and an aspect of the sensorium emerges as either a communication or an action originating from God. This in turn has effects on the broader scenario.

But if we suspend the imposition of a causal order on the diagram, then we can see how it would be an adequate frame for other Pentecostal/charismatic phenomena. As we will also see in the next chapter along with specific examples there are moments when God speaks to a believer apparently unbidden; biblical models for this include the moment when Saul became Paul on the road to Damascus, or when Jonah received his commission to Nineveh. These moments of unbidden divine speech can be seen as expressions of the lines of force in the diagram as well: as the divine part of the sensorium works on them, a sundering in the sensorium causes some aspects of the person or collectivity to be seen as willing and others (internal or external) as willful.

The simultaneity of expression of forces in the diagram means that what appear to be differently ordered causal sequences are accounted for by the same concurrent set of relations. This occurs even when the forces are experientially ordered as part of a chronological sequence. The felt sense of ordered sequence raises the question as to how the expressions of forces can be simultaneous in the first place, or, more to the point, what are the benefits of thinking of these as occurring simultaneously. After all, the sense of a causal sequence would seem to indicate that we should see petitionary prayer and prophetic messages as different routes with separate starting points and destinations. Under the presumption of a sequential unfolding, petitionary prayer starts with the individual and a scission in the will. By contrast, prophetic experiences start with an unexpected event in the sensorium, which then hails a willing subject in an almost Althusserian manner, compelling the subject to go on to battle an unwilling remainder.

The counterargument to this commonsense reading is that found in any discussion of structural causation: each aspect of the structure in some way presumes or relies on the existence of other aspects of the same structure for this to work as a specific kind of event. But if this is predicated on a simultaneity, what gives the *sense* of sequence? Recall the discussion of Vineyard time in the first chapter. It showed time has various constituent aspects that work in a disjunctive synthesis. On the one hand, both past and future are only available in the present, but likewise the present encompasses both a *becoming future* and a *becoming past*.[30] This is because the past is never past and the future does not exit. For either the past or the future to have effects, they must be active in the present, making each one a part of the present despite the fact that the present is always splitting into past and future.

When thinking about it through the lens of the diagram and the unfolding of the event, this seeming contradiction can be accounted for by looking at the temporal direction of the coeval forces at the moment under consideration to take into account their tangent, the instantaneous "rate of change" in the moment; this is what controls which elements seem to be past and which seem to be tending toward the future. Forces whose tangents are positive are growing and hence are experienced as future-facing; those forces whose tangents are negative or flat are seen as receding into the past. However, both receding and growing are qualities of forces that exist in the now.

This approach, which sees the experience of linear time not as an orderly sequence of presences and absences but as an emergent effect of the coeval relations and rates of change as they occur in a single present moment, allows us to address another temporal objection. Not only are there cases in which a causal sequence seems to be sequentially realized but there are also times when only particular parts of the diagram seem to have been actualized. There is prayer but no reply; there is the sense of a divine message, but it neither causes any actor to be constituted as willing nor targets other aspects of the actor or another external part of the scenario as unwilling. Can such moments, such assemblages, be considered instances of the diagram if important parts of them are missing?

There are three answers to this, or to be more exact, three ways of couching the same answer. One comes dangerously close to metaphysics and another to tautology, but both the metaphysical and tautological answers must be understood as variants of the more empirically grounded responses. The tautologically leaning answer would be to state that everything that exists exists; thus as long as one grants there is a potential, then that potential exists and the "missing" element of the diagram is present but only as *potentia*. The seemingly absent aspects of the diagram are at the very least present as promise, even if that promise is never fulfilled. This bleeds over to the answer that comes closer to metaphysics: the argument that the opposition between potential and the virtual on the one side and extensive objects on the other is not a binary one. Rather, as processes take place potential becomes fixed by degrees and the virtual becomes obscured by fixed objects.

Therefore, what may seem to be missing objects, scissions that have not occurred, or fields that have not been disarticulated are phenomena that are still there. They simply exist more on the side of the fluid and incipient.

Again, this is metaphysics, rather than social science, unless we can point to some more empirical variant of this formula. For this we have to lean closer to the "actualized" world that is an expression of the lines of force of the diagram. Here the appearance of one aspect of this diagram raises the expectation that other aspects will appear as well, priming the senses for their being uncovered. Believers who pray to God in a petitionary way look for signs of an answer; someone who has heard from God in an unbidden or prophetic manner wonders about both the import of the message and a proper response. To the degree then that "unrealized" aspects have effects not just despite their apparent absence (lack of a divine response, uncertainty about how to react to a message from God) but because of and through their absence, then they do work and must be accounted for. This absence is a presence.

Of course there are times when some forces may simply be absent in the register of both the actual and the potential; nothing is so immutable that aspects of it cannot disappear, that variables can be removed from the equation as their rate of change becomes indeterminable. When these things happen, however, what occurs is not a diagram with lines of force absent but, rather, *a mutation to another diagram altogether.* Differently constituted lines of force give rise to different fields, and the nature of the religiosity changes. Instead of being a charismatic diagram for the miraculous, it becomes (depending on exactly what is exhausted and under what circumstance) the diagram for more authoritarian or more voluntaristic forms of religiosity or alternately becomes something else instead (perhaps a diagram for an existential ethic). But in most cases, the presence of one aspect of this diagram suggests the presence of the other lines of force and of other fields, either fully realized or as potentials that despite or because of their incipient status have very real effects.

METHODOLOGICAL ATHEISM AND OCCLUDED DIVINE ASSEMBLAGES

For many, issues of time, potential, and absence will not be the greatest stumbling blocks to this argument. Rather, it is the presence of God through signs that is troubling. This presence may be troubling for different reasons to different constituencies.

This diagram is dependent on the appearance of the miraculous; and in a mode of religiosity in which angels and saints are for the most part stripped away as possible agents, the active force behind the miraculous aspect can only be God. This presence is unusual. In most of social science, God's presence is unnerving because his existence is either denied outright, or, alternately, because he is foreclosed through the social science analytic technique of "methodological atheism." According to that technique, the question of God is "bracketed" so that human social activity can be brought to the fore of the analysis.[31] Actual and methodological atheists are not the only potentially offended parties. There will also be those who are offended if God appears only as an expression of relations of forces. For those theists, this form of appearance seems to suggest that God is an effect and not a cause, a disturbing proposition for those who see God as an ontological, eschatological, or ethical guarantor. In sum, one side may feel that social theory has been abandoned for applied theology, and another side may feel that divinity, rather than being bracketed off or exiled by social theory, has been enslaved by it.[32]

Both of these potential readings are incorrect. What I propose is not a renunciation of methodological atheism but a way of making God present as an autonomous force in such a framework. Further, this is an approach that makes only the most threadbare metaphysical claims about God and makes none that would *necessitate* God being made subservient to social processes, or for that matter necessitate God's being granted some foundational ontological status.

God's presence in the diagram is the same proposition that said churches and denominations are real; and those entities are real despite the fact that they are constructed from or partially determined by other subsidiary objects, such as people, institutions, tax laws, customs, and networks of communication. If all objects are objects, then denominations have to be acknowledged despite their being constituted from heterogeneous material.[33]

The same is true of God; God is an object by virtue of the various lexical items that reference him, by the exercises (theological or otherwise) in thought that take him as an object, and finally by the way that people rely on him. God exists even if he doesn't. The question is not whether God exists but in what specific modality he exists, how his existence is expressed and with what degrees of *clarity* and *insistence*. He is certainly expressed in the miraculous elements of the sensorium: in anything from hearing God's voice to a coincidence that suggests a divine hand. The nature of the mechanism that constitutes God, though, is occluded to the degree that elements behind the particular expression are not capable of immediate investigation by those who experience them, or at the least that they do not habitually expose these messages to rigorous tests. (As we will see in the next chapter, however, these messages are often subject to *discernment*, a term for a mix of procedures and sensibilities that is used either to ratify or to discount the source or content of these messages.) The miraculous voice, the untimely knowledge that arrives seemingly by itself, the feeling of divine peace or love, the unexplainable healing are all forms of the miraculous that also serve as events obscuring the means through which the specific instantiation of the miraculous comes into being. Believers tend not to try and look inside the miracle to see if they can spy the clockwork.

What happens when someone does try to look inside the miracle? Probing can produce some sense of the occluding mechanisms and open up the nature of God: that is, the sort of being God is in that instant. However, the attempt to look inside to see if God can be broken up into heterogeneous materials produces what are in effect differently constituted divine assemblages. Looking inside the miracle breaks open the black box, importing the occluded elements into the diagram and thereby making it a different diagram with different emergent effects.[34] The sort of God produced by this "looking inside" is to a degree a function of the form of probing that one is engaged in. A metaphysical meditation on the miraculous can produce a divine ontology. For example, theology would posit a set of propositions, axioms, and deductions behind the miracle. Likewise some forms of Pentecostal intuition, particularly the prosperity gospel, would uncover binding rules about forms of exchange and repayment that serve as controlling limitations on divine potency. A phenomenological investigation might identify embodied imaginaries, while a psychoanalytic one would uncover some sublimated or substituted familial theater. A classical Durkheimian search would claim to identify God as a coextensive emanation of the social. Even neurological investigations would have suggestions that isolate God as a misfiring agency detector or some other neurological spandrel arising from the human cognitive architecture.

All these approaches are true, or are at least are all the products of their own (mostly) internally self-consistent truth procedures. This is not a relativist position but an empirical and positivist one; different findings will result from different investigatory methods. This is not to say that they are all equal in the resiliency of the truths they produce. Different truths have different resiliencies when they are being exposed to different kinds and increasing levels of pressure or probing; there are specific situations, in which a phenomenological, neurological, or theological account might break down or be less resilient than other truths. Likewise the issue may not be that some truths fall apart but that others have more promise. Some truths may go further than other truths; rather than quickly ending up in a tautological bind, they might lead to new horizons and questions. But in searching for where these truths decohere or open up the world, we are departing from our ethnographic problem and the diagram for fire is left far behind. Again this may seem to be a discussion set in the register of nosebleed metaphysics, but that is not the case; this is an anthropological problem and an ethnographic phenomenon. In the Vineyard, the nature of the divine assemblage shifts from moment to moment; sometimes God is a person, sometimes an idea, sometimes a hypothesis, and sometimes a fiction. This is not to say that God is not real but, rather, realty has a shimmering quality as the footing of believers shifts between various naturalistic and supernatural frames.[35] Anthropology must find a way to express this phenomenon.

GENERIC AND MULTIPLE ASSEMBLAGES

Focusing on how the diagram transforms and collapses through the appearance of differently calibrated and previously occluded virtual forces can give the illusion that this is a fragile and not readily transposable set of relations. It is true that the intensities that constitute some of the lines of force can wane to nothing; lines of force can also bifurcate depending on the qualities of the intensities, resulting in the expression of multiple fields.

But change is not necessarily dependent on a lack of robustness in the diagram: change can also take place while the same set of topological relations perdure. We have already claimed that at points of inflection the variation in the quality and intensity of lines of force results in differently constituted fields; however, that is not the only way this system can express itself with different results. These relations are also capable of being transposed, accelerated, or decelerated in ways that change the fields that are expressed. As we shall see, the *generic* nature of this assemblage and its capacity for being carried out with differently constituted scales (including temporal scales) is just as important as the capacity for changing into specific, differently constituted diagrams through the addition or subtraction of lines of forces.

What sort of variation comes with the play of scale? Earlier I suggested that at least some mutations in this diagram could lead to what is in effect the architectonic expression of an existential ethics. A global deceleration of the play of forces, however, results in something completely different: a religious ethics along the lines associated with the late Foucault, according to which external elements are selected and internalized (or in our parlance a relation between the scission of the sensorium and the willing) so that other aspects (the willful) can be mastered. When this diagram has such ethical effects, a subject takes the unveiling of the miraculous through an event—what would be called in a different language *revelation*—and as a result reworks what is willful and willing in relation to this miraculous aspect of the sensorium. There are also some slight shifts in the likely position of the willing and unwilling; when working in an ethical register, the willing and willful here are most likely to be aspects with loci primarily internal to the person—habituations, desires, and the like. Over time a different relation with the miraculous is produced; either through a submission or an identification, a different set of capabilities arises, placing the subjects' habitations and inclinations more in line with what is seen as the Good.

The ethical is not the only permutation. There is a different result when deceleration occurs with an expansion of scale beyond the individual to where there are multiple individuals constituting the willing field. Singular composite ethical subjects made of two or more discrete individuals may exist.[36] But when the qualitative features of the willing are being transformed in the play of forces, what we have is a politics, the collective becoming of a people as they simultaneously cohere and metamorphose. This is the miraculous as an important moment in a process of fabulation, catalyzing the creation of something bordering on a new polity—a people who are yet to come but may be brought into being by the miraculous.[37] As we will see, here the call of a people yet to come is the call of the already/not-yet, of a transformation that is at once immanent and present and yet is also a part of the future.

We should be clear that this is not the only form that a politics can take. The lines of force, the relation between affective energies and the forms that they engender in the fields they express, can work not to catalyze but inhibit the transformation of the set of relations. Such a program is rarely structured as being of the future: the various positive and negative transformations in the rates of change are attempts to make the future and the past the same. This can be complicated as it is sometimes a "return" to a virtual past that never existed. In certain moments there can be a great deal of transformation that functions to inhibit transformation more globally. This politics of return is a form of politics that is also found in enthusiast religion, though it is by no means unique to it; these two forms of politics sharing the same diagram can bleed and blend into each other even though at other times they can differentiate themselves from each other, not merely bifurcating, but also warring with one another. The same phenomenon can also be found in ethical practice; in addition to ethics of transformation, there are ethics of stasis, which are concerned not with deterritorializations, expansions, and transformations of the diagram but with territorializations that lock in certain sets of relations.

The nonsublating dialectic formed by stasis and change, territorialization and deterritorialization, is not the only way in which the lines of force that constitute this diagram can stay in the same topological relation and yet have different effects. As was stated earlier, no diagram ever stands alone—every instantiation of a diagram not only cuts through various "planes" or "strata" of language, bodies, and other materials but also shares these fields with other diagrams. Here what is the willing, willful, or unwilling is construed by other diagrams as citizens, laborers, consumers, and family members; at the very least, willing and willful aspects or moments instantiating this diagram are also aspects of persons and collectivities, who are in other times also capable of being classified in these other ways. And the transformations in fields effected by the play of intensities in these other diagrams that invoke these other categories are "communicated" to the charismatic diagram, just as the transformations effectuated by the charismatic diagram are relayed to elements of these other diagrams as well.

These two dynamics, that is scalar and qualitative shifts on the one hand and the imbrications of diagrams on the other, are the subjects of the following two chapters. These chapters will chart how variations in scale and global shifts in temporality, as well as the iteration of the diagram in differently constituted locales, result in the numerous forms that are common to the Vineyard and other similar enthusiastic religions. Chapter 7 addresses how these diagrams and the assemblages they express couple with other diagrams and assemblages. Through the traversals between various strata and diagrams, the diagram has effects beyond the immediacy of a moment of prayer, healing, prophecy, or deliverance; after all, for a social science, it is the effects beyond the religious moment that are as vital as the diagram for fire itself.

WORSHIP AS AN EXPRESSION OF THE DIAGRAM

We will see this diagram "operationalized" in the next few chapters, but the discussion in chapter 1 already showed the ways the diagram can be expressed in the various dimensions through which worship music unfolds. With worship music, there is the cocreation of a sensorium and an audience; this occurs through forces communicated during worship by words and the bodily and musical rhythms. These forces have feedback effects and build to certain plateaus, which means that at a certain point worship music, the worship leaders, and the worshippers temporarily become a single self-sustaining system. At times, aspects of the sensorium, supersaturated with affect and shot through by intensities that are markedly different from the quotidian world, seem to be indexing the presence of the Holy Spirit and therefore functioning as the miraculous sign. At the same time, these worship sessions have effects on the willing aspects of those present. The high-energy moments of worship can serve to increase the levels of their ardor; by contrast, the introspective moments can change the quality of that willingness, shifting or expanding what one is willing as reconsiderations of their relationship with God are catalyzed. And to the degree that the shifts effectuated during worship simultaneously summon up forces the will is arrayed against, they also create the willful and unwilling; the tiredness and distraction from God resulting from a week of work and family stress are set in relief at the same time that they become undone by the fervor and repentances that often come with worship.

This play of forces and movement points to worship as an assemblage. But worship is also imbricated with several categories of assemblage: familial; church organization and governance, which constitute the space where the charismatic diagram can be actualized; and the larger worship-music production and distribution complex (which is itself dependent on numerous other business-derived assemblages). Further, the expressions from these assemblages appear in other assemblages as different energies and enthusiasms are fed into those that constitute work, politics, recreation, and ethics. Even the body as an autonomous assemblage affects and is affected by the overlap between the forces it organizes and the forces organized by this diagrammatic worship. And each assemblage is an extensive concrete realization of the intensive lines of force that constitute the diagram that is particular to that constellation.

But worship is not all there is. There are actualizations of the diagram, in which the miraculous is more stark and the divisions expressed are more clearly delineated. These range from moments when the Bible itself speaks, instead of being merely read, to thunderous visions that come from God himself. And even the demonic can be an effect of this diagram, as in the moments when the miracle and the unwilling appear to have a darker and commanding edge. It is to all these varied instances that we turn next.

4. *Tolle, Lege*
Talking, Reading, and Hearing

The goal of this chapter is to trace how the charismatic diagram is actualized through some forms of talking, reading, and hearing from God. This is difficult because this diagram seemingly provides both too little and too much leeway. As we saw in the last chapter, the set of variables for the actualization of the charismatic diagram could seem rather limited; we are, after all, restricted to scale, site, qualitative affect, and speed. This limitation is made up for by the fact that this is an open system linked to a host of other diagrams that range from biology to the family and from capitalist practices to ecclesiological forms. In short, the question is not simply what the variables are but what other diagrams the Pentecostal-charismatic diagram is linked to at any particular moment as a result of these shared variables. While these are not technically variables, since they are situated "outside" the abstract space of the diagram, the traversing energies and affects carried over from the other diagrams that are also in the process of being actualized as assemblages have effects; they are what modulate the quality and constitution of the particular variables that are a part of the charismatic diagram's actualization (and vice versa).

BEING ALONE WITH GOD

We also discussed how on a larger scale, the diagram may have political effects, while on a smaller scale, its actualizations can work at the level of the person to function as an ethic in the Foucauldian sense of the term. Speaking of actualizations at the level of the person is not quite right, of course; no matter how small in scale a particular actualization is, it will never become an entirely private concern, in that it can never be solipsistic; an entirely private religiosity is just as impossible as a private language was for Wittgenstein.[1] The diagram always draws on material (including discursive material) that originated from outside the subject and has circuits that at least temporarily exit the boundaries of the physical body, even if they often loop back to the body.

Placing scare quotes around "alone" here is also applicable because under the logic of the diagram the person is also either presented with, or has his or her unity interrupted by, the miracle, which is a virtual index of the presence of God. This is not by accident. Through sermons, books, and advice, Vineyard believers are constantly encouraged to spend time alone with God, either during periods set aside for dedicated prayer (the start and end of the day are both good times for meditative prayer) or while they are out in the world. In the second case, one talks to God during quotidian activities—while on a walk or during the morning commute. Listening to recordings of praise music can also be done alone; while praise music may sometimes just be doing the work of creating an ambient atmosphere, there are other times when praise music can be personalized religious devotion.[2] Regardless of the method, regularity in practice, schedule, or both facilitates the process.

Just as spending time with God takes multiple forms, it also draws from multiple sources. First, the Vineyard understands the evangelical imperative to mean having a "relationship with God" through American presumptions of intimacies of affect and informalities in self-presentation. Those are not the only means, however; there is also a surprising amount of interest in *spiritual formation* in the Vineyard, a term used for self-disciplines that are intended to allow one to grow as a Christian. Because of the nature and historical source of a great deal of this literature, the pain and tears of medieval and early modern mystics exercise an imaginative force in the Vineyard. This may seem unlikely to those familiar with early Protestantism's anti-Catholicism. This interest, though, is still laundered through a Protestant sensibility. The historically inflected material usually appears as bits of popular evangelical self-help literature, or through the somewhat unsystematized free-range and omnivorous Vineyard imaginations; it does not usually appear in the actual texts authored by the mystics or through the wholesale adoption of their systems of spiritual discipline.[3]

When speaking to God, what do believers say? For some Vineyard believers, the statements are expressions of intents and anxieties, salted with requests. When recounting their prayer practice, some people make them sound like the sorts of casual conversations one holds with intimates. More common, though, people's accounts suggest that their conversations have an air of unrestrained drama to them. The latter talk about throwing themselves down on the floor, shedding tears, and experiencing feelings of submission and surrender. At times, accounts of prayer even reference attitudes of pride and resistance, reminders to God of perceived promises or claims of unfairness. These conversations run along the lines of protestations to God that the person was being faithful in taking up a ministry, job, or relationship on the basis of a perceived sign from God; in such cases, external difficulties, interior feelings of frustration and lack of fulfillment, or even instances of impending or outright failure, suggest that God did not hold up his part of the bargain. And finally, there are often complaints over a prompting or calling in the form of a sign, dream, or vision, in which it seems that God is making unreasonable demands, perhaps asking a person to shift careers, tithe a great amount, or confront someone about a topic (such as a compromised ethical position or moral lapse) that the person would rather not address.

There are reasons to suspect some rhetorical excess in these accounts of prayer as negotiation or complaint. The logic of the excess is to stress human limitation and divine sovereignty, with resistance highlighted so that later submission to God can stand out in proper relief. But as we will see, there are enough hints during forms of slightly larger-scale but still informal and intimate collective prayer to suggest that it is not entirely theater; the play of will and the unwilling seems inescapable. There are also enough accounts of people praying this way while in the process of struggling with some event—a familial illness or death, an unexpected career setback, or social or romantic isolation.[4] Given the unfolding and chronic nature of these issues, praying about them cannot be presented solely as a rhetorical moment in a larger narrative because often there is no real overarching narrative, only an ongoing, unresolved ordeal. Even in such cases of prolonged difficulty, ardor and energy will ebb at times; every evening or morning of prayer cannot be the Garden of Gethsemane in miniature. It is also common to hear people complain about a hollowness to prayer, which they speak about metaphorically as being in a "dry season." The people complaining about hollowness are often the same ones who in other times present accounts of the sort of emotionally charged prayer just discussed. When discussing these dry seasons, they say that when they pray, they are sleepy; their prayer feels formulaic and lacking in emotional investment; or there is no sense that anyone is listening.

There are also forms of prayer that are not structured (explicitly or implicitly) in a dialogic manner. In these instances, prayer involves quietness and an almost meditative attention to God, without verbalization or the production of a real-time, stream-of-conscious internal narrative. Sometimes it appears to involve a dilation of the senses and a lack of either policing or imposing order on mental associations. Other times people speak about prayer not as a relaxation of mental processes but as an exercise in constant intention and focus. This form of prayer can sometimes seem like a test of will; I remember speaking once with a parachurch organizer in his late twenties, who told me that he was trying to be constantly in prayer for an entire month, focusing on Jesus *whenever* he was awake. This is exceptional, but it suggests the elasticity of this kind of devotion, as well as the degree to which it can be carried out while someone remains engaged in the broader world; there is no particular reason to think that he was lying or exaggerating, but neither did he seem distracted or in other ways disengaged from the world around him.

READING THE BIBLE, AND LETTING THE BIBLE SPEAK

One of the most common ways of spending time with God is to connect with him by spending time alone with the Bible. Individual Bible study is a long-standing, though varying, evangelical discipline.[5] Devotional reading, which again occurs usually but not always either early in the morning or late in the evening, has specific methods to it. First there is the question of which sections of the Bible are to be read; some people will go over a particular section, cycling repeatedly through, for example, the book of Psalms (a perennial favorite); others use scheduled readings, such as the thematically oriented "Bible in a Year" or "New Testament in a Year" reading schedules that are available in Christian bookstores, online, or as smartphone and tablet applications. Many, though, let mood and chance determine what they will read and they may continue reading from a particular section or on the same theme as long as they feel that it is fresh or alive for them.

The specific version of the Bible that is relied on is not that important. There is a great deal of openness about which translation to use. Unlike some (rapidly shrinking) strands of English-language fundamentalists or classical Pentecostals, who have a "King James only" position, or denominations that lean toward translations they may have formally or informally endorsed or sponsored, people in the Vineyard choose their translations themselves. The choices are not unlimited, however, as was brought home at a Bible study in Southern California when a concerned and respected founder of the group pulled me aside to let me know that the apocalyptically orientated red letter Scofield Bible that I had brought to the meeting was, in his words, "dangerous."[6] Even so, his admonition was cautionary rather than a command, and not everyone in the Vineyard would have shared this view and offered this warning. Likewise, I never saw anyone using a Bible translation that was associated with forms of Christianity that most Vineyard members and a wider Evangelical movement find suspect; for instance, people did not whip out copies of the Seventh-day Adventists–affiliated *Clear Word Bible* or the Jehovah's Witnesses' *New World Translation* Bible.

These minor and implicit limitations on specific translations and editions of biblical texts aside, this openness suggests the kind of infinite translatability of divine texts that Walter Benjamin mentioned in his work on translation.[7] This runs against the fact, however, that Bible translations are not generally fungible. In choosing Bibles, many Vineyard believers are concerned not about the provenance of the various translations but about the scale of the translation: is it lexically oriented, working for a word-by-word level of exactness ("formal equivalence"); concerned with transmitting concepts ("dynamic equivalence"); or an effective reimagination of entire passages in scenes reworked to sound more natural to contemporary, American English–trained ears ("paraphrase equivalence")? What is striking is that not one of these modes of Bible translation is preferred. Rather, they are all available options.

This kind of variability is allowable because of the Bible's doubled status. On the one hand, the Bible is a public text, a set of universal truths that are valid because of their general applicability regardless of the vagaries of history or status. On the other hand, in the Vineyard, the Bible also has an equal and complementary status as an individual, albeit textually mediated, ahistorical and decontextualized speech act originating with God, and as addressing a particular reader at a particular moment.

An example of the Bible as both decontextualized text and individualized speech was recounted by a church member in his late twenties after he returned from a short-term mission trip. When I met him, he was a little frazzled.[8] He was soon to resume work at his postdoctoral clinical position in a laboratory, even though he felt as if he had just barely returned from Southeast Asia. While there, he had spent some time doing mission work with a population of Karen Christians, who were caught in a no-man's-land between the Burmese and Thai border. He was eager to speak about what he and the rest of the mission team had learned about the sociopolitical position of the people, the Karen's openly hostile relations with the Burmese military, and the peculiar personal dynamics that arise whenever one travels internationally with a large group. He even talked about the rather heavy bout of traveling illness he started to exhibit on the long return voyage from Chang Mai to Southern California. He was especially eager to tell about receiving what was for him a new gift, "prophetic scripture."

For this man, prophetic scripture had a meaning different from the usual one. Most evangelicals use the phrase to reference either historical events occurring after the date they were supposedly written down (e.g., the suffering servant passage in Isa. 53, which is read as predicting elements of Jesus's person and ministry) or narratives of eschatological events, the completion of which will occur in the future (e.g., elements of the books of Daniel and Revelation). Instead, he used prophetic scripture to describe receiving during prayer a "sense" (the word he used repeatedly) of a passage of scripture that was appropriate to the situation. As an example, he stated that before he and the rest of the team had visited the Karen, he had been drawn to Psalm 91, which he described as communicating "a sense of God's protection and provision through times of war." When the team arrived, he was surprised to discover that the Karen claimed to have had experiences that, as he described them, mapped almost perfectly ("verse by verse") onto the Psalm and had incorporated them into what he described as their "deliverance story" from the Burmese army.

This sense of prophetic scripture was not necessarily oriented around momentous events, experienced either by others or oneself, which were immediately fulfilled. Although he had received biblical passages regarding the Karen and biblical passages referencing issues that affected members of his mission team (he declined to reveal what the passages or the issues were on the grounds that doing so would breach their confidentiality), there was one instance of prophetic scripture whose referent was unclear until the very end of the mission trip. The first bit of scripture he received during prayer was Ezekiel 37—the famous "dry bones" verse, in which the narrator is commanded by God in a vision to prophesize over a field of desiccated skeletal remains, which God clothes in flesh and reanimates. My informant only realized the meaning after he had returned from his mission trip. On the way back, he fell rather sick and required medical attention both in transit and on arriving in the United States. One of the problems that was immediately identified during treatment was dehydration. As the fluid flowed in through the IV, he reported, "It literally felt like life was being put back into my veins so I kept thinking about this passage, because it pretty much captured what I was feeling so I felt that God gave me a sense that it would happen, that the end of it was the bones get restored back to life." This divine warning was more than a medical prognostication because it also spoke to his larger circumstances, specifically a sort of ennui that he had been feeling ever since he had moved to the suburbs of Southern California, which he had previously felt was monotonous and overly conservative. "It was significant to me because outside of the trip, I had been dealing with a loss of hope which I don't really know why, it was just something that I was dealing with, mostly because moving here is just not really realizing where I fit into . . . so the sense it was encouraging to go through the experience, to come out the other side I saw it as an affirmation of a hope that I had, basically that God is a good God who's doing things you know . . . so that's kind of the personal level." In short, there was an isomorphism among three elements—the scripture in question, the medical circumstances that had followed on the heels of a somewhat unusual short-term mission trip, and a longer period of general unease that had followed a change of circumstance.[9]

This is an elaborated example; the circumstances here obviously set everything into sharper relief. Still, similar transactions with scripture occur all the time when people read texts devotionally. A passage, sentence, or even at times just a word or phrase from the Bible will resonate with someone, capturing his or her imagination. This occurs at different speeds. A bit of scripture might affect someone like a thunderclap when it is read; for others a fragment of biblical text might increasingly nag the believer as he or she goes through the day without him or her immediately knowing why. Whether slowly or all at once, the decontextualized bit of text will map onto the person's life, providing clarity and pointing the way forward.

This mode of engagement with passages of scripture is not just different from the way the Bible is used as a general ethical charter in Christian communities (including the Vineyard), where it serves as a guide to what is proper individual and collective conduct. This style of reading is striking because it is also different from how most texts function generally. Usually the meaning of texts is structurally underdetermined as a result of the way the technology of writing is necessarily predicated on the absence of the author; this absence means that writings can be reread in all sorts of contexts that were unimagined by the author, producing combinations that do not relate to the original intent, since the veracity of an interpretation cannot be immediately affirmed by an author.[10] Therefore, the risk exists that new meanings may be imposed on the same text, set against multiple backdrops over time and space with each act of reading.

This acquisition of new meanings as a result of the displacement and recitation of texts may seem to be what is occurring with these Vineyard believers, but to rely on such an understanding would be to ignore an essential aspect of how this mode of reading functions. The difference between the personal meanings discovered during devotional readings and the usual practice of discovering or creating latent meanings through interrogating texts in situations and manners that the author did not take into account is this: In the Vineyard, these meanings are not accidents that come from the absence of the author but the opposite. These are *intended* readings, ratified by a presence. These individualized readings are not thought of as being part of the intention of the original author—there is no claim that Ezekiel was thinking of saline solutions when he penned the passage referenced above. Rather, the Holy Spirit is "speaking" through these passages, giving them the immediate intentionality of a personal communication.[11]

This sense of presence is not isolated to specific revelatory moments of individualized biblical reading; a similar consciousness of presence can be seen in moments when the Bible is "read" in a group. One example is church meetings, where it is common for a pastor to read a biblical passage aloud either before or during the course of his sermon. If the passage is longer than a line or two, and especially if the text will be the main focus of the discussion, the pastor will commonly improvise a short invocatory prayer immediately before the reading. A typical, and in fact almost architectonic, exemplar of the prayer is the one below:

> Father, again we invite your presence, again we say, Lord, come, and anything that I might say is that from you, that you would bring it close to the heart, make it change us, God, and anything I say that is not from you, Lord, that you would not allow them to remember at all, so that it would just be about you today and what you desire, and Lord I know that your spirit is the convictor of truth; Spirit do your job, do your thing, we pray this in Jesus name. Amen.[12]

This short opening prayer communicates the desire that the biblical passage about to be read find an effective re-expression in this particular moment through a doubled agency: that God, acting on the pastor as he exposits on these biblical passages, allow for written language to work as spoken language is often imagined to work: as an immediate transmission particular to the moment and in line with the intent of the speaker. This guaranteeing or ratifying presence also returns us to the question of the multiplicity of acceptable biblical translations; various translations are all considered to be workable because these transformations of the original biblical text do not vitiate the guiding hand of God or the Holy Spirit. This is a situation unlike that found in translations of conventional texts, for which the problem of recontextualization that comes from authorial absence during the act of reading is exacerbated by having the material reconstituted in a foreign language. By way of contrast, in these cases the ultimate author of the books of the Bible, the God who inspired and informed whatever earthly scribe is credited with originally penning a particular book, is still able to exercise influence directly on the reader as he or she takes in the text.

It is important to note that the means through which this supplemented communicative act is being effectuated by God or the Holy Spirit are mysterious. No earthly mechanisms identify divine speech in biblical writing; there is no indication of divine presence in speech outside an otherwise seemingly unaccountable saliency, an insistence at the level of emotion or a seemingly statistically improbable fit with a particular personal circumstance that no early author could have anticipated. This is a miraculous intervention or, rather, a reterritorialization of texts, affects, and circumstance as a miraculous sign and a cleaving of the will into willing aspects that are either catalyzed by, or working in accordance, with the miraculous sign and the willful and unwilling aspects of the person and the circumstances that would resist it. For the young man undertaking the short-term mission, that unwilling element is either a lagging body or a lack of enthusiasm springing from the stultifying conformity of the Southern California condominium suburbs.

In this, though, these moments of devotional reading are no different from what is brought about by other means of private prayer, such as quietly soaking in the presence of God or of prayer as a long discursive exchange, as discussed above. Quiet solitary prayer is often not all that solitary. It is common for people to experience the presence of God, Jesus, or the Holy Spirit during prayer. This can occur both in more meditative forms of prayer and in discursive prayer, in which there is an *imploring* of God. What is striking is that sometimes there is not merely a presence but also an *answer*. God speaks, at times audibly and at other times in ways that are even more decentering than hearing voices. The next section discusses how these other forms of prayer and the seeming presence of an active response from God open up similar actualizations of the diagram.

SURPRISE, VOICE, AND VERSE

What of the times when God initiates the conversation on his own?

The first time he heard from God, he was at a party. God's message was this: "Do you, do you feel lucky?" Years later, he would become an influential Vineyard pastor at a successful, midsized California fellowship, but at the time God spoke to him, he was a freshman in a large Southern California university. He had left behind his family's conventional mountain-state evangelicalism and rather rapidly developed a drug and alcohol habit after he arrived in California. During his first year at university, he'd started using drugs even before breakfast; his level of habituation was such that he had to drink during class simply to maintain his equilibrium. He even had to drink to get to sleep at night. While he was not experiencing full delirium tremors, he would have the jitters if he was unable to drink.

This was his situation when he was attending a party in one of the suburban communities that skirt the fringes of major Southern California research universities. Years later, he offered the following account of his experience of hearing from God that evening while he was standing in the back of the house, near the beer keg:

> I was at a party one night, and just felt that God was speaking to me kinda out of the blue, you know. The specific thing I thought he was saying, it was funny, "Do you, do you feel lucky?" I had always felt that this [his use of drugs and alcohol] would not catch up with me and all of a sudden realizing you know, I think that this is gonna catch up with me, all of a sudden it was like my confidence was shaken and I certainly don't think that God's out there protecting me when I'm doing this I don't, I don't, a deep confidence shaking . . .
>
> It has the communicative component in that it was time limited, I know where I was at his party when it happened, it wasn't a general impression through the night. I was standing on the back porch of a house in [the neighborhood]. I know a couple of the people, who were right around me, I can still remember where I was and it was a powerful gut kinda, yah, impression. It wasn't an audible voice, it was no shining light.

This was not the only time he would hear from God in this way. Shortly after this event, a university counselor at this secular institution took the unusual step of praying with him; as the future pastor recounts it, from this point forward he completely stopped using drugs (though he mentioned that he also started attending substance-abuse support groups). This same counselor also brought him to the Vineyard church that he would end up pastoring nearly fifteen years later. After becoming involved in this church, he found that his grades improved radically. His original plan of going to law school was coming closer to being realized as he approached graduation.

He was at the cusp of graduate school when God spoke to him again:

> When I felt called into ministry, I felt God speak strongly enough that I to this I day, like I almost, I wonder if someone was standing next to me would they hear something. I think no, they wouldn't have, but it was very much an in the ears kind of thing. I was planning on going to law school, I had applications in my backpack, I was walking by Central Library in [a] grove in late spring as the Sun was going down, and I know where I was and I felt God say "Go To Seminary." Went home, threw away my law applications, called my parents, said forget eight years of preparation for law school, I'm going to seminary! It was pretty decisive [laugh] so in that case, very radical, but even then, was it

audible, no, was there light, no, but it was, it would seem strange to use the word impression, I would want to keep some vocal aspect in the language, I heard God, but I don't know that the membrane in my eardrum resonated.

To his mind, the variations between the two experiences were not a function of a growing ability on his part to discern God but, rather, a function of the different type of communication that each situation required in order to best effectuate God's intent:

What it reminds me of is when I speak to my kids, I use a lot of different voices, I convey tenderness, I convey priority, I can convey emergency. And when I felt called into ministry it was gallant, a huge loud strong call to follow Jesus that I understood that these were the words clearly. I would give my life to ministry. And I've never doubted since that day ever that I would be in ministry my whole life. Um, and that was, ninety-three, so that was a while ago, ten years, and I haven't considered other career options, really, they're not open [laugh] they're not open to me, that's what I'm doing with my life. But the rededication moment, that was more of an invention or a question moment from the lord in the same way that I would ask a question, it wasn't a command, it was, you know, do you feel lucky.

Variation for this pastor is just voicing. Like other speech, it is intent and context that control expression.

What should we make of this account? The previous section was concerned with the phenomenon of talking to God through prayer and biblical texts, whereas here the question is what happens when God speaks. There are some similarities between the two. Recall how the former process functions: A bit of writing becomes personal communication instead of generally directed text when it is decontextualized from the larger scriptural passages, in which it is embedded. This text becomes joined to a "divine" assemblage constituted out of God (as an ideational or actual entity), ideas about God's immediacy, and a psychic or physical sense of presence. Further, the appearance of this assemblage is triggered by crossing the saliency thresholds separating, on the one side, a sense of the quotidian and of what are merely odd chance occurrences and on the other, occurrences so unlikely that they are subjectively understood as divine action indifferent to a natural order. The salient text becomes a miraculous sign that determines what is proper will and what is willfulness or being unwilling.

The two events recounted above about the experience of hearing from God may appear to be different from regular, solitary prayer practice, or from the use of biblical material as an individualizing mode of communication. Here, instead of a scrap of text located in an exterior, consensually recognized book becoming salient, we have unbidden, disruptive moments where something experientially close to a voice breaks in, hailing the individual but in a way in which other bystanders presumably would not hear. Further, this kind of immediate "vocal" event seems to have a capacity for greater transformation. The first event, a backyard communication during a party, made the man a believer at least in the sense of becoming *devout*, in that it seemed the conceptual and linguistic materials necessary to mark material as miraculous were already present, most likely gathered during his childhood (note that *who* was communicating with him was never really in question, at least not as the narrative was presented). The second communication was equally transformative, causing an immediate departure from a long-planned life course.

Now the quasi-vocative nature of the event may make it appear dissimilar from the kind of personally oriented saliency seen with reterritorialized biblical verses; believing a passage of already-sacred but otherwise sensorially and commonly accessible text might have some supplemental relevance is different from hearing voices. This is to a degree true in that we are dealing with what is perceived as different media. But the difference between divine voice and biblical text is less apparent when we consider the fact that the incorporation of voices is the result of crossing thresholds similar to those found in reading as a form of divine hailing.

The first threshold governs the confluence of forces that must act together to effectuate something *like* a sound. In others words, there must be an intensification of processes—internal, external, or both—that will allow some experience to capture a person's attention and be recognized and attended to as a sensation.

The second barrier, though, is a crossing of the evidential threshold necessary for something to be adjudicated as proximately being caused by an agency situated outside the body rather than within it. It is a threshold not regarding the *saliency* but, rather, *exteriority* of the experience. The quasi-vocal events narrated above, even as they are presented by someone convinced of their divine origin, could counterfactually have been given a psychological explanation by the subject; indeed, we can see that the first speech event involving God could have been characterized as effectively an internal realization. However, despite its description as a "gut impression" without an "audible voice" or a "shining light," it was still understood as the immediate product of an exterior agency.

It is that final attribution of origin that marks another threshold. Causation in most cases is effectively an automated or passive phenomenon, one that requires little effort, or at least little effort that is available for conscious introspection. Therefore, to view the attribution of causation as a deliberate decision would be a mistake (though there is of course the possibility that a later conscious elaboration could recode a phenomenon). If we see the attribution to divine causation here as also being a passive phenomenon, as we do the attribution of other causations, we still have to ask which elements mark the communication as different, as exterior. In the two accounts given above, what stands out about them both is that the events *were contrary to the will and expectations of the individual at the time the individual experienced them*. At the party, the content of the communication was contrary to the future pastor's stated sense of the state of affairs: that is, there was no risk associated with a particular lifestyle. The content of the communication certainly went against his will, which he described as being ensnarled by substance abuse. And there was also an element of temporal restriction. Even if the instances of hearing from God had lasting effects and thus in a way persisted, they were both isolatable as happening at particular moments. Finally, this was in a sense an unanticipated communication. The same could be said about the communication on campus: a message surprising in strength and clarity but also in the way that it demanded the sudden abandonment of a very long-term plan and hence a reconstitution of what was willed and willful.

In total, both were taken as being divine communications having an external origin, even though one was merely an impression and the other was classed as *effectively* a vocal event. What marked these events as being of external origin was actually the crossing of a series of subsidiary thresholds (degree of variance with the will, degree of suddenness, relative lack of anticipation); these thresholds demarcated an affective space of *surprise*. This is important because surprise travels light. It would be wrong to say that surprise and associated phenomena like the startle reflex are never culturally elaborated; there are ethnopsychological conditions, like latah in Southeast Asia, for instance, that suggest surprise is an emotion that can be elaborated along very specific lines and actualized in different ways.[13] This aside, though, it seems clear that surprise, however elaborated, is a candidate for consideration as an effectively transhuman affective register that further responds to an event not anticipated at the moment of its occurrence.[14] This is important because it means one of the properties of surprise is that it is relatively transportable, ranging from nineteenth-century Methodist wilderness camps to turn-of-the-twentieth-century urban Los Angeles, from Latin America and Africa to, finally, the suburbs of Southern California.

A correlation between surprise and outward causation should not be that surprising. It is difficult to "surprise oneself," or at least to startle oneself intentionally. It should also be noted that one of the characteristics of surprise as an affect is its capacity to be bundled either simultaneously or sequentially with other affects so as to give it a number of generally eudemonic or anxiety-provoking valances. But what is also telling is the larger correlation of charismatic/Pentecostal-type experience with surprise more generally.[15] As the Pentecostal philosopher James K.A. Smith put it, Pentecostalism is characterized as "a position of radical openness to God, and in particular, openness to God doing something differently or new."[16] Even more to the point, this is not just a valuation of surprise but a practice of surprise as well: "One of the reasons Pentecostal spirituality is so often linked to spontaneity is that Pentecostal worship makes room for the unexpected. Indeed, we might say that, for Pentecostals, the unexpected is expected, the surprising comes as no surprise."[17]

A correlation of charismata with surprise also fits in with what Vineyard believers say about the "character" of God. As mentioned earlier, it is common for people in the Vineyard to say that God is "messy," a statement that covers a lot of ground; not only does this suggest a disruptive element to the work of the spirit during collective prayer and worship but it is often used as a shorthand to refer to the belief that acting as an ethical Christian complicates rather than simplifies life. In the opinion of Vineyard believers, ethical problems ramify rather than become more simple as one tries to "act like Jesus" in a world where it is not always clear what Jesus would do.[18] This concept of messiness is also used to suggest that God often acts in ways that are contrary to expectations. God is not necessarily concerned with human plans; he often makes requests or imposes situations that go against the expectations and desires of believers. And while this messiness is not limited to the kind of practices that can be considered actualizations of the charismatic diagram, the somewhat wild ways that charismata are carried out are certainly a large part of what people mean when they use this term.

Therefore, at the level of the ethical, experiential, and ontological, God is about surprise. And this centrality of surprise is why biblical verse as conscious divine communication is not that different from hearing God speak directly. Recall that what set biblical verses apart as a special form of communication was an unanticipated relevance not just to the current age but to a particular individual at a particular moment. This too is a function of surprise. It is admittedly a less heightened form of surprise, but as we have argued throughout, what gives specific events their particular grain is that much of the affect and many of the energies involved are on a relative gradient with one another. The lessened gradient for surprise works in combination with the fact that even at its most deterritorialized text naturally has a slightly different temporal window than vocative divine communication. Biblical texts preexist at the moment they are read, and believers often will have had prior contact not just with the Bible in general but with that specific snippet of text in particular; further, unlike vocative events, texts can be revisited after the "salient event," when it has been sutured to a specific life or situation. Finally, the capacity to arrange the circumstances so that a salient event occurs with text lies more with the readers, even if they cannot control it; people can turn to the Bible looking for answers, though it should be remembered that answers are not guaranteed. Contrast that with the divine vocative event. One can choose to listen to God, engaging in prayer or opening oneself to his message, but one cannot decide to *hear* God; it is by definition something that happens to a passive recipient.

In each case, surprise is an aspect of the diagram's actualization, a necessary aspect of the scission of the sensorium (what is and is not divine action) and the scission of the will into the willing and the unwilling (the surprise of the unanticipated semiotic force of the message). This suggests a more general statement: given the primacy of surprise, we can see that it is to some degree the controlling element. For the diagram to hold together, therefore, there must be *at least a mild amount of surprise or, at the minimum, a feeling of an absence of individual causative agency by those beings heralded as at least in part* willing or unwilling/willful. Again, as the comparison of verse and voice suggests, there does not always need to be a high *level* of surprise. The levels of variance are not just in the intensity of affects involved or in the speed with which things occur but also in the various thresholds as they exist for a particular person in a particular circumstance.

If surprise is what indexes events as divine in causation and if gradients in affect and in the temporality of the media used allow for the difference between, say, the Bible and the voice of God as a communicative modality, we still have a pressing question. While we have explained the difference *between* how voice and verse is expressed, we have not accounted for different actualizations *of* voice. To look for patterns in the various actualizations, we need to turn to another set of experiences of "hearing from God." This example is taken from a Korean American Vineyard pastor, who at the time of our conversation was employed overseeing a local branch of a nondenominational national parachurch that supported undergraduate Christian university students. This narrative relates how after drifting away from the Church he heard from God, which resulted in a renewed dedication to a charismaticized evangelicalism:

> I had come home in the middle of my freshman year and uh, I guess I didn't realize it then, but my parents could see something because they were trying to get me to go to this retreat that their church was holding, and I didn't want to go, and that was actually the first time really I had ever said anything like that to my parents, and so I think I jarred them a little bit, and they said, hey um your friends will be there, and I'll pay for it and, just kind of sell it. And I decided to go, 'cause my friends are there, you know, my old church friends. And then when I got there, the person that was asked to speak that weekend was terrible, absolutely horrendous two hours on stuff like de—like think about your death, really boring, completely had no point except to make us feel bad, it was typical Korean American spirituality you know, guilt you into wanting Jesus so bad that you'll feel some catharsis at the end of it.
>
> And they turn off the lights, and the pastor starts praying for people individually, and it's a pretty crazy scene, the pastor, apparently, hits you on the back, pretty hard, and, uh, I don't want a piece of that at all. It does not sound fun. So, I uh, when he came close to me I just moved to another corner, I continued to avoid him, they caught me once and asked do you want me to pray for you and I said no, no I'm fine and they went to another person, so I went away as far as possible. And when I finally got a place to be alone in the quiet at just staring at what's going on, I swear that I, uh, I heard a voice but it wasn't an audible voice, it would be as if my own consciousness was speaking to me but it felt as if it was coming externally and not of my own, um, it's like you hear it as your own thought but you know that it's more than your own thought, and I hear you've been far from me and it was just that sentence that undid me, and I started weeping and realized, well, that's right, [chuckle] at that point I was going to try to be different.
>
> The voice doesn't sound any different. Doesn't echo, doesn't boom, doesn't sound like thunder, it sounds like your own voice, the pronouns were switched, but I can do that to myself, too, it's like '"Jacob, come on, get up, get to it,"' you can give yourself a pep talk
>
> It's not a hunch. There is a certain certainty.

This account is not unlike the first one. There are obvious situational differences (this venue being a religious retreat rather than a party) and similarities (the two people are close in age, and both have recently begun their undergraduate university educations). But even more notable was the understated nature of the voice in both narratives: distinct, unanticipated, and punctual but notably similar to the sorts of sensations and internal monologues that constitute a great deal of day-to-day, late modern subjectivity.

What is also worth noting, though, is the way that this contrasts with a later experience of voice, which also occurred at a retreat:

> So, the other story then, my sophomore year, it's the fall semester, and um I'm fired up, I'm back on the [inaudible—road?], I'm back in the saddle, trying to figure out what I should do with my life, I'm an electrical engineer at the time, I was studying to be one and I'm at this retreat and it's the last night of the retreat and it's a Korean American setting, so when they ask you to pray, everyone's praying all at once, it's a loud, ecstatic [inaudible] and uh it's so loud actually that it's, it's a little annoying, but it's loud and people are going for it, and I feel I should go for it uh, and then in the middle of all that, and again I get an impression, and that's really the best I can say, like a hunch, that somebody's looking at you, a feeling of "I need to get out," 'cause I feel that God wants to tell me something. So with that I go okay so why not, right? It doesn't hurt, actually back then I probably would have— there was a certainty about that—I just got up and left, went upstairs two level floors, a very quiet place and then I said I remember praying God what do you want to me to know? And I saw in my minds eyes while they were closed, I saw the word ministry, just the word ministry flash like white on black, just flashed in my mind and I understood that to mean full-time vocational ministry, give up your uh give up your current training the direction you're going and head in my direction head into ministry. So I couldn't shake it, right, it could have meant anything at the time but that was the meaning that I received from it and no, I said no, there's no way I'm going that, I did not come to Boston to do this that's the honest conversation no! I don't think so that is not why I've come and then I see the word ministry flash again whoosh [flashing hands] like this in my mind's eye and I said ok, so let's say that its true, kinda reasoning with God if that's true I'm gonna go in the trade if I think it should be, and no one else thinks I should be, so at the time I said if this is from you, you're going to have to let me know from somebody else, sorta like golden, like putting up a fleece and seeing what happens.[19] So that's what I did and uh I stopped praying and went back downstairs and they were getting done and uh there was a campfire thing and uh, I guess at this campfire they asked me to tell a story so I just told a story, telling a story around the campfire about people coming to God, there were parallels. Stupid short story, people were digging it, loving it, and at the end of it, at the end of it, we're all milling around and this senior from, uh, the same college group that I was a part of, she's a few years older than I am, came up to me and said Jacob, uh, kinda looked at me kinda puzzled and said "Have you ever thought about going into full-time ministry? You'd be really good at it" and I just looked at her thinking, and uh in that moment, knowing that was a confirmation, at least that's what everything felt like just the fact

that—I asked her "Who told you to say that?" And she just said "I just felt like I was supposed to tell you that so."

There are three things to note about this particular set of accounts. First, the sensory element seemed to be more elaborated. The original vocal event that led to the man's rededicating himself to Christianity took the form of something that he perceived as the continual patter of an interior monologue only more striking, which gave him the impression that its origin was external. The second is that instead of being verbal, the sign itself had a visual component: a word that not only flashed onto the field of vision but did so repeatedly.

The other thing to note is there was something somewhat trope-like about the call to the ministry. Observe that, with the exception of the switch from a vocal to a visual modality, the call to ministry was not that different from the call to seminary in the earlier case. This is not too surprising; in the second case, we have someone trained since childhood in an ecstatic form of Christianity. Even if there were a dip in enthusiasm for the practice at the time the first summons took place, he was presumably more familiar with the form than was the future Vineyard pastor, who heard from God from the back porch of a party. This suggests some form of typification occurred in the expression of the diagram. Yet typification would seem to threaten a routinization of these experiences and therefore would be a nullification of the aspect of surprise that was just posited as an essential affective tone for the diagram's realization. This will become important later on.

The third observation is that this experience was not taken at face value. Testing its validity required additional confirmation, a process that is usually called "discernment" (though discernment can also be used to refer to a broader set of practices).

While discernment is an aspect that will be dealt with shortly, we must first address the elaboration and typification of charismata. These two phenomena also pose a particular challenge to the line of thought that we are engaging in here. After all, if we can say that something is "typical," then this opens us up to judgments made on the basis of comparison. The idea of "better or worse" instances suggests there is some sort of telos or goal internal to the diagram. The idea of a telos suggests that we can use the internal structure of the diagram to make judgments about better- or worse-realized instances of the diagram; for instance, we could say that the more audible voice commanding "go to seminary" and the visual manifestation of the word *ministry* are both more *complete* expressions and thus closer to the *ideal* expression. While this makes a certain sense, remember that the diagram was produced so that it could be adequate not just for the American charismatic Christianity of the early twenty-first century but also for the long line of enthusiastic religions that led to the Vineyard, exist in parallel to the Vineyard, and came after the Vineyard. The attraction of diagrammatic thinking here is that it allows for infinite variation while not allowing just anything to be counted as an instance of the diagram. This feature would be undone if we could in theory rank the various manifestations along the lines of more or less, better or worse.

If as seems to be the case with the two narratives related here we are going to have something that appears to be in effect a telos, either in terms of its elaboration or its typification, this can only be an effect of the other diagrams that the charismatic diagram is imbricated with at a particular moment. This at once sharpens and limits the charismatic diagram's scope. There are practices that train the mind and body, preshaping the likely trajectories that form the interactions of the constitutive lines of forces. In other words, it is not that there are purer expressions of the diagram but that the forces being threaded through the diagram in this particular milieu tend increasingly to urge the expression of the diagram in a particular direction. It appears that what we have is the working toward a purer expression, but what we actually have is a general drift toward one particular expression that is framed as the end, rather than as just another potentiality in the field assayed by the diagram. No particular telos preexists but is rather imminent on the activation of the diagram, that is, "called forth by the conditions."[20]

That was the case here. In both accounts, the second time the men heard from God was arguably different because the various thresholds for what count as salience, surprise, and external origination of material in the sensorium had been recalibrated; simultaneously, both the affective states involved and the capacity for the men to be affected had been increased. There had been in a sense an education of the senses, which was the result of the idea of a pedagogy of the spirit that goes back to the charismaticization of the church growth movement. The questions of course are how did this education occur and what other work do Vineyard typifications and elaborations perform.

5. The Living Room Seminars
Pedagogies of the Spirit, Typification, and Elaboration

This chapter takes up where the last chapter closed. Chapter 4 ended with the observation that pedagogy, particularly as typification and elaboration, is important in sharpening and constricting the form in which miracles appear. There has been a great deal written in anthropology on how Pentecostal experience is the result of a pedagogy, an attempt to craft an ethically valued self.[1] Similarly, there has been work that shows much of Pentecostal practice is in effect the result of material-technical means and therefore presumably is open to mastery by way of attention to technique.[2]

The idea of a pedagogy of the spirit is an acceptable conscious framing within the Vineyard as well. As we saw earlier, the Vineyard is predicated on the idea that gifts of the spirit are in essence teachable: an important turning point in the Vineyard's history was John Wimber's seminar on miracles as an applied practice at the Fuller School of World Mission, which was a central institution in the development of twentieth-century evangelicalism.[3] This tradition continues today. A small coterie of experts, often pastors but sometimes gifted layman, circulates through the body of the Vineyard, stopping at a church for a day or two to give talks or run seminars on the subject.

These seminars are mostly didactic, but like Wimber's original class, they are shot through with hands-on moments. During one Friday night conference I attended, we sat on folding chairs in a rented grade school auditorium as the speaker paced excitedly back and forth. He told us that hearing from God was possible if one could simply focus on what God has to say in the same way that you have to purposefully tune into a radio station if you want to hear it. God, he explained to us, does not have trouble speaking; rather, we have trouble listening. As a preliminary practice, we were told to first clear our minds and then attend to what thoughts bubbled up. Those thoughts, it was suggested, might be from God. After about a minute or two of awkward silence, the speaker asked for volunteers willing to relate what they had experienced. A woman in her early twenties said what sprang up for her was the Hanna-Barbera cartoon character "Grape Ape," adding she "thought it was cool" that God knew that purple was her "favorite color."

Conferences of various sizes are vehicles for training people to engage in hearing from God, but the more effective training is often done one on one or in small groups. During my fieldwork, I saw an example of what this looks like while I was attending a weekly Bible study, prayer, and discussion session. Over a two-month period, I saw a group of well-educated believers in various stages of what the Vineyard would call spiritual maturity. These believers would wrestle with the techniques taught as they shifted from having them modeled for them to being asked to engage in this work themselves. While not everyone ended up adopting these practices as part of how they engaged with both God and the world, many did. These sessions not only allowed us to understand what this pedagogical arc can look like but also helped us to get a better grasp on how typification and elaboration sculpt actualizations of the diagram.

Almost all of my fieldwork with the Vineyard occurred in office parks, coffee shops, repurposed school auditoriums, or condominium living rooms. My time with this small group was no different. The small group meetings sometimes took place in a suburban living room or a family room in graduate-student housing, but most were held on the fourth floor of a condominium in a pseudo-adobe, Southwestern-style development with palm trees lined up in regimental fashion on the crowded streets that circumscribed it. The condominium itself was owned by a telecommunications engineer, but the group was run by a married professional couple (he was a research psychologist, she a lawyer), who had been attending Vineyard churches since they met in college. Membership was made up of various counselors, social workers, physicians, graduate students, campus ministers, scientists, nurses, political activists, charity nongovernmental organization workers, white-collar office workers, and even an aspiring theatrical dancer. Like most small groups (sometimes called "community groups"), it was formally affiliated with a specific Vineyard church, and most of its members attended that church on a regular basis. In this case, the label "small group" was a bit of a misnomer. Even though it was not even a year old, it had grown quickly; sometimes more than fifteen people would crowd into the living room.

The topic this evening was on hearing from God, something that the other meetings had been working toward for several weeks. The church itself had just finished a weeklong prayer vigil, with church members gathering in various public spaces at dawn, noon, and dusk to pray collectively for their community. The two small group leaders had started organizing the group to shift away from Bible study or discussions, which had been the typical concerns so far, in favor of a focus on what they called "evenings of prayer and praise." This passage from my field notes records that April, one of the co-organizers, would typically start out these evenings with a short prayer and some instructions. She began by encouraging people to

> take chances, to stretch [yourselves this evening] if God wants you to do something different. She discuss[ed] prophecy, stressing the fact that if you get [a] prophecy for someone (this seems to be what she was primarily interested in), you should first pray over it to see if [you] should share it and then . . . if you're the person receiving it, you need to be the judge of whether it is "from God" or not. She [did] give one pointer, though—"If it is in any way discouraging, that's not God."

After these instructions, the organizers took a few prayer requests from the group. The idea was for people to ask for prayers regarding issues that were bothering them and receive some solace that would allow them to focus their minds on what was to come.

April then initiated the central part of the evening of praise and worship, addressing God directly while praying out loud. That night her prayer was a plea for members who felt guilty because they hadn't talked to God in a while (or hadn't ever talked to him, she added as an afterthought) to ask her to petition God to have the block removed. She encouraged people to "soak in the spirit," a phrase that means to relax and let the Holy Spirit course through you. As she encouraged people to do this, she started to weave into her conversation/prayer a very quiet, subvocal form of speaking in tongues that was common among more experienced members of the Vineyard. Her soft breathy rustling never interrupted her speech but padded out the normally silent moments between phrases. In the background, her husband played praise music on acoustic guitar; his playing was not performed in a highly structured verse-chorus-verse manner but in a purposefully droning, rambling way that did not have the structure of pop music but rather sketched out what the anthropologist Gregory Bateson called plateaus: climax-free zones of sustained emotional tonalities.[4] Slowly April's prayers shifted almost entirely to tongues, and the group started to decohere. People broke off from the circle and scattered throughout the living room. Some sat or stood by themselves in meditative prayer, often with their hands half raised, as if they were receiving grace directly from the heavens; others formed smaller groups of two or three, where they prayed over someone who had earlier voiced specific concerns. One cluster focused on a woman who was working for a fiscally faltering, local Christian charity that assisted the poor (weeks later, the charity would suddenly close its doors for good). Laying hands on her, another women called out loud that "God is a God that is for the poor, we know that from scripture, we know that from the work of [name of charity], God is the God of the poor, the oppressed, the prisoner!" As she said that, she drew money from her pockets and threw it on the ground as a "free public donation" (as the night went on, other members of the group also contributed to the charity, some in similarly dramatic ways and others in a much more understated manner).

At one point, April walked up to where I was sitting and said she had a word for me; she asked if it were all right if she shared it and I nodded. She then said God had let her know he himself would answer whatever research-related questions I had. She said she did not know what this meant; she then prayed over me, asking God to assist me with my dissertation and that I would get my questions answered.

Later in the evening while he was still playing the guitar the other coleader, David, leaned in and asked me sotto voice if I would be comfortable praying over one of the younger group members, who was named Emma. I said no. He smiled and nodded in a nervous agreeable manner. At that point I knew full well I was going to have to do it anyway, but I got up to go to the bathroom first to get up the courage. When I got back (feeling not unlike a junior high school student asking someone to dance for the first time), I asked Emma if it would be all right if I prayed over her. She agreed, smiling, and I laid my hands on her back; I noticed as I did so that I unconsciously chose to stand behind her, where I could not get a good look at her face as I prayed and so that I could stretch my hands out flat, getting the most skin contact possible. After a brief pause, I decided to center the prayer on her upcoming visit to New York City, one of the few things I knew about her. I then tried speaking in the same manner I had heard other Vineyard believers use so many times during my fieldwork—an odd mix of the colloquial and the biblical that is often built around chiastic inversions of common phrases. Awkwardly opening with "Father God," I requested that God "help Emma go to the city, to let her swallow it whole." I asked that "you [God] assist her in not disappearing into the crowd, in not letting her feel like a one-in-a-million face but that you instead find her a one-in-a-million job, a perfect job that is reverse engineered from her resume to match with her perfectly, and that when she has problems, and she will have problems, she doesn't forget who she is" (later in the evening, I apologized to her for my "bush league prayer"). After about an hour, the energy in the room sank, the guitar was put away, and people started talking about more plebeian topics, including a sustained discussion about basketball.

Evenings like these were surprising to many of the people, who were new to the small group, this church, or the Vineyard in general; I was even a little taken aback by them myself because of the degree of involvement that was demanded of everyone present (including the anthropologist). But for the coleaders of the group, the level of participation they were seeing still fell short of what they had hoped for. In conversations outside the group, they kept saying they wished that group members would "stretch" more. They were also worried that members of this group were too cerebral, to scholastic, to throw themselves into the experiential deep end of Vineyard religiosity.

THE SHABBAT DEBATES

After a few more weeks went by, the small group leaders decided to follow Vineyard tradition and make the problem more explicitly pedagogical; they dedicated a special session of the evening group to learning how to "hear from God." The buildup to this was considerable. This particular evening session was telegraphed by the leaders a few weeks in advance, which was rare as they usually claimed they did not have overarching plans but would follow the day-to-day promptings of the Holy Spirit. This topic also seemed to capture the imagination of the small group itself. A group consensus even emerged that hearing from God should also be the discussion topic of the next "Shabbat dinner," an irregularly scheduled Saturday evening communal dinner that many members of the group attended. This dinner, while not in any way formally affiliated with the church or small group, had a good deal of overlap with small group membership (such rituals, consciously modeled on Jewish practices, are not uncommon in American evangelicalism).[5] The next Shabbat fell a few days before the planned small group session that inspired it, so it was a good way of identifying where people were in relation to the topic.

Saturday evening came. In a rented house designed in the arts and crafts style and located in a formerly rough but rapidly gentrifying neighborhood at the edge of downtown, some of the more conservatively attired small group members rubbed shoulders with guests with nose rings and tattoos. Many of those from outside the small group could be generously classified as "Christian hipsters," a part of the first wave of what is called the "Emergent Church" movement.[6] The first thing I saw when I walked through the door was a beat-up laptop sitting on a thrift store desk; the laptop was covered with "free the slaves" stickers, which had been slapped onto it in what looked like a purposefully careless manner. Piles of books were scattered about. A few people in a corner were excitedly discussing agricultural dumping; they considered it to be a social justice issue, and though none of them had a social science background, they were batting about ideas for producing a study to back up their arguments. At one point, they turned to me with a question about how to construct a statistical survey. During that exchange, I fell into a discussion with a recent addition to the group, a law school graduate from Guatemala, who had converted from Catholicism and moved to the United States with his wife, an American, who was being trained as a nurse-practitioner; he mentioned that his family members, who had a lot of ties with Opus Dei, were not happy about these recent decisions.

The sun finally fell, the signal for the Shabbat dinner ritual to officially begin. Everyone sat around a series of small tables, jury-rigged together to give the illusion of everyone waiting at a single long table. The Shabbat opened with a small ritual, which mostly consisted of lighting and extinguishing candles and reading aloud excerpts from the psalms and bits of various biblical accounts of the Last Supper (beforehand one of the hosts had helpfully mentioned, almost as a prophylactic against complaints about heterodoxy, that the liturgy was taken from a messianic Shabbat ritual). Everyone present was ripping off chunks of peasant-style bread, and bottles of red wine were being passed around.

The conversation drifted, and at some point Mason (the male half of the husband-wife team that was hosting the Shabbat) started the discussion by saying that tonight the subject was "Hearing from G-D"; he spelled the final word out, omitting the middle vowel in a way that indexed practices in "religious" Hebrew. As my notes for the evening read,

> Mason acknowledges that he has been trying to hear from God his whole life, and that he has not succeeded. He says that God is present in his life, citing a psalm about God guiding every step, tweaking these steps so that it turns out right. Everyone seems excited about the idea that Mason doesn't directly hear from God, and the questions focus on his relationship with God for a while until, a bit tired, he says that he wants to hear how others hear from God.
>
> Claire [an enthusiastic Asian American, who had just recently graduated from college] says something about consulting God before decisions, conversing with him; Ethan [one of the two group members who worked in campus ministries] chimes in, in a more nuanced way, and mentions that these conversations sometimes occur through the mediums of words, sometimes through visions, and sometimes through other means. [During the group conversation] I press him on this, asking him how he knows something is from God and not from him[self],

seeing how it all occurs in the space of the head. He says that if the thought comes out of the blue, if it is something that he couldn't have known, then it is God. I then ask how he knows in other cases that something is from God, and he acknowledges that there appear to be different categories—the openly supernatural and areas like making a job decision that seem less clear cut.

Sergio [the recent immigrant from Guatemala] starts speaking, saying that there are supernatural incidents. He mentions a time in Berlin when he walked outside of his residence, felt that he had to go back and get twenty euros, and then had a twenty-euro fine levied against him for not getting something stamped that was required to use the subway system. How could he have known that? It must have been God. He also mentions feeling thoughts that are out of character (e.g., an insistent thought that he should be nice to someone whom he normally wouldn't feel obliged to be nice to—illustrated by pounding his chest with his fist) are signs of God speaking to him. Jessica [the other host] says that God often speaks to her "descriptively" rather than proscriptively.... Explicating what she means by this, she says that instead of telling her what to do, looking back she sees God saying that this was him acting in her. Oddly, Claire agrees to this assessment (though it seemed to stand in opposition to her earlier discussion of how she goes back and forth with God in making decisions).

This discussion drifts over who has responsibility for hearing God—Ethan feels that we live in a divine-suffused world, and that we just need to turn to God, that this is heaven, and that it is people that turn God off (particularly in what he calls the "global north"). This is from the Dallas Willard book that Jacob [the other person in campus ministries] has been forcing down everyone's throat, as Ethan acknowledges in more polite language (this book appears again in the pastor's sermon on the weekend).[7]

This [personal responsibility to hear from God] doesn't sit well with Mason, who makes two points: (1) that even if everyone were fully directing their energy to hearing from God, the world would still be a sad place (as an example he claims that most of the modern church in America is pushing policies that penalize the poor, all the while sincerely believing that they are doing God's work); (2) that Ethan's claim suggests that people who desperately want to hear from God but can't are themselves to blame.

Building on this, Mason says that the blame is God's because he made mankind, even hinting that God made mankind because he was lonely. Ethan asks if this means that the Trinity wasn't enough and then suggests man was created because of an overabundance of love, like a child made by a family.

Returning to the question of *not* hearing from God, Sergio takes the "who are you to demand answers" tack, saying that Moses couldn't even look at God and we aren't like David, who was intimate with God in the sanctuary of the temple. But Mason counters that God owes him because he was made in God's image and also Abraham and God spoke face to face as a friend to a friend. Ethan doesn't like Sergio's subtext and asks if they aren't as much in God's presence when they worship in church, citing an epistle that says each worshipper is like a brick in the temple [1 Peter 2:5]. Gail, Sergio's wife, seems a little disturbed, too, asking aren't we even closer to God than those Old Testament figures because of the sacrifice of Jesus?

The conversations start to overlap, and in the background I hear the hostess say, a little nervously, something functionally equivalent to "It's nice that we can present multiple points of view and ask questions." As the conversation starts to settle down, Ethan becomes apologetic for presenting what he calls "standard evangelical arguments" but then adds that he holds the "unfashionable" position of believing there is an actual truth that he can work toward . . . even if he doesn't possess it or won't get to it in this lifetime. Jessica balances the desire for intellectual questioning against the fact that the "truth" is the Gospel message that Jesus died to save us from our sins. She discusses this as a question of faith, and she quotes her husband in saying that faith is just a failure of knowledge, a decision to go with a message that the person isn't entirely convinced of; Livi [another small group member] objects strongly, saying that this prioritizes one kind of knowledge—head knowledge instead of heart knowledge. This again raises the issue of whether the small group is a little "heady" and doesn't really reflect other modes of approaching god; in response, Ethan admits getting tears in his eyes watching Emma [an aspiring professional theater dancer] dance during some worship sessions.

By this point, it was eleven thirty in the evening, and the conversation drifted away from the topic of hearing from God. People (including me) started to break off, though I later heard that the final guest didn't leave until one in the morning.

The evening may seem surprising for those unfamiliar with American evangelical culture, and it is true that debate of this sort is not typical of everyday Vineyard conversation. But that does not mean the discussion was a complete outlier. While there were elements of Messianic Judaism in the ritualistic opening of the supper, that night could also be seen as an instance in which a desire for *authenticity* over *orthodoxy* meant both turning to previous Christian forms with a less evangelical patina and also charting other imaginable positions that exceed a strict evangelical understanding.

Indeed, this drive for an authenticity that is corrosive of evangelical axioms and aesthetics is sometimes seen as definitive of the Emergent Church as a movement.[8] Also, while much of the Emergent Church is apolitical, the politics that were evident that evening could be understood as being at least partially a sharp counter-reaction to the usual right-leaning politics common in American evangelical circles (though as discussed in the concluding chapter, even this left-leaning mode of politics can be an expression of the charismatic diagram).

Many of the younger members of this particular Vineyard church were interested in the Emergent Church movement, though this interest was expressed more as an occasionally voiced sensibility than a concerted organizational motif. But more than "emergence" is at play here. Mason, the cohost, who placed the blame for hearing from God at God's own feet, was not new to the church by any means; his father had spent several years as a missionary outside the United States, and for most of his childhood Mason had attended Vineyard-style churches. His stated inability to hear from God was not a function of a lack of opportunity. This points to a frustration that often lies right below the surface: when capacity to hear from God is framed as an issue of being willing to listen, or just of willing in general, failure can feel like it has an ethical dimension, one that in this case Mason reacted against quite strongly.

PROPHECY, THEORETICAL AND APPLIED

The following Wednesday, the "hearing-from-God" session began. Usually the leaders of the small group, either singly or as a couple, led the discussion; this time, however, they chose Ethan, one of the participants in the hearing-from-God Shabbat meal, to lead the group. Ethan was attending a local interdenominational seminary part time and made his living working as a staff member for a parachurch organization, so he was a smart choice; his ratification of evangelical orthodoxy during the Shabbat meal suggested that he was also a *safe* choice.

Despite these strong qualifications and the level of buildup that had been under way for this event, the actual discussion that night was slow to start. Ethan was hesitant in the beginning, having the mannerisms of a teacher who is afraid that the class might have started off with his pupils already bored. Again, from my field notes:

> Ethan launches the discussion with the question about hearing from
> God, mentioning that he is "in a season" that is dry—he's not hearing

from God the way that he wants to. Claire is called on (a "plant," as Ethan refers to her, acknowledging that this part of the evening was preplanned) and recounts a time when she was at a Bible camp and her group got a prophecy that another group was being disturbed by someone who was not "being a team player"; later, that prophecy turned out to be true. Apparently, true prophecy (from the Bible camp, about the Bible camp) was going around, and there was a "checklist" that by its end was "completely full" of correct intuitions.

Mason repeats his discussion [from the Shabbat dinner] of not hearing from God but [acknowledges that he is] still certain that God made his path straight; Min-Seo, citing [again] the ubiquitous Dallas Willard [a University of Southern California philosophy professor and author of popular books on evangelical spirituality], says that hearing God is something that everyone can do [she repeats the radio channel metaphor that was used during the Shabbat evening]. Livi mentions in contradistinction that she hears from God, usually when she is furthest from him, in places where she thinks she can "do it alone"; [other people bring up biblical narratives of hearing from God like Saul of Tarsus on the road to Damascus]. Ashley [a professional social worker and recent transplant from the Midwest] mentions that when she hears from God it is like a thought—a thought that is alien because it is not like her normal thoughts, comes out of the blue, is followed by a sense of peace; she mentions a time when she was a sixteen-year-old, [a] cousin of hers that she was close to, died [and] she had an experience [of hearing from God]; she [states that] at another time . . . she was taken by a sudden thought to move into her parents' house [which she understood to be another message from God]. April concurs, referencing her experience in opening up an eating disorder Bible study group at college [this out-of-character action is something she now understands as divinely inspired].

Jessica instead talks about how to distinguish being in the presence versus speaking—her husband, Mason, is a presence and often lets her know that he loves her [though not always through speech]. This point is contentious, and some people have trouble catching up with what she has to say. Somewhere in here Ethan trots out the [biblical] discussion of sheep and the shepherd [(John 10:27)]: the sheep know their shepherd's voice.

Benjamin, a lanky bioengineer, mentions the words and pictures question that April usually poses at the end of small group worship [April would traditionally close prayer by asking if anyone received any "words or pictures" during prayer]; he mentions that it is something that was new to him. David discusses this, saying that he usually doesn't get a lot of [images during prayer] and [when they do occur], they are like flash images [quickly fading away]. April basically concurs, mentioning that she also doesn't usually get a lot of them unless there is a night of worship and prayer, when they tend to come on more; I think David says that he knows other people get them a lot, so that is why the two coleaders ask [the group].

Ethan lurches on to the topic of barriers to hearing from God. Mike mentions that his guilt and fear keep him from hearing God—fear that he isn't as good a Christian as everyone else, fear that he isn't worthy. Claire mentions that when she "isn't real," she can't hear from God.

Jacob gives another confessional, mentioning that there was a [previous] relationship with a girl (I think that this is the actual phrase), who wasn't Min-Seo, his current wife. When he was seeing that girl, at the peak of a worship service he got a feeling that he should marry her . . . which was a mistake, he quickly added. This "mistake" added five years to the relationship (three years followed by a two-year period of "Are we broken up or aren't we?"). That relationship was misery, they fought all the time, they had nothing in common, and his friends all had doubts about the relationship. He mentions that he suffered under the Christian notion that relationships are hard work—that's what pastors have to say, after all, they're preaching to married people—and while that's true, he didn't know that they aren't supposed to be *that much* hard work. He also mentions that this image was as strong as the one he got when he was called to ministry—and that afterward, he was depressed for a year and a half because if he got that wrong, maybe he got all his calls wrong. He says that what this taught him was, don't throw your head away when you pray (his exact words), and that you should also go through community ["going through community" being an abbreviated Vineyard way of stating that it is important to get outside confirmation of prophecy from fellow believers and particularly from members of your church community].

Building on Jacob's emphasis of the importance of going through community, I ask a question about testing prophecy—is it smarmy to test to see if a message is from God or is it stupid not to test? April and Jessica talk about confirmation, April on her decision to date David (this could be "the one") and Jessica on her choice of careers. [In both cases] after-the-fact confirmations seemed to have three parts—internal (a sense of peace), outward (success), and confirmation from the Word, some sense of the message being in harmony either explicitly or implicitly with scripture (which is something that Jessica stressed earlier in the discussion). April also mentions that her life was more or less transformed at that point, with everything coming into alignment with her choice to date David. Jacob continues with his story, saying that the year and a half of being depressed was worth it because when he met Min-Seo he didn't want to pray on it at first but went to chapel, where he asked God whether he should date this women, and God said, "I think you already know the answer." He did this apparently only a week after meeting her.

Ethan then picks on Harrison and Evolyn [respectively, an insurance worker and a pediatrician], who haven't spoken [so far that night], with the idea that they should tell a story. Harrison recounts that he talked to Jacob a week or two after [Jacob prayed regarding his future wife], and that he was impressed because he had never heard about God speaking to someone—he asked, "Does God do that?" Evolyn recounts that when Harrison converted she didn't believe that he really had become Christian—when Harrison first ate the communion bread at a service, she questioned him afterward asking why he did it and whether he was simply hungry [laughter]. She didn't trust the motives behind the conversion. She mentions that at one point when she was leading a Bible study she came across the story of feeding the five thousand and realized that she had been putting God in a box, God was bigger than she thought, and he could indeed touch the life of someone that she cared about. In this case, it was through the Bible verses that he spoke to her.

This was a good discussion, but it was about this time that we were reminded that we were going to engage in more than discussion. We were going to "do the stuff," as John Wimber would have said, which is to say, attempt to perform the miraculous ourselves.

We then pivoted to the hands-on section of the evening.

Hannah gets up to leave and is prayed over by a bunch of people—about six. Livi and her two friends leave as well, and we wind up in three groups of five or so. Jacob and David in the back room, with April in another (forming an all-female group). The final group consists of Ethan, Claire, Stephanie, Luke [and me]. Ethan just wants us to talk about what we want from God [which was another difficult moment for me as an anthropologist who needed to balance a certain honesty while not letting my status as a nonbeliever throw the group dynamics out of whack].

As part of this process of saying what we want from God, we take turns going around in a circle. Natalie starts: she is a graduate student in sociology [at a nearby university]. She had wanted to get a PhD [in order to] help her in a ministry she wants to establish in China. But during the summer, she was there [in China] and she doesn't feel right—she recounts looking at a thunderstorm in Shanghai and saying "God, if you want me to go to China, then have the lightning strike here." The lightening didn't strike. She wants direction from God.

She moves to the middle of the [small] group [of us], and everyone turns their attention to her—hands resting on her shoulders, head, or back or merely extended in her direction, with palms facing her: in short, the usual arrangement for someone who is receiving prayer. Ethan starts off with an introductory prayer, addressing God in the second person while recounting Natalie's problem and resulting prayer request. Quickly, Claire gets an image—of Natalie. A bunch of windows are going past her very fast, she is screaming, and then things slow down, like a [decelerating] subway [car]. Ethan asks Natalie if that resonates with her. She says, yes, a little. Immediately afterward, Claire gets another vision of iron bars coming down and sidewise, blocking off a view, followed by something sharp drilling a small hole; Ethan asks again if that resonates, and she says not really. Trying to salvage this, Ethan says that there is a mention of iron bars in Isaiah. [Though I did not recognize the verse at the time, it was Isa. 45:2: "I will go before you, and level the mountains, I will break in pieces the doors of bronze and cut through the bars of iron."] He takes out a worn pocket Bible and starts reading aloud from that chapter, which is mostly about God using Cyrus the Great, king of Persia, as an instrument of his vengeance. Natalie responds again that it doesn't resonate with her at all, and Luke dryly observes that this "sounds like a miss to me."

Turning back to the vision of windows rushing by, Ethan says that he thinks the initial vision is about God having her slow down, that it is time for her to rest, and at this moment Natalie starts to cry. Luke motions for me to grab a napkin from the game table. [Natalie] says that she has been in four different cities in three years, that because she is from [another Southern California city] she hasn't really put down any roots here since she can always go back up to [her home city] to visit. She says she feels like she has no home church for fellowship and she wants and misses one. Someone mentions that there is a graduate Christian fellowship, and she says that while she was an undergraduate, Christian fellowship groups took all her time, with activities occurring every day, and that for this reason she was avoiding them now that she is in graduate school. Ethan says something about *this* group, and the church that sponsors this group being her home. While all this is going on, I think I hear someone from April's group crying—April is explaining some vision of a fire, talking excitedly about seeing a lit fireplace.

Luke's turn. During this period, Luke has been taciturn, and what he wants addressed this time is all the issues that he had flagged before, both in prayer and personal conversations: he is feeling distant from both God and people, craving intimacy but also feeling he can only be liked if he is perfect. Luke moves to the middle of the circle, and people lay hands on him or stretch their hands out in his direction. Again, silence and waiting on the Lord for what seems like minutes but probably is not that long.

Ethan eventually gets a vision, something about a pearl, which he thinks is a reference to Jesus being the Pearl of Great Price and Jesus being inside of him. Claire gets the word "beloved"—this affects Luke, and Ethan pushes this line. Ethan says that often when he gets something like this, he wants to repent publicly of the lie that he believed, a lie he received from the enemy or the media, or whatever, which said that he isn't loved or valued. This lie, Ethan adds, is shown to be wrong by Jesus's sacrifice on the cross. Despite all this, Luke is hesitant. Ethan does lead Luke in prayer, voicing these things on Luke's behalf. Luke, saying "well, you heard me," endorses the repentance in a lukewarm way. Ethan insists that Luke has some sort of a ministry inside him, something to share. Luke mentions that he has been thinking of something like this, and I remind him of a conversation we had had weeks earlier about Luke's possibly going into teaching, which is, he admits, one of the things that he has been batting around.

I am the next person sitting in the circle; as I often do when I'm in one of these situations, I ask people to pray for my research. [It's a useful ploy, in that it reminds them of my status as a researcher and of my project while also giving them a way to address it in a framing that is cogent to them.] I explain a little of what I'm doing, specifically mentioning the difficulty of having to address such separate audiences. Ethan says it must be hard having to live "in two worlds," but I say it's one more world than I normally have, so I'm happy.

They pray over me.

Being prayed over is an odd experience; whenever I am prayed over, I feel self-conscious; at the same time, I become incredibly aware of my body since everyone is oriented toward it. There is more touching in groups like the Vineyard than in a lot of other circles. Hugs are an almost obligatory means of greeting each another. This is even the case when the partners greeting each another are of different genders, though in order to keep it from being misconstrued, it's often a "side hug." (Side hugs are so ubiquitous in evangelical culture that they are often the object of in-jokes.) Even exposure to these more open levels of physical affection does not prepare you for being prayed over, as multiple hands are either laid on you or held just an inch or so away from you. The latter is in some ways more uncanny as those hands are still perceptible by the proprioceptive senses that are normally tuned only to internal bodily sensations and usually fall below the level of consciousness. There is also a certain kind of mental blankness that occurs when you are prayed over. The attention is so concentrated on the bodily sensations and what is transpiring that it is impossible to really forget the self; but at the same time, the pressure of a continual internal monologue fades away almost completely.

As previously mentioned, when praying like this, the wait for the first word seems to take hours instead of the half minute or so that it objectively does; it seems even longer when you yourself are being prayed over. After an interminable spell, someone talks:

> Ethan starts; not letting go of his earlier observation, he prays that there be some peace for the warring ideas in my head, for time off, a sabbath from my research. Luke, uncharacteristically, says he has a vision of—well—vision—and he prays for sight, which he glosses as insight into what I'm doing and an ability to see something new (for some reason, he focuses on the Pentecostal aspect, and I wonder later if that gloss is a way of religiously recoding my project, thereby containing it). Natalie prays about how hard it can be in academics, for protection, and for a filter for my committee—for me to find a way to write so that even nonbelievers will understand. Everyone is working with the metaphor of truth. Ethan calls my work a ministry and prays for allies (strong men and women) to be my lieutenants; I think he is referring to Judges, the story of Samson maybe. Afterward, even though I remind him again that I am not a "believer," Ethan says that this is why they have groups like his campus ministry: to affect academics. He's impressed with Luke's vision, which he says is "spot on." In doing this, he mentions that he doesn't really get "visions" that much—that they are very weak for him, as though he can only just barely see them. Luke meekly mentions it was more the concept of vision that had struck him, but that the difference doesn't matter.

> Ethan's turn to be prayed over. He's seeing his girlfriend—a [ministry] team leader in Davis, California [who is a part of the same parachurch organization that he works for]. This is a fraught visit for him as it hasn't been a good week between the two of them, and he's at an emotionally unbalanced point. What he would like are prayers about whether or not he should marry her. Luke gives a typically careful covering prayer, the sort of prayer that restates the problem through directly addressing God, and usually precedes anyone reporting any prophetic intuitions (Ethan had been giving these introductory prayers for our little group beforehand). There is a period of silence.

> We wait for a while. Sitting there, I have an image briefly flash in my mind of Ethan in a plane, flying to Davis, and the plane landing. It has no particular force, and there is otherwise nothing to distinguish it from any other sort of daydream, but to fill the silence, I recount it anyway. After briefly sketching out what I "saw" [there is an awkward bit of silence], I give a loose metaphorical reading of what the image might be "trying to say": that while things are "up in the air" right now, soon things will be grounded and Ethan will have arrived. Almost immedi-

ately Claire counters. First, she offers an apology ("I don't know how this goes with that, but . . .") and then describes an image of Kenny from South Park sledding cartoonishly up and down hills (she demonstrates the exaggerated heights and depths of the hills with her finger). Then there is a cutaway—or, maybe, a circular hole is carved in the picture—and Kenny is on his back in a green field under the sun, relaxing. Ethan takes this as a reference to his emotional ups and downs and sees it as a chance or opportunity for peace. He breaks form by praying aloud while the prayers focus on him, taking a turn and praying for himself in the ways that others do. Working the metaphor of grounding, which came up in his prayer (carried over from my "vision"), Claire mentions him being focused on the "rock" of Jesus.

At this point the evening began to wind down; most of the groups were done practicing to hear from God, and people, including myself, broke off to get some snacks or wait in line for the bathroom. When I came back, a few people were praying over someone face down on the carpet, asking God to set her vertebrae in order so that her scoliosis, which she had been complaining about earlier in the evening, would no longer bother her. Most people, however, were heading to the door—it was pushing midnight and the next day was a workday for almost everyone.

TYPIFICATION, ELABORATION, PEDAGOGY

So what can we make of this attempt to introduce this relatively loquacious set of differently experienced believers to the phenomenon of hearing from God? What sorts of activities were they engaged in, did David and April's pedagogical project work, and what does this entire situation tell us about the problems of typification and elaboration of the diagram?

The first thing to remember is that with or without pedagogy, not everyone was capable of hearing from God. Mason, for instance, did not receive any visions and afterward felt that he was no closer to communicating with God after the series of discussions and exercises than he was before.

Not everyone who has trouble hearing from God is willing to hazard going down that road, however, and they find other ways of reading moments in their lives as hearing from God. Often people discern communiques from God in the ways that their lives unfold, in their career turns, or when they meet their partners; they use these signs as a way of forging an implicit divine conversation mediated through the Holy Spirit. They retroactively understand moments of their lives as signs and see their wills and sometimes the wills of others as being in either harmony or tension with those signs. Others take advantage of the polysemous sensibilities present in the language used to discuss charismatic phenomena. The language of gifts is used with varying levels of precision at different times, and people may associate gift with specific charismata like prophecy when they are discussed in contexts like the one that dominated this multiweek initiative on hearing from God. In other framings, gift can be used more loosely. Beyond just referring to specific Pentecostal/charismatic miraculous phenomena, gift can be used to describe capabilities and character traits that are considered integral to the person and are often understood as divine inheritances—things bequeathed to the person by God. This is particularly the case for characteristics that are collectively positively valued. An example of this was a conversation I once had with the wife of someone who was well regarded in the church for his charismatic gifting; she stated that despite her husband's supernatural gifts she didn't feel jealous because she had the gift of "encouragement." This phenomenon is also given some weight with respect to the previously discussed dependence of most Vineyard churches on volunteerism. People gifted with the spirit necessary to propose directions for the church by identifying "what God is doing right now" are put alongside those people who have the gift of various forms of organizational genius, as well as those who are simply willing to plug away at the various repetitive tasks that are a part of the day-to-day management of a church. This results in a loose leveling of these different capabilities and to some degree a charismaticization of quotidian abilities.

The gap between those who are capable of hearing from God and those who are not is also mitigated by an understanding that the core charismatic gifts are never fully realized. Except for certain peak moments, quotidian-style hearing from God in the Vineyard is always presented as attenuated. We should note that, even among those who regularly receive visions, there is a sense that the real exemplars of fully effectuated visions occur either at some other place or time or to some other person; recall that April and Ethan, who were some of the chief visionaries of the group and had the greatest pedagogical roles, saw themselves as lacking. They claimed they were basing their expertise not on their experience but on what they had seen other truly gifted individuals do. This makes sense. Lessening the power of particular instances makes them seem less otherworldly, while acknowledging their kinship with more fantastic events maintains their ties to the realm of biblical miracles. Finally, there is also a wisdom in downplaying the sort of miraculous phenomena that took place in the small groups over a series of weeks. After all, these experiences had none of the commanding affect or life-determining effects that were present in the earlier discussions of those nearly vocative instances of hearing from God that resulted in conversions, rededications to the faith, or dedication of a life to ministry.

Despite these protestations of weakness, we can still see that what was going on in that fourth-story condominium living room was just as much an instantiation of the charismatic diagram as those more full-throated moments of being directly addressed audibly by God; the same scissions are present. The situation is organized in such a way that the production of signs is seemingly out of the control of the subject who is receiving them; and the signs (when they are effective) cleave aspects of the broader stage of affairs as that which is actually, or potentially, in harmony with the sign, and willful and unwilling aspects that either resist the sign, or are extinguished by it. The reason these living-room prophecies seem so different from those in which God's voice is experienced as almost audible is because even though the diagram is constituted similarly the particular instantiations of the diagram involved the "summoning up" of surprise in a controlled and intentionally created situation. Because surprise was intentionally brought up in a pedagogical setting, more subtle intensities and different sorts of affects were in play: this was a willed passiveness.

This tells us something important. First, surprise, or the temporary abeyance of an intentional agency, is both relative and time delineated. In a way, hearing from God is not surprising when one is conducting an exercise in hearing from God. The necessary element of surprise and the unexpected can only be located in the particular free associations that come up. This resembles in one sense the sort of presence-supplemented exercises that are used when reading the Bible. While hearing from God may be expected, what is not *specifically* expected is the particular sense-making potential that is found in certain unintentional, combinatory juxtapositions of image and circumstance. Remember no particular combination of image and circumstance was considered sufficient to validate a message from the Holy Spirit; people were asked if messages resonated or struck home; messages that catalyzed some sort of nonvolitional affect (such as Natalie's tears) tended to be seen as particularly on point.

The relative and situational nature of surprise is also facilitated by what might be called a recalibration of thresholds. Controlling the environment, setting aside a particular moment for the exercise, and purposefully encouraging watchfulness mean that aspects of the sensorium that would not normally come to conscious attention are given psychic space and allowed to appear and participate in the series of syntheses that clear the way for the miraculous scission.

Such recalibration of the senses can become habitual in the same way eyes learn to focus and scan in particular patterns in written text. The embodied and reflex-like segments of these actualizations of the diagram transverse the other more neurological and biological diagrams with which they partially overlap, shaping the ways in which those embodied aspects themselves will be actualized in future instantiations; those shifts will in turn torque the way that, for these bodies and minds, the charismatic diagram will be actualized in the future.[9]

This is the explanation for the seeming elaboration we saw in the spontaneous, vocative-style moments of God speaking in the last chapter. What we have is not a greater realization of the diagram but rather a realization of the charismatic diagram in which various threshold levels have been dialed down and certain realizations have become effective attractors as a result of prior sculpting of the subject. Earlier we suggested that the diagram is never partially realized; though not all elements in the diagram will necessarily convey the same degrees of force and some aspects may be more sharply drawn than others, the presence of one of the elements necessarily implies the presence of the other. This suggests that in moments when the diagram is summoned up by an affective intensity (again most likely but not necessarily by the one involving agency), the full habituated form of the actualized diagram, including the habituated sensory and embodied elements, rise up fully formed as well. When something with the intensity and quality needed to be registered as a divine voice occurs to someone who has been playing with the charismatic diagram, therefore, the thresholds will drop to habituated levels. In these recalibrated instances, a voice that might normally seem to be merely an "impression" might come across as closer to an actual voice or be taken in through the form of actual written words that appear fully formed (and enflamed) in the psychic field of vision. This is to say, the more pedagogy that one is exposed to, the more the miraculous will not just take on a surprising face but will also be a clearly delineated face; this is what distinguishes the sharper from the more fuzzy moments of being hailed by God in the last chapter.

This brings us to the issue of typification. The second thing to observe from the living-room seminar is that the insertion of multiple subjects into the circuit at once *multiplies, intensifies,* and *domesticates* the sort of surprise that we are dealing with. It multiplies surprise because what is surprising enough to indicate a causal link with a divine assemblage must first be considered surprising to the person who relates the message to the person the message is for; further, the message must also be conveyed to and decoded by the ultimate recipient in such a way that it counts as surprise.

This might suggest an intensification and filtering of what is necessary to count as surprise. Candidate moments for God's voice might be expected to be incrementally or exponentially more surprising because they have to have effects on two people. There are moments when that is undoubtedly the case; some people who hear from God on a regular basis are quick to recall instances when no cause or content for a message occurred to them while they were talking with someone (in typical versions of this story, the interlocutor was often a stranger); they often feeling a pressure—sometimes nervousness, anxiety, or a sense of urgency—to pass this information along. In these stories, seemingly random information ends up having incredible unforeseen relevance: for example, if someone mentions a color to the recipient while he or she is in a prophetic mode, then the color might be associated with a beloved family member who has just passed away; if someone reports a number coming to mind unbidden, that number might be the street address of a location where the recipient just applied for a desperately desired job (examples along these lines proliferate).

These tales are related for the reason that most tales are told: they are rare enough to be worthy of interest but prototypical enough to be immediately comprehendible. It follows that that most instances of hearing from God are probably not like that. What is more likely to happen is the suspected divine transmissions run the risk twice over of being considered the equivalent of noise, that is, they do not appear with enough force and surprise to be agentive and therefore signs with the proper scission effects. Rather, they come across as essentially underdetermined, instances of pure chance that should have no effects at all—what Luke called "a miss."

This gives us a sense of the workings of one of the two engines of typification. Surprise is what cannot be anticipated in advance. And surprise is considered to be sufficiently characteristic of God so that he is often described as possessing the seemingly undivine trait of being "messy." Remember there are multiple ways for God to communicate: he can access believers through vocative events, images, or other sensations that are either classified as internal or ambivalently situated inside or outside the body; he also acts through coincidences so perfectly situated to circumstances (Sergio's euro notes) that they appear to be statistically improbable according to folk heuristics.[10] Given these various modalities, determining how God can communicate in advance seems impossible. Further, much like the channel the content also cannot be known in advance. Typification works on this swath of possibility not by controlling surprise but by denaturing the miraculous, creating an implicit sense of what are not signs of a supernatural agency but merely the effects of more quotidian forces. Certain affects are given a negative moral evaluation, for instance, and are never seen as having the sort of intensity that indexes God. Anger, jealousy, and the like, even if they seem to be without cause or are surprising, are not signs of God's hand (at least not in the Vineyard). Further, images that have obviously erotic connotations, even when they are sublimated, are not routinely considered of divine origin. (Recall the embarrassment occasioned by the "sea phallus" prophecy that was given before the pastor could stop it. While it became a source of amusement, it was never treated as divine communication except by the speaker.) Likewise, at least in the Vineyard, negative, castigating, or violent communications are not considered to be a part of God's character; people may have visions of a sword suggesting, perhaps, that someone is a warrior or some problem will be cut in two, but the vision will never show the sword being used on someone in a graphic or gratuitous way.

This refusal to see God's character as negative is obviously not a logical necessity; there are enough examples of negative or violent prophetic communications in the Hebrew Bible and apocryphal New Testament texts that someone would not have to look too hard for a model for prophetic missives from a wrathful God (Catholic charismatics, for instance, have historically not seemed to have any difficulty producing violent and negative visions, or regarding them as being in harmony with scripture).[11] My suspicion is that in the Vineyard such potential divine communications are discounted for two reasons. First, they are associated by many in the Vineyard with a more Pentecostal mode of spiritual practice and, in particular, a tendency in some Pentecostal churches to have authority centralized in particular (and often pastoral) figures, who use prophecy as a method of moral policing.[12] By way of contrast, prophecy in the Vineyard forecloses authoritarian structures by decoupling and redistributing the production of the sign and the sense of surprise from both the intermediary and person or persons the prophecy is for. At a second more speculative level, I believe the Vineyard is sufficiently saturated with folk Freudianism to ensure a prophecy that was sexual, violent, or off-putting would raise anxieties and doubts about whether it was actually an act of God or an instance of repressed ideational or affective material coming to the surface. Basically, potential prophecy would not be interpreted as prophecy if it were easy to see the id rather than the divine hand. These two processes—a class- and politics-inspired egalitarianism and a shadowy Freudian folk theory of the drives—create typification, not by making authoritative statements about what God is, but by chipping away everything they implicitly assume God is not.

TYPIFICATION AND THE LINGUISTIC IDEOLOGIES OF SPEAKING FOR GOD

Typification does not occur only by fixing the form of surprise. Typification is also an effect of the language that is relied on in a community to discuss both Charismatic phenomena in the abstract and linguistic norms that exist regarding specific instances of hearing from God. What we are dealing with here are the questions of which groups of lexemes are relied on and what the language ideology of the group is.

Let's take language ideology first. In the broadest sense, language ideology is a discussion of what sort of language is considered both efficient and effective; it can be used to favor one language or another in contexts in which there are multiple possible languages available for use, or endorse one dialect or register of language over another in specific situations (think of discussions about what sort of language is appropriate for the workplace, for the home, for politicians, and for popular media figures).[13] At a more abstract level, language ideology can concern not only the type of language used but a proper form for language as well: Is formulaic language to be favored, since it has an authority having to do with historical depth and an origin outside any specific immediate context? Alternatively, is language that suggests sincerity and spontaneity a better choice because it is thought to be authentic and to express the actual thoughts and emotions of the (valued) speaker? A parallel issue can be found in questions concerning the materiality of language: Is meaning located primarily in words and language, with material objects being mere inert referents? Or does meaning inhere in material objects themselves, making them as much a means of communication as language itself? If the former question is considered the right way to think about the interaction of language and materiality, then seeing meaning as inhering in material objects at the least incorrectly locates agency and sense. At its worst, it constitutes a moral crisis because people who choose incorrectly end up bound to and enthralled by material objects when the true meaning resides in themselves. If, however, the latter question is more on point, then there is something dangerous about people who see material objects only as representations or symbols of things, rather than direct instantiations of principles and ideas; they imperiously claim powers for themselves and their words that actually reside in the world around them.

There is a consensus that Protestant Christianities are more likely to favor sincerity and authenticity in language and be suspicious of any view of language that identifies meaning with the material.[14] This referential logic can also be found in the Vineyard; their break with forms of Pentecostal speech they consider showy and overly elaborated is about keeping speech *real*, a term used to express sincerity. I remember that one Vineyard pastor with whom I was discussing the differences between classical Pentecostalism and the Vineyard mimicked the speech styles of a generic Pentecostal pastor, speaking in a hysterical tone and with strange rhythms and intonations; at the end of his improvisatory performance, he asked rhetorically if that was the way Pentecostal preachers spoke when they ordered a hamburger in a restaurant.

In contrast to this (hypothetical) Pentecostal mode of speaking, Vineyard pastors try to talk in natural cadences during worship. That said, there are obvious difference between their actual day-to-day speech and how they speak when they are in front of their congregations; preaching is a structured and prepared activity not a spontaneous speech act, and listening to someone speak from the pulpit with the hesitations, false starts, and malapropisms that characterize everyday speech would be unbearable. But the shift is not in word choice or patterns of intonation. Rather, preaching differs from quotidian speech in being polished and organized like a monologue, as well as being accompanied by a different set of gestures and movements (pastors often exhibit wide-ranging back-and-forth movements; they sometimes walk partway down the aisles in a way that is referred to on occasions as the "pastor walk"). Still, other than these technical changes, pastors have roughly the same personae when speaking on or off the pulpit.

This is, of course, a consciously made and elaborated decision. These pastors consider "being real" a response to "religion" or "religious culture," which is their way of speaking about what they see as a formulaic set of practices intended to segregate spirituality and keep it limited to church; the examples of a religious mindset I was given again and again were wearing one's "Sunday best" or publicly reciting prayers in a formal style. According to the Vineyard these practices, which they believe have more to do with concerns about human status than with what God desires, suffer from faults ranging from mere wrongheadedness to a demonically assisted attempt to vitiate God's presence.

To the extent that Vineyard members prize this sincere informality, they stay true to their evangelical semiotic inheritance; it certainly resonates with a broader ethic of authenticity that supersaturates the Vineyard as a whole. But the Vineyard's take on what is ethical and effective speech is more complicated than simply adhering to a common Protestant language ideology. While the Vineyard would like to break with certain theatrical aspects of Pentecostalism, their worldview is predicated on the possibility of authoritative communiques originating from outside the person even as the messages must traverse the person. In other words, God talks to people not only through forms like church tradition or the Bible but also by playing with human thoughts and emotions. And this is a problem because thoughts and emotions are, at least in most of European American metaphysics, considered elements internal to and constitutive of the person as an autonomous subject.

The question this traversing of the person raises for linguistic code is a simple one: given the Vineyard's valuing of sincerity and framing language as representative of internal thoughts specific to a particular speaking person, how does one use language to express the divine traversals of the bounded person? There are three rough approaches in the Vineyard that tend to blend into one another even though they (roughly) inhere in different generations. Thus, at the risk of seeming to violate the imperative that equal weight be given to all the differential forms, I consider one of these forms to be more common across the various demographic groups in the Vineyard, suggesting a direction in which the Vineyard is trending as a whole.

Of the responses to the problem of representing divine speech, the historically earlier variant, which I will classify as "non-Vineyard," is a Pentecostal/charismatic inheritance. It is non-Vineyard not because it is never found in the Vineyard but because it precedes the Vineyard and is relatively rarely used in the contemporary Vineyard. It occurs when the person reporting supernatural activity presents her- or himself as the animator of the speech but not as the author. Usually during moments of charismatic excitement when the level of affect in the room has been building up for a while through means, such as worship music or extended exhortation by a speaker, someone will shout out. What they say varies wildly, but the structure is the same. First, the statement is in the first person but is obviously not meant to be read as the vocalized thoughts and opinions of the person speaking. Second, this speech act (to various degrees of success) uses lexical and grammatical forms associated with biblical language, meaning terms that are effectively folk impressions of the King James Bible's style and vocabulary are used. At times, this style of speech will go as far as to use entire biblical thematics or metaphors to structure a sentence. In short, this is a moment of a "return" to religious language, which is excusable because it is not supposed to be an expression of the speaker's interiority and therefore does not violate an imperative for sincerity. Third, there is often a great deal of repetition with the same phrase or sentence sometimes presented several times in a row. This is sometimes a mechanical repetition, in which each iteration is the same. At other times there are purposeful variations on subject-verb-object sentence structure; if there is a noncontrasting conjunction like "and" in the original sentence, the speaker will play with reordering the first and second clauses or sentences, going so far as to make a chiasmus. (Since chiasmus is a common biblical trope, its use could signal a special case of the "King Jamesing" of speech.) These speech events may be very short: a woman shouting out, "My children, do you know how much I love you, I dance and rejoice over you?" At other times, they may be fairly elaborated: for example, "So the country suffered! So with my church! As the rulers of the people bring their ears back to me, miracle-working power, authority, power, destruction!" or "I am coming and I will restore my church, and the whole world will now see my glory!" Often these statements are semishouted in a rolling, somewhat frenetic intonation with all the syllables stressed as if the statement were an imperative, regardless of the actual grammatical mood.

While the animator of this speech act is the fleshly person present in the room, its author is God. Not simply hearing from God but speaking for him as well are practices that go back to Pentecostalism, if not beyond, and it should be no surprise that it seems to be more present in some of the people who cross over to the Vineyard from certain strains of Pentecostalism (though as we will see in a later chapter, some of those individuals see the Vineyard as offering a chance for them to retain a certain kind of Christian religiosity while jettisoning Pentecostal practices, including being ventriloquized by God in a manner like the one just described).[15] For others, this is not tied to Pentecostalism by inheritance but the result of the conscious modeling of Vineyard speech on Pentecostalism during the early days of the Vineyard. At that time, Pentecostal genres were the only obvious and available templates for those moments when God speaks to a believer, who then speaks for God.

There is something in speech derived from Pentecostal practice, though, that runs counter to a Protestant aesthetics of speech favoring sincerity. Presenting language that supposedly originates outside suggests one is "playing" God; this isn't compatible with a sincere speech ethics calling for the identity of inner states and outward linguistic expression since one's words are reporting the inner state of a divine being. A kind of ventriloquizing is seen in some forms of "sincere" Pentecostal speech, of course, as all speech has external precedents that are parasitic on prior speech acts.[16] Alternately, for those who reject a vision of prophecy as a sort of performance, one is still being interrupted by another spirit—the Holy Spirit—who is speaking in one's place; and this temporary evacuation of agency is also hard to reconcile with sincerity as a virtue. Recognizing that this is not a binary, either-or choice of language ideology is important. There can be graduations and indeterminacies between prophecy as performance and prophecy as an interruption, where what is uttered is a psychic or situational truth that resonates with the history and problems of the speaker, making it a sort of sincere statement, though in a more abstract sense of the term.[17] Still, the sudden eruption of the voice of God, speaking in unnatural notes and using a biblically inflected language, is odd when set against a Vineyard preference for naturalistic speech.

For perhaps this reason, this particular Pentecostalized form of describing what it is like to have God speak through you is on the wane. It is found primarily in older generations of Vineyard believers, and I would say that even among that set, it is relied on less and less often. What has taken the place of more Pentecostalized speech is a different form of reported speech, in which the speaker recites what he or she has been told by God but does not quote God or speak in such a way that the speaker and God as first-person narrators are conflated. In this mode of prophetic speech, God is generally less likely to be presented as reliant on the sort of quasi-biblical language that is a hallmark of his Pentecostal mode of communicating. Presenting God's speech this way also places limitations on when it can be presented. Unlike the direct Pentecostal style, ventriloquized prophetic speech, the reported speech style is ill suited for shouting out spontaneously during a worship service. Unplanned outbursts do still occur during worship services but often in a controlled manner; a lead speaker, such as a pastor or worship leader, will either announce something that he "just heard from God," or the microphone will be passed to someone from the congregation who spoke to that lead speaker about receiving a message from God. An example of this can be taken from a 1985 Vineyard pastor conference, where during an improvised part of the meeting someone recited the following words from God to the entire conference:

> You [the various pastors present at the conference] were doing this task [professional ministry] of quote-unquote serving God, and the way God looks upon your heart, because of how you treat the things you are doing, you speak to your associates in the coffeehouse or restaurant after the service or whatever, the attitude of your heart when you're talking about it is like a harlot, like a prostitute talks about the trick that she just turned.

While the language here has biblical resonances (note the use of the word *harlot*), this reported speech style is different from a full first-person channeling of the King James Bible.

This mode of divine reported speech is more easily assimilated by contemporary evangelical ears because it is not a lamination of the human voice onto the divine, or an overriding of the human voice by the divine. But there is another way of articulating the divine message that creates even more space between human and divine speech while also underscoring the intimacy between the two actors. This other method is basically a public presentation of the communication through imagistic sensations that we saw practiced in the small group; in this third language ethic, God is presented as communicating through visions instead of words; the message is still transferred, but the need to translate between media creates a sort of semiotic insulation.

INVITATION, GLOSS, AND FREEDOM

In this third mode of presenting divine speech, the general template for relaying what God has to say runs along these lines:

(invitation):evidence:gloss:qualification

What are the elements of this formula? The *invitation* is the opening moment when someone redirects an exchange that is already in progress toward "what they think might be" a message from God; if the speaker is addressing someone whom they believe either is not Christian or belongs to a form of Christianity that is unfamiliar or hostile to the idea of charismata, this element in the construction may include a statement to the effect that "this may seem a little strange, but...." This is usually followed almost immediately by a statement asking if it is all right if the speaker shares this message with the listener. While it is hard to know how this invitation will play out in the full panoply of circumstances in which it is exercised, I have never heard of someone who asked to share a prophetic word with someone being told no. Perhaps this is because no one wants to revisit a story about someone who declined to hear prophetic words (if they ever do) because the exchange was awkward; in addition, it would make a rather short, embarrassing, and not particularly compelling narrative. My own view is that for the invitees this would probably be an "offer they can't refuse." Believers are backed into a corner. They have to claim an interest in what God has to say to them even if they are suspicious of either the manner the message is relayed or the abilities of the messenger; and nonbelievers are most likely thrown off by the unexpected nature of the communication and disinclined to say no right away because they may not even have a firm grasp of what is being requested. Intrafamily communication between believing and nonbelieving kin is a different issue; it is easy to see how divine intervention might run afoul of tacit agreements that keep familial fault lines from erupting. Also as we'll see the danger that divine communication can come across as overweening might make it far too toxic to invoke in these spaces.

Evidence, the second term in the template, is the description of the image or word constituting the "root"' of the message; examples are the vision of the Grape Ape experienced by a believer in the prophecy-training session described at the opening of this chapter and April's sense that God would himself answer whatever questions I have in my research. The *gloss* is the unpacking of the image when the person who experienced the prophetic word hazards a possible interpretation, and *qualification* is the implicit or explicit message that the recipient should evaluate to determine whether the message is intended for him or her and if so whether the gloss is accurate or God meant something different.

Gloss and qualification to some degree work together. The gloss is the reading that the person relaying the prophecy gives; since prophecy is often imagistic, it has to be assigned a more conventional meaning. Qualification is the reminder that the gloss is not necessarily part of the prophetic communication and the accuracy of the prophecy, as well as its underlying meaning, are ultimately for the prophecy's recipient to judge.

In the *(invitation):evidence:gloss:qualification* sequence, the invitation is in parenthesis because it may be pro forma, or absent. The reason it may not always be present is a function of practicality; if the audience is a large group, permission may not be sought, in part for logistical reasons and in part because presence in the group implies tacit or implicit willingness to receive these kinds of communications. Besides, when the individuating and to a degree private form of the message is blunted, as when the group is addressed, the fact that the communication addresses a collectivity at large undoes the personal edge to this speech act.

Even when speaking to large groups in a church-scale setting, however, the speaker will often extend an invitation by saying something along the lines of "I hope it's all right if I share something with you." This is a rhetorical question that presumes the answer; circumstances when someone in the audience would shout no are hard to imagine. Often when this pro forma invitation is not sought, there is still acknowledgment that formal permission is a normal element in the speech act. The speaker will turn to the audience and say something along the lines of "I'm sorry, but I just have to share something that God is telling me." When permission is not available as a warrant, compulsion as an overriding imperative is relied on to authorize this sharing, even as an apology is simultaneously presented.

Sometimes at a church service, but more likely at a conference or special evening service devoted to hearing from God, individuals are publicly given a specific message that is meant just for them. An individual who has been invited because of his or her special capability for prophecy might choose, seemingly at random, one person from the audience, usually identifying them by a feature that is sartorial ("you with the red glasses") or positional ("you, the woman in the back row sitting between those two large men"). Interesting and relevant are that phenotypical features, especially skin color, are never used as designations; individuation is determined by those attributes that people can control, rather than those that are a function of genetic inheritance. This custom is not consciously articulated, and it may be that people who engage in the practice have no conscious knowledge of it even though they follow it all the same.

In addition, when people are called out for prophetic attention in a crowd, it is highly unusual for simply one person alone to be singled out in this manner. Usually such individually directed communications occur as part of a sequence, in which a series of seemingly randomly selected people will be given prophecy publicly for anywhere from fifteen minutes to an hour.

Even when people are publicly given prophecy in this manner, an invitation is extended if only to the group as a collective; the speaker tells the group that he or she is going to be giving prophetic words to individuals and explains that the addressees must judge for themselves whether the words are accurate. This occurs despite the fact that in most settings almost everyone present is already well aware of the conventions. An explanation would, therefore, be superfluous. No one says anything along the lines of "As you are probably fully aware, we're now going to be given individual words. You most likely know the drill, but for those one or two people who do not. . . ." This presumed familiarity means the explanation is not intended to be informative but is offered only to secure implicit consent from the audience that they are willing to be addressed both as part of a collective and as individuals.

An invitation, even a pro forma one, is important; otherwise, what occurs when prophetic words are shared is something quite different. Prophecy transmitted without at least tacit consent generally does not occur in Vineyard churches. It is, however, common in many churches that are not affiliated with the Vineyard but have been deeply influenced by Vineyard-like forms of spiritual practice and may share a genealogical link with the Vineyard. Often in churches whose practices do not include an invitation, there is little development of the idea that the recipient of the message, the subject of the prophetic transmission, must ultimately ratify both the truth and the sense of the message. In these other churches, the messages are presumed to be true—the recipient can *accept* the truth or not but cannot in any way *judge* it. In these other churches, it is also common to claim not just that different people are differently gifted but also that the *degree* of gifting is sometimes radically different and that certain individuals, almost inevitably leaders in the congregation or the movement or people who are extraordinarily close to leadership, are gifted to the point of being in effect infallible.

The Vineyard had brief moments in the mid-1990s when it gave space to supposedly infallible "prophets," but this practice was quickly abandoned on the basis that it was a challenge to Vineyard norms.[18] Even though most Vineyard members are unaware of this part of the movement's history, many of them are aware of other Pentecostal and charismatic churches that are dominated by this more autocratic style of prophecy. Many people I talked to (primarily women who spent their teenage years in some of these Vineyard-style authoritarian churches) have sharp and sometimes painful memories of pastors or other church leaders receiving words of knowledge about their purported immorality, "prophecies" that were often shared in semipublic church spaces. This is so common there is even one successful East Coast, urban Vineyard that for several years presented itself specifically as a place where people could come to recover from exactly these sorts of overweening practices; these practices were always associated with religion as opposed to spirituality, which is what the Vineyard purports to offer. Absent both the invitation and the subsequent qualification, prophecies carry the specter of this other kind of charismatic authority in a way that is all too palpable. But what is noticeable about this overweening form of prophetic authority is that it is far more likely to be structured along the lines of the direct communication, in which the underlying impression is presented as laminated onto a divine verbal speech act.

The above discussion suggests there are three ideal types of prophetic speech that exist on a continuum:

1. Speech acts that present the individual as in effect speaking *as* God and in which the sensory phenomenon the speaker interprets as a prophetic message is obscured by the entextualized quote.[19] While no one believes the individual speaking is God, at the moment that the speech act occurs the speaker is structurally presented as animating a divinely authored statement. This is not treated as a case of possession; I have never heard anyone use possession as an explanatory frame, and the few times when I proffered its possible

applicability, I was told possession is not in any way analogous. Still, similar issues relating to the temporary abeyance of human agency and human or divine responsibility are applicable even if the individual is understood as having some control.

2. Speech acts that present the person as relaying a message from God. Such messages may or may not be contemporaneous; "God told me that" and "I hear God telling me now" are both typical formulations. Since these take the form of reported speech, there is no lamination of human with divine agency or language; it is easy to disaggregate animator from author in these cases, and issues of human agency and responsibility are far less pointed. However, the phenomenological nub, the element of the sensorium that is divine rather than human, is still linguistically overcoded to the point of being effectively erased, with the entextualized statement obscuring its traces.

3. Speech acts that attempt to avoid an overcoding of the original aspect of the sensorium by separating the moments when the experience is narrated from the underlying message. This goal, of course, is to a degree impossible because even though the messages are not presented as direct, divine discursive statements, the events must still be presented in and through language. But language is also indicative of an underlying lack of identity between the interpretation and its proximate divine cause. Here some of the issues of human agency and responsibility that pertain to the first speech act, such as when God speaks directly through actors, return though in a different form. Rather than the subject having a moment of what appears to be an abeyance of human agency and responsibility, there is a fracturing of the subject with various divine stimuli introjected inside the perceptive and cognitive economies of the prophesying subject.

All these approaches, but particularly the first and third, pose problems for sincerity as a value. Furthermore, they are distinguishable from one another to the degree that very different relations to authority are implicit in their structures; this suggests that these moments of spirit-affected speech can be considered internal counterideologies, forms of ethical and effective speech with a telos that is orthogonal to the standard, regnant Protestant speech norms. Also these counternorms, which are again about form not content, are effects of *concerns* regarding authority. These different forms are not directly shaped by anxieties about different abilities to hear from

God, or speak as representatives of God, but they affect the way this content is expressed.[20] Still since different narrative conventions emphasize or de-emphasize a verbal or imagistic coding of the event, these worries about authority serve as another engine for typification and elaboration.

We should note that while these structuring concerns about authority and linguistic presentation affect the specific ways in which the diagram is actualized and expressed, none of these assemblages of enunciation *denature* the diagrammatic aspects of prophecy. Remember the discussion of the temporal aspects of the diagram: that the diagram is expressed in the ratio and structure of forces being actualized *whenever the prophetic account is being repeated* and not merely in those moments when it occurs. Each moment of recounting the effects of the diagram is also a moment when the diagram is actualized yet again.

This may sound counterintuitive because it seems to presume that talking about visions is quite different from having visions. But this presumption does not hold together. While it is being recounted, a narrative about prophecy or another form of hearing from God will have a moment in which God's work as language, image, or coincidence appears. It is a sign and hence an act of God. This moment of divine action has effects only in its implicit juxtaposition against forces that are not animated by the Holy Spirit. The fact that this moment is mediated by language is immaterial twice over. First, there is still a direct causal chain that leads back to God, so everything, including the narrative itself, can be seen as an effect of the miracle through which God appears. This may seem to be special pleading, but recall we have already established that biblical texts have features not common to other texts. This means they have the same potential to operate as direct speech as anonymous written language.[21] We have also seen that prophetic events are prone to being entextualized when recoded as language, to become fixed and iterable occurrences that can be recounted with much of the supporting context (such as the haptic, kinesthetic, and visual elements of the divine aspect of the sensorium) folded into writing. This ironically means there is a tendency for the biblical writing inspired by God to act like speech and for the speech of God to have aspects that make it like writing. Biblical and charismatically mediated prophecy are never so disembedded from their original forms, however, as to be interchangeable with each other. This means divine prophetic words, even though they are recounted later on, can be charged with a speech effect and produce presence in the now just as biblical written material can.

Proof for this can be seen in the prelocutionary effects that Vineyard speakers hope for when they recount prophecy and other events through which God acts in their lives. Charismatically oriented Vineyard believers often recount miracles to each another, either in informal spaces or as part of sermons and other pedagogical and inspirational talks and exchanges. But at times they also share them with nonbelievers, most often through charismatic media, such as books or videos, or in moments of general address, such as in a church service where nonbelievers are present as guests. (Many Vineyard believers tell me that speaking to individuals about things like this in person is awkward because they are afraid they will sound "crazy.") In circumstances like these, stories about miracles and hearing from God are reported because believers hope these stories will have an effect on those who do not know God. They also hope accounts of miracles will act as supplemental presences that are distinguishable from other aspects, encouraging the listener to be willing to work in harmony with the message and on those aspects of the self that are unwilling. These miracles are not countenanced only because they lead individuals to God, though that is their chief purpose. Rather, they are also prized because of their status as signs and wonders, evangelical tools that lead believers to better know God or renew the faith of those whose faith is waning. Accounts of miracles have potential to bring about new constellations of willfulness and will; in short, they are miracles themselves. This does not mean that we should consider each renarrativization as identical to, or as an aspect of, the original event. Different affects and intensities are being threaded through the diagram each time, and shifts from, say, a primarily visual or physically palpable aspect of the sensorium to one primarily centered in language are important. Whatever continuity there may be between a retelling and the original event, there is also considerable difference. But each time people recount God acting in the world, God is acting in the world yet again and the diagram is actualized one more time. And this repetition of stories is at once another mode of typification *and* elaboration and an instance of the miracle on its own; hence, it also bears the capacity to order things anew.

6. The Body, Tongues, Healing, and Deliverance

In our discussion of language and sincerity, we mentioned but did not dwell on the idea that none of the elements of the diagram necessarily maps onto the categories that constitute the person. We discussed this as a problem of enunciation, but it is also a problem regarding the boundaries of the self. The willing and the unwilling/willful may at times be identical to a person or persons; we have seen moments when people were commanded to do something they did not desire, making the miracle-inaugurated contest between the willing and the unwilling aspects a struggle "internal" to the self. There were also moments of "spiritual warfare," in which those who were unwilling were entirely external or absent persons whose sensorium is not at issue in this moment of prayer; this is certainly the case in more politically conservative churches, where "liberal" or "humanist" political figures are considered appropriate targets rather than beneficiaries of prayer. However, most of the time both variants of the will are to differing degrees present within the same person and between persons, and the willful and unwilling aspects must struggle against each other wherever they are located; subjects may eventually be unified by their responses to such internally mixed constitutions of the self, but they are sundered the moment they have contact with the divine sign.

Just as the willing and willfulness can be ambiguously positioned in regard to the perceived boundaries of the person, so too can the miraculous sign. There are moments when the appearance of the miraculous in the sensorium is unproblematically positioned outside the subject. These are often providential moments, amazing coincidences that run counter to any folk sense of how probability functions. However, as we have seen, most often the divine part of the sensorium is at best only ambivalently situated "outside the head," and sometimes it appears to be clearly a part of the inner world of the self. Recall voices that are sensed *as if* they were audible but not entirely; these voices are examples of an ambivalently situated edge of the divine assemblage. There are also imagistic and spontaneous thoughts that occur to some believers. These are clearly mental pictures internal to them, but they are also unquestionably an effect of an exercise of outside divine agency. Likewise, prophetic speech, whether presented as being ventriloquized by the Holy Spirit as reported speech or as an interpretation of an imagistic event, plays with language, expressing an unproblematic relation between an individual's own internal thoughts and the external reference.

In this chapter, we will trace how the splintering of the self is brought about through a miraculous event that is indifferent to an internal-external divide and has effects that often divide the person into willing and unwilling aspects. We will also track how this splintering destabilizes another opposition: the Cartesian firewall between mind and body. It is no secret that Pentecostal and charismatic Christianities are embodied.[1] But there is no emphasis on the foregrounding of the body as just one cascading effect of a miraculous diagrammatic that can also spill over into practices, such as divinely inspired reading or contemplation, that tend to be understood in most of America as hypocognizing the body, as opposed to hypercognizing it. We start by discussing how speaking in tongues expresses the body and the person in the Vineyard. Beginning with a linguistic practice may seem counterintuitive, but speaking in tongues is about the embodied and sonorously material aspects of voice and speech, in which the external aspects of language rise to the fore. We then work toward healing, for which the body and mind act on each another through a miraculous circuit. Finally, we take up deliverance from demons, a moment when the miracle-effectuated circuits between inside and outside, body and mind, and will and willful work to temporarily challenge the ethical charge of the miracle and create a space for the demonic.

TONGUES

Speaking in tongues is not a universal Vineyard ability. In many forms of classical Pentecostalism, speaking in tongues was "initial evidence" of a person's receiving the Holy Spirit and hence was the chief indicator of salvation. In the Vineyard, though, glossolalic activity is not a requirement for any kind of spiritual status. It's not surprising, therefore, that some have not noticed its presence in the Vineyard. Many Vineyard believers are themselves unaware that tongues are relatively common in the Vineyard; once or twice when speaking with Vineyard lay members I mentioned tongues, and they were surprised to learn it took place in their church, even though I had repeatedly seen the same individuals in prayer circles with people who were speaking in tongues while standing next to them. I have even seen a pastor stop a seaside baptism midcourse when someone attending the baptism started speaking in tongues out loud; obviously anxious that this display might unnerve people, he briefly paused the baptismal ritual to take time to explain to everyone present what tongues were, making clear that it was "just another way of worshiping the Lord."

Speaking in tongues, however, is not rare. While not everyone I knew spoke in tongues, many of the most charismatically engaged members did. For some, tongues took place primarily in private devotion, but just as frequently, it was done publicly in a subaudible style: a quite breathy murmur, a stream of sibilant phonemes that sounded like a cross between some lost Semitic language and the sound of rushing water. Speaking in tongue was not a trance state. Sometimes people seemed to be carried away when speaking in tongues, while at other times they seemed as alert as in any other moment. One church leader said even when speaking in tongues he had no problem scanning a room full of people engaged in exuberant prayer and keeping track of what was occurring and who was praying for whom. Still speaking in tongues was not something that could be done with any kind of automaticity; no one was able to just "perform tongues" at the drop of a hat. Rather, tongues existed as an index of charismatic activity the same way a barometer predicts rain.

Speaking in tongues can be framed as a skill. Vineyard members who grew up in Pentecostal families where speaking in tongues has a salvific and eschatological importance remember struggling to speak in tongues as children. They recall it was difficult but they also believed it was achievable, even though at least one member retrospectively doubted she was "really" speaking in tongues. The sense that tongues is not necessarily a true expression of the spirit is not an artifact of childhood. A young adult member, who came to the Vineyard from a more fundamentalist-leaning church that was skeptical of the charisms, earnestly desired tongues and prayed for them regularly. But he only slowly and haltingly acquired them. Even though he was apparently speaking in tongues for a while, actually "receiving" tongues was a gestalt achievement that only occurred when the entire practice finally came to him fluidly as opposed to intentionally.

Speaking in tongues is the only charism I failed to successfully participate in as an anthropologist. This was not because of any outside restrictions placed on me but because of my own inability. As mentioned earlier, I was able to engage in what by Vineyard standards were considered effective acts of "hearing from God," at least during a few prayer sessions; I also prayed for healing a few times and once was credited with curing a headache. I was always careful to pray only for people who knew who I was and understood my ethnographic project; there were admittedly some gifts, such as casting out demons, that I was too nervous to invoke because of their degree of seriousness and my concern I might psychologically damage the person I was praying for. I had enough skill that I was even told at a particularly poorly attended Sunday morning summer vacation season church service that I could be part of that day's prayer team; I declined because I was afraid it would open me up to praying for people who were unaware I was an anthropologist and not a believer. Still, although I was not "religiously musical," as Max Weber phased it, I was at least "good enough" to be invited to take part take part. Despite all this charismatic experience, though, I was never able to speak in tongues. Even so, all my attempts at glossolalia, despite my trying for long awkward periods of time when I was alone in my bathroom, felt halting, artificial, and a little guileful.[2]

Tongues does not always feel "fake" when a person first attempts it. Every so often someone claims that speaking in tongues came to them all at once. The clearest version I heard was from someone whose background was solidly evangelical rather than Pentecostal. As a teenager, this person claimed to have suddenly started "fluently" speaking in tongues at a Christian summer camp while praying alone in a tent with a particularly loved counselor. A similar narrative was shared with me by a member of the generation that joined the Vineyard in the early 1980s. While praying alone at the solidly evangelical Wheaton College, he suddenly started speaking in tongues. These two stories are in some ways the inverse of the other narratives, in as much as these two people neither desired nor apparently had to labor to acquire the ability. They also did not gradually achieve the capacity to speak in tongues. A shared sensibility, however, does unite those who struggled for tongues and those to whom tongues came all at once: speaking in tongues is only considered "authentic" when it is not the result of concentrated, purposeful human activity. Whether the ability is the result of multiple attempts or is acquired suddenly and unsought, genuine tongues do not feel labored. The glossolalic subject ultimately must be passive.

Fluidity is important because of the way glossolalia is typically understood in the Vineyard. Unlike classical Pentecostalism, tongues are not xenoglossy, that is, communication in unfamiliar foreign languages through supernatural means. To be more exact, the default assumption is that tongues are not usually instances of xenoglossy. Every so often I heard someone tell the congregation about a friend, often someone who was on a short-term mission trip or something similar, who spoke in tongues in the local language; I repeatedly heard a similar type of tale centering around someone speaking in tongues domestically, who was asked by an emigrant to America where the friend "learned" the emigrant's language.

For the most part, though, tongues are described as a private "love language to God," the sense of privacy and love stemming from the peculiar intimacy of tongues; in turn, this intimacy results from the way tongues thread through the subject. Tongues are a gift from God but also a capacity of the person. More peculiarly, people do not understand what they are saying when they speak in tongues. I have never heard anyone gloss or translate what they "said" when speaking in tongues; when asked, they almost always denied knowledge of any semantic content.

There is an exception to this rule. On *very rare occasions*, someone with the gift of interpreting tongues will offer a translation when tongues are spoken in a semipublic space like a church (already a rare event in the Vineyard). In both tone and content, the translation will be very similar to that spoken by someone engaging in the ventriloquizing mode of prophetic speech. An interpretive event is so rare I have witnessed it only a handful of times and only at the Yorba Linda church where John Wimber preached; this crowd was charismatically seasoned and for the most part the members were older. While I did not often discuss public interpretation of tongues with people in the Vineyard, the few times I did, people were surprised; one time I received an intensive grilling from someone, who was obviously fascinated. This person acted as if I were recounting an encounter with some incredibly rare and fantastic animal that he had read about but never seen.

But usually glossolalia is treated as if it has no referential content, functioning like an interjection or divine phatic speech. Obviously, speaking in tongues is something that can be overheard by others, but having others overhear it is not a necessary aspect of the speech act. The real question is this: Who is the intended recipient of a speech that cannot be understood by others? There are definitely performative or atmospheric effects associated with tongues.[3] Speaking in tongues both makes and marks the moment it takes place, and there is something decentering and, to my ears, slightly uncanny about the murmur that tongues create if there is a sufficient mass of glossolalics present. The people present when tongues are spoken are part of the audience, but they are at most intended overhearers rather than addressees. In addition, they are not usually hearing a particular locutionary act but the press of tongues in general.[4] Rather, tongues as a "love language to God" are formally directed to God. This is curious because tongues come from God only to traverse the subject and return to God; the subject does not understand the language and this languages has no semantic content. The language is one of pure sensation and intensity, which the subject can either constrict or let flow but cannot create or shape to particular effect.

The lack of semantic content means tongues are also a language of pure embodiment. Tongues have no content other than the sensation of speech, the rhythm of breath, and the affective load created and conveyed. Hence the common association of tongues and tears. Individuals praying in tongues usually do not cry, but crying is often mentioned. Crying is not tied to sadness or grief, however. Like tears during praise music worship, tongues are an affective *too muchness.*

HEALING

In one way, tongues are an extreme case of what we have seen with prophetic speech: language as pure divine force, as nothing but intensity, as something both predicated on and indifferent to the believing subject. In another way, there is nothing odd about how language operates here because of the nature of language itself. Consider again the discussion of the "Protestant language ideology." There are historical reasons for the existence of this vision of ethical and effective language, reasons that the anthropologist Webb Keane ties to early modern efforts at religious reform.[5] But there is another formal reason for protestant language ideology. Protestant language ideology is concerned with proper language use, rather than with valorizing particular languages or dialects or connecting specific language forms to particular social or political formations. It exists because of ambivalence about language itself: socially coded yet internalized, stratified by lexical contents and grammatical rules yet capable of play and innovation, functioning as a way of referencing the world but also working as a form of expression, or of transforming circumstance through language's performative capacities. It even relates to whether language is cognitive or embodied, earthly or otherworldly, even as it functions not just to create these differential categories but to negotiate the position and permeability of the boundaries between the categories it creates.[6]

Healing similarly crosses such boundaries, but its continuing importance in the Vineyard's self-narrative means it works to far greater effect. Healing was an important part of the kinds of global Christianities that were influential when John Wimber was shaping the Vineyard; healing also played an important part in John Wimber's early experiments with this hands-on charismatic activity.[7] Reports about healing circulate throughout the Vineyard, though the forms of reported healing run along a continuum. On one end, pastors at times allow a believer to testify during Sunday morning services about long-running back pain that was healed through prayer or a worrying tumor that inexplicably disappeared by the time the doctor performed a biopsy. On the other end, one occasionally hears, usually not from the pulpit, about someone raising the dead. Like xenoglossy, this activity is almost always told thirdhand by someone who had heard about it from a person who had been traveling in a foreign place like Africa or Southeast Asia. The *idea* of raising the dead in itself is sometimes enough. On a few rare occasions I heard (again, always thirdhand) people recount stories about people *attempting* unsuccessfully to raise the dead in the United States; in the relatively early days of the Vineyard, John Wimber would say, usually with an excited grin, that he could "hardly wait" until he himself had the chance to raise someone from the dead.

Raising the dead, the prototypical New Testament miracle, is a limit case, the far end of a continuum of divine healing that runs from the serious to the frivolous and from the overtly supernatural to the merely divinely guided conventional medicine practices. This providential form of healing is exemplified by a common type of healing prayer, in which the petitioner may bring about the success of a medical procedure by, for example, requesting that God guide the hands of the surgeon; similarly, someone may pray that naturally existing bodily capacities for healing be divinely catalyzed for a quick recovery.

This type of prayer may seem a step down from raising the dead; in some ways it is the inverse of praying for resurrection. That does not mean there is not a continuum running from a radical supernatural intervention to a particularly pleasing outcome of a medico-technical or biological process. Factors influencing where on the continuum a particular type of healing falls are the forms and measures of space and distance involved. Prayers for successful medical procedures are usually marked by a double absence or distance—a physical and temporal gap exists between the person or persons praying and both the object of the prayer and the medical procedure. In a typical prayer taking place in private conversation or during a small group meeting, someone may mention they have an ill family member, such as a sibling or an aunt in another state, who is having an operation; people will then take turns conceiving of various positive scenarios, expressed as prayer requests. People may suggest different outcomes and improvise out loud, though they usually pray for an expedited and successful procedure. In contrast, when people recount attempts (successful or otherwise) of someone raising the dead, they always involve the proximity and presence of the petitioner. The person who is cast as the miracle worker is adjacent to the body and often touches the corpse while he or she commands the deceased person to rise. The miracle worker addresses the dead, rather than God, ordering the dead person to "stand!," "rise!," or "get up!"

The vast majority of prayers, though, can be located somewhere between two poles: (a) entirely verbal prayer at a temporal and physical distance, in which the intended beneficiary is not directly addressed and the prayer is routed between the petitioner and God, and (b) physically and temporally proximate prayer directly addressed to the intended beneficiary (often in an imperative grammatical mood) that is usually supplemented by direct bodily contact. Here is a somewhat typical example from my field notes of a middle-range healing I experienced one night while attending a small group.

> [It's my turn to make a prayer request as we go around a circle, and] I mention that I'm unwell, and I'd like some prayers for my health. Rather than praying for healing right there, in the way that we normally would handle a prayer request, Jacob insists that we get David to do this because he has the gift of healing [David is in another prayer circle in the next room]; his basis for this is that David "straightened [the pastor's] spine" when he prayed over him a few weeks ago. I mention that it is odd that different people have different gifts, but Jacob likens it to people with different athletic skills (he uses Sprewell, the basketball player, as an example). I ask why that should be the case, and Jacob says that it's for the sake of community—if everyone had all the gifts, there would be no need to pray together. Sergio says that it is interesting that people with the same gifts are often attacked by the enemy in the same way (his example is tellingly about healing and lust), then moves smoothly to how God wants to work on people's character in the same way.

> When everyone else is done [receiving prayer for their prayer requests], Jacob grabs David from the other room. I'm led into a bedroom, where I stand while everyone gathers around me; my hands are down at my sides but rotated so that the palms point straight up [though I'm not certain how I found myself taking this stance]. David is behind me to my left, with his hands on my back; Jacob is to my right; my front left shoulder is taken care of by Ethan; Harrison is standing nearby; and Sergio and Luke are sitting on the floor looking reflective. David places another hand on my chest, right on the solar plexus. He is speaking in tongues softly, though more audibly than normal, and the pressure of his hands is gently though surely straightening my posture. He is saying things like "illness go to Jesus," "immune system, be strong—not overly strong—be right—in the name of Jesus," "Body be strong." [This particular language is telling of how individually crafted these seemingly formulaic prayers may seem; I had mentioned weeks earlier

in passing that I had a history of autoimmunologically related skin disorders, though I hadn't brought it up that evening; I credit this for the otherwise strange request for a vigorous, but not too vigorous, immune response.] Jacob "casts out" the illness using those exact words, as if the disease were a conscious entity. After what seems like five to ten minutes, they ask how I feel.

I say better, but not all better, so Jacob and David decide to finish the work, and the praying goes on, the congestion is commanded to drain. There is some drift, at this point, in what is being prayed for; I believe it may be Ethan, who starts it off, asking for sadness to be gone (which is odd, because I hadn't mentioned sadness), that I be filled with joy, that I not be a "sustainer" but an "advancer" (the last was again Ethan's). At a few points I feel faint, I think at a moment when Jacob says something like "come Holy Spirit"—is this just the weirdness of the situation, or the fruit coming from the story Jacob previously told [me about someone who fainted a few days ago while Jacob was praying for him]? Waves of warmth pour over my body. For a second I feel myself on the edge of being really disorientated, but then I come together again as I start following my breaths.

After another pause, I'm checked [again]. David asks me how I am, I tell them I'm better—I actually do feel much better, hardly troubled by my cold symptoms at all now. I thank everyone, telling them that I'm at a loss for words. They laugh, and one of them (I forget who) tells me that I'm not done; David then asks if it would be all right if they pray for blessings for me. I express some nervousness about taking up too much time but agree, and it's more of the same, that I should be a man of the Lord in my department, that I should be blessed in my upcoming marriage (Harrison's request). Eventually it tapers off, and we go to the other room, where everything degenerates to a discussion of movies (much talk about having an all-day *Lord of the Rings* festival when the extended edition comes out) and discussions of half-price sushi, and I fall into a conversation with April about her legal work at the volunteer juvenile legal aid program.

This was a somewhat modest and impromptu healing session; I chose this example because it was the most extended healing session I experienced firsthand on which I was able to make at least passable field notes. What is of interest here is the way in which the forms of address shifted during prayer; during the prayer circle before the healing, people asked for divine intercession for concerns like marital harmony and success with a new job. (One office worker prayed he would not be distracted during his work week by thoughts of an upcoming golf game he was looking forward to.) During the healing session, though, the mode of address shifted, with the addressee no longer being God but disease, which was given as series of commands; for a while prayers for my physical and psychological health were again addressed to God, returning the address to a more deferential footing only to return to the imperative mood with Jacob commanding "Come Holy Spirit." After the part of the session centered on healing was over, however, prayers involving my impending marriage and my position in the anthropology department were again presented as petitions spontaneously made on my behalf to God.

Another important element is the language used to address the disease. In my discussion of glossolalia, I mentioned that not only was language ambiguously positioned between the incorporeal and the corporeal—the subjective and the world outside the subject, the social and the self—but it was also an important element in creating those differences and structuring how the barriers between the incorporeal and corporeal operate. Language achieves this in part through a play of what is addressed in these requests or imperatives and by shifts in the vocabularies that are invoked when these statements are made. The same is true for healing. Let us take the vocabularies of healing first. Most forms of healing have a moment when, as either intention or order, the object being healed or the source of the illness has to be described. The challenge is there is no specific vocabulary set aside for this; rather, there is a wealth of vocabularies taken from technical, expert, or lay discourses that are repurposed on the fly for the activity at hand. For instance, when someone prays for healing, it is not uncommon for the person to invoke medical and anatomical language. Prayers often invoke features, such as muscles, nerves, neurons, white blood cells, and even neurotransmitters, as the person describes or orders diseased parts to remake themselves. Alternately, these biological objects are described as the battleground in narrations of combat with and imminent victory over various enemies, such as abrasions, tears, ruptures, viruses, bacteria, and tumors. Likewise, metaphors can be presented in which chronic pain is figured as "water putting out fire," or affective or mood disorders are referenced as "clouds being lifted and the sun coming in." There are also speech acts, in which the object of the healing is addressed not as a particular metaphorical or actual object but as the "spirit of" something (the "spirit of pain," the "spirit of illness," or the "spirit of depression"). Sometimes as in the prayer session described above the disease is depicted as something that has both agency and volition and is therefore something that one can command to be "cast out." Sometimes if the conditions and inspiration are right, these accounts of disease occurring during prayer can become quite elaborate. I heard firsthand detailed descriptions of pus draining and viruses retreating, of swollen muscles and inflamed nerves calming, and sometimes even of body parts (including organs and other bodily material that are invisible to the naked eye) shifting their colors from red or black to a more calming shade like pink. I heard people invoking a metaphorical sunrise bringing light to a landscape and burning off an obscuring fog or telling various spirits, all with proper names referencing the symptoms they cause, one by one they are not welcome and are being thrown out "in Jesus's name."

People shuttle between these descriptors. Much of healing prayer occurs in semipublic places, such as churches or prayer groups, and several people may pray over the afflicted person. This form of prayer unfolds in a manner similar to the kind of collective hearing from God discussed earlier; the same person not only begins the prayer by addressing God, referring to the prayer patient in the third person as he or she describes the problematic condition and the relief being sought, but also closes the prayer by addressing God and restating the general nature of the request. However, in the middle, people take turns praying over the person, and this often functions like a sort of impromptu verbal jazz, in which a petitioner takes an earlier reference (such as a command for back muscles to reknit themselves) and either elaborates on that reference by redescribing it in greater detail or with shifts in register. In practice, as registers and vocabularies shift, there is also a continual change of focus, a leaping back and forth among the biological, psychological, existential, and spiritual as the locus of action; the person being prayed for at times comes into sharp relief when he or she is discussed as a psychological entity, but when the biological is discussed, the person appears as an assemblage of parts and processes. Later on in the same prayer when the difficulties are discussed in a spiritual framework the person may be discussed as a terrain over which otherworldly forces and energies battle. Like speaking in tongues and healing from God, the diagram when actualized as healing is at best indifferent to the normal boundaries of the person as demarcated in most of middle-class America culture; it often acts to dilate the borders of the person, allowing forces, metonymic chains, and intentionalities to traverse the subject.

It may not initially be clear that healing is an example of the diagram: the presence of imperatives, such as the willful acts of the person as the trigger for prayers and not as something delineated by the miracle, may suggest that the sets of relations that constitute the diagram are no longer in play. If the divine aspect of the sensorium is dependent on surprise, in what way can an imperative, a purposeful act, *a request*, be the engine of surprise? Will, in this case specifically a desire to heal, precedes divine action, which goes against the general sensibility of the instances of the diagram seen so far.

This would be to forget, though, that the charismatic diagram either has all the elements present—albeit in different qualitative intensities—or it is not that particular diagram; if an element or elements were completely absent, it would instead be a diagrammatic expression of some other constellation of forces. This means the appearance of the will and the divine aspect of the sensorium always occur simultaneously and only the sense of import, sense of proportion, or shifts in ratio create the illusion of sequential action. Therefore, even these requests for healing are diagrammatic in the sense that we have been using it, since the requests set out a will for health in harmony with the potential healing miraculous, set against an unwilling aspect of the ill body or mind or of an invasive natural or supernatural agent. Finally, in the moment of prayer and healing, we have a divine event that makes this difference visible even as it transforms the relations between the willing and unwilling. Given the indifference of the diagram to the conventional boundaries of the self, it makes no difference at all if it is the will that "appears" to originate in a human request or imperative. As long as it is either a will that is in harmony with the miracle, or a will that is transformed from (or to) being unwilling by the miracle, the dynamics of the diagram are in play.

DELIVERANCES

All these issues, of temporality, of will and willfulness, and of the shifting boundaries of the self, came into sharp relief when the prophet visited the small group.

The news about his impending visit was broken to the small group well before he arrived, and there had been weeks of anticipation before the prophet came to town.[8] But whatever the group had been expecting was certainly different from what ended up taking place. The prophet wasn't originally labeled as a prophet by the small group participants, and it wasn't particularly clear exactly how and when he achieved that status within the small group. He was first described by the married coleaders of the group as someone who was "gifted at hearing from God," a Vineyard-renowned individual with a particular blessing they had first encountered at a leadership retreat earlier that year. A high school educator by profession, he shared his gifts on the side, driving up and down the state to present seminars to churches. Impressed by him, the coleaders had requested that he come to their small group so the fifteen-to-twenty people, who had been cycling in and out of the once-a-week informal meetings over the past year would have an opportunity to "hear from God" in a new way.

As we have seen, the act of hearing from God had been a thematic touchstone of the small group for some time. But this was new. At some point, the word *prophet* had become the way to identify this upcoming guest. During interviews, invariably held in one coffee shop or another, the small group members I met with would ask me about him. Because I had seen him teach a seminar during the previous spring, I was at times asked by the leaders to describe his supernatural abilities, something I did with a guilty conscience, torn as I was between my anthropological skepticism and my desire to support the small group leaders.

Finally, the day came. When I arrived at the meeting at seven o'clock in the evening, the prophet was sitting on the couch, and seeing him was a bit of shock. When I had first seen him giving the seminar in the auditorium of an elementary school, he had been a flamboyant, energetic presence, darting across the basketball court with a wireless microphone gripped tightly in his hand as he interrupted himself with anecdote after anecdote. Here, he was more inert, sitting glumly on a couch, a balding, goateed white man in his late forties. Slowly the members of the small group and several guests, who were drawn by the unusual nature of the evening, entered; over the course of roughly an hour, twenty people showed up.

When all the chairs in the living room were filled and people had started to sit on the floor, one of the coleaders picked up the guitar, prayed "come, Holy Spirit," and started playing plaintively and slowly the songs that were familiar from church services and worship music CDs and downloaded MP3s. The prophet covered his face with his hands as he started rocking back and forth in time to the music. In the background, the rustling whisper of the "polite," subvocal speaking in tongues could be heard. After a while, the prophet joined in speaking in tongues with his eyes closed, though at times he would open them, stop speaking in tongues, and check his watch—a sign not of bad faith but of nonchalance. As the singing went on, people drifted from the lyrics, with women singing the counterharmonies and one man rushing in improvisatory prayers in a rhythm almost akin to scat singing during the gaps between the lyrics.

After a good forty-five minutes, the prophet started giving what he styled a "fireside chat" (like, he said, the one given by Nixon on the projection screen at the Richard Nixon library). All his taciturn worry had now been washed away, and he was his prior self, the rightful center of attention. He started his talk by speaking haltingly about the vitality of "the kingdom" and about "justice," though he slid off topic rather quickly, discussing instead how God's power would "flip your little theology around." From this point forward, his talk, which was a mixed account of various instances of supposed spiritual warfare with both demons and Jehovah's Witnesses, attacks on Christians for being "religious," and heathens for being heathens, was only so well received. He repeatedly made references to broad categories, such as "Westerners" and "suburbanites," who don't get the message, making comparisons to Africa, a place of (supposed) genuine belief that—he frequently mentioned—he had visited. "Why do we hear so many stories of people being raised from the dead in Africa (after praying for them for four days)? Because they don't know any better, they haven't been educated any better." Realizing this was a faux pas in front of this audience, he quickly repackaged his statement as a claim that Africans, not being awash in a consumer culture, are not schooled in the sorts of empiricisms that serve to preclude belief—something that afflicts Westerners in general and him specifically (as he confessed, "I'm like that too; my brain is my worst enemy"). As was usual for that evening, he rescued himself by going off on a tangent, asking, "Why are there so many civil wars in Africa? Because it's a place of spiritual warfare. It's a land where Christians stand next to people who go to witch doctors." He ended with another change in topic, saying that if you wish to reach the world through evangelical outreach, "Go to the university." One of the campus ministers hissed a loud yes at that minute, but on the whole the audience looked uncertain and restive (later on, his talk would be charitably remembered by some of those present as the weakest portion of the evening).

What he announced next was "ministry time," starting it off with the statement, "First we talked about the kingdom, and now we're going to demonstrate it." That, he clarified, did not mean everything he said would be correct—the person who receives the prophecy is the measure of whether it is right, and the prophet is as likely to be wrong as he is to be right . . . except, of course, when he is right; when one prophetic revelation comes in, other revelations start to vibrate like adjacent guitar strings, making it more likely he will receive messages that are true. After another brief verbal waiver (the prophet doesn't predict death, marriages, and babies—not because he doesn't receive information about them but because of the disruption caused by passing these revelations along), he asked the group a question that seemed to be as much a casual aside as a dramatic presentation, "Is anyone here named Sarah"? There were ten seconds of anticipatory silence. No one in the room was named Sarah.

The prophet smiled and said he was relieved—he was worried that there would be someone named Sarah in the room and she would automatically assume the prophecy would be about her. No, this was a message about a promise, a promise that had been made and that someone had been waiting on, longing for, and is there anyone here sad because they have been waiting on a promise? After another ten-second wait, a blond college-aged student, an active and very charismatically orientated member of the church (but not a regular attendee at this small group) slowly raised his hand as he closed his eyes in angst. Starting to slowly sob to herself, a woman in the back, who had complained in the past about her stalled career and single status, raised her hand as well. Unsteadily, the female coleader said she had a vision of a geranium, or perhaps a tropical flower, atop a snowcapped mountain that looked like Mount Fuji, but there was no response—all eyes were instead on the prophet as he prayed over the college student, his voice a mix of sing-song tongues and a whispered speaking voice as the college student cried. He moved over to the single woman, his hands on her head as he told her, "You are loved by God, as a woman, you are valuable to his eyes as a woman." Casting an eye over the rest of the audience, he issued them a directive—"You know that the prophecy is for you if your first thought is that the prophecy is for you, and your immediate second thought is that it couldn't be you." I looked around and noticed that this one evening, I was not the only ethnographer—three other people were taking notes.

He worked his way around the room dispensing prophecies. The prophet told one man he wasn't meant to have a McJob and he wanted to bless the man's hands because they'll "write songs to the Lord." The prophet then turned to the man's wife, asked if they were together, and after hearing the answer told her "You aren't just some accessory for your husband. I see you taking in and teaching wayward and lost girls, you have value apart from standing in your husband's shadow . . . it's okay not to dust immediately, to let the dishes go undone for twenty minutes." He walked away from her as she cried, ending the exchange with the communication that God wanted her to be creative.

Eventually, he worked his way to a dark-skinned, dark-haired, college-aged man named Justin, who was also not a regular member of the group. Justin sat there, worry and obvious consternation sketched on his face, as the prophet walked up and held his hands. The prophet got his name and his occupation (he was a student at the nearby university) through a little banter and after that brief introduction told Justin, "The Lord wants you to know that he is real, and that he's not the author of your problems. I declare the cross that redeems, you have value to the father, the father knows everything that you're thinking, that he still loves you." He threw out a phrase that he used earlier in the evening: "You don't need to call the psychic friends, you just need to call 1-800-Jesus." The prophet told Justin that he was "not wasting his time," that he was "not stupid," that he didn't get to the university "on some quota." Justin sat there, not particularly moved but not any less anxious either. The prophet asked whether he did computer art, but Justin muttered that he worked in biology, to which the prophet answered, "The arts and the sciences are very close." Another small, uncomfortable pause and then the prophet said to Justin, "Those hurtful things in your family, God wants you to know that it's not your fault." As if he had been waiting for the moment, Justin started to cry. "The Lord knows your heart, the load of guilt we take it off now." Justin continued to cry as the prophet continued his work, saying that he "senses girl problems," but Justin was off in another world, at first slouching forward on his plastic dining-room table chair and then slowly sliding off it. Walking away to pray over someone else, the prophet called out to Justin over his shoulder, "That's the healing of the Holy Spirit, enjoy it!"

Almost everyone paid attention as the prophet went along his way, but to those who stayed with Justin it soon became obvious that he was in no way enjoying his healed state. Finally falling clear of the chair, Justin crashed to the floor, where he began coughing and moaning. A friend of his, the blond student who earlier had been prayed over because he had been waiting for a promise to be fulfilled, now prayed over Justin. From the back of the room, one of the college ministers joined him in prayer with a moving gentleness and concern; the college pastor's genuine caring did nothing for Justin's immediate condition, however. Interrupted from dispensing prophecy, the prophet called out in a mildly annoyed tone that all the blond student had to do was "break the familiar spirit of death." The blond student brought his face right up against Justin's as he snapped his fingers repeatedly in front of Justin's fluttering eyes, rapidly repeating a command for the spirit to leave "in Jesus's name." Justin's moans became louder. Someone rushed a metal bowl from the kitchen as Justin started coughing into it with more force. Justin was by this point being cradled like a pietá, and a charismatic, gentle-voiced Korean American college pastor came up to assist. Justin's face was by then covered in phlegm and specks of blood because he had split his lips. His eyes were glassy and red. A paper towel wiped his face clean, but it didn't stem the mess. The newer college pastor, holding Justin's hand with an obvious tenderness, asked in a calming tone what Justin wanted, and Justin said he wanted "to kill myself." Nervous, I asked one of the coleaders whether we should consider taking him to a hospital, but she didn't reply (the next day she told me she would have taken him to the emergency room if she had felt at any time that he was in danger, but since the attack "seemed pretty clearly spiritual in nature," she thought it was "important to try to get to the root of what had been happening for him personally"). People gathered around Justin encouraging him to cough it out of himself, and some of the bystanders flinched from the moisture as Justin started to violently double over on the floor. The prophet interrupted, saying as if in passing that the church had lost the symbolism of water and then sprinkling a little over Justin's head to no obvious effect before he walked away. As if to continue the theme, someone took a plastic Aquafina water bottle and poured some water down Justin's throat, but the water didn't stay down. The gentle-voiced minister squatted in front of Justin and after a pause continued to talk to him in the same soothing voice he employed earlier, telling him that Jesus died for him and it "isn't a guilt thing," but Justin "has to make a decision to reject" his sins, as well as whatever else has hold over him. Justin bellowed a "No" that, smiling, the gentle-voiced pastor took as a rejection of whatever had a hold on him up to now. Behind them, the female coleader read softly from the Psalms. She passed the college pastor a small plastic bottle of oil, and he anointed Justin's forehead. By now, well over an hour had passed; Justin's eyes were less red and heavier, as if he were about to fall asleep. He mumbled that he couldn't feel his legs, and the gentle-voiced pastor prayed for "wholeness and feeling" to return to his body—as he did so, he touched each of Justin's limp legs, which suddenly twitched with the contact. Justin was led stumbling to a sofa, where the prophet, busy the entire time, came up to him and said in a forced, chipper manner that "It wasn't the worst deliverance I've seen, though you did toss your cookies." As the evening wound down, people prayed in thanks over the prophet; just past two a.m., everyone went home.[9]

What occurred that night was not an exorcism, or at least would not be understood as such in most forms of Pentecostal and charismatic Christianity. And what Justin experienced was not a possession either. An exorcism involves the disembedding of a demon that has usurped the conscience and volition of the person, a state in which the demonic entity enjoys not only complete control but also sole possession. This is a state of affairs that most Pentecostal and charismatic Christians believe cannot occur, or at the least cannot occur to believing Christians, who are under the protection of the Holy Spirit and thus immune from this high degree of demonic predation. It was for this reason that despite their readily granting the existence of demons many forms of early Pentecostalism rejected the idea of possession, and hence exorcism, out of hand.

For other forms of Pentecostalism, though, the allure of engaging in the prototypical New Testament miracle of casting out demons was too much. A secondary understanding of the demonic was slowly developed, according to which what occurred was not possession but, rather, a degree of demonic attack on, and interference with, the person. In this form, although the will may have been severely hampered by demonic attack, the human subject was never eclipsed and the exercise of human agency could never be completely discounted. Generations later, John Wimber encapsulated the Vineyard's version of this model of the relationship between demons and human agency by saying, "I do not believe that demons may own people absolutely while they still live on earth; even when demons gain a high degree of control, people are able to exercise a degree of free will that may lead to deliverance and salvation."[10]

The state that occurs is therefore not *possession*, a term with intimations of the individual as a form of property, but rather domination.[11] Likewise the act of disembodying the demonic is not exorcism, with its sense of expelling an entity in the way one evicts a resident, but rather deliverance, which brings with it undertones of liberation, that is, of rescuing a human under siege, rather than ousting a supernatural other. The importance of agency in a possession is evident in one aspect of the deliverance that occurred in the small group that evening; the turning point in many explicit deliverances often is a moment of *decision* by the demonized individual. A person must make a choice and exercise (as opposed to exorcise) the will. This is done either by accepting Jesus or by rejecting demons or a category of sin that the demon is leveraging to exploit the person (these sins are often associated with a lack of self-control like substance abuse or consuming pornography). This makes sense. Most of the symptoms of demonic attack point to a lack of control. Facial contortions, bodily thrashing, and production of body excretions and effluvia that are usually not discharged in public all suggest a body that is not being governed; and the wails, distorted speech, and often incoherent pleas point to a mind that is not well ordered and is not practicing the usual methods of self-restraint. In contrast, a decision indicates the first moments of a self-control that was not evident earlier in the improvised ritual. It is the point of inflection in the ritual, the moment when the movement of the deterritorialization of the self is overtaken by the reterritorialization of the self, and a harmony of speech, body, and connect begins to reemerge. It is a moment of will over willfulness.

As suggested by the story of Justin's ordeal, the circumstances of a deliverance can be florid and deliverance is unlikely to be a daily event, at least not in the life of an average church member. For a pastor, however, or someone who focuses a great deal of his or her attention on charismatic practice, events like these can be more usual than one may expect. The pastor of the church affiliated with this small group estimated that during two years as head pastor and about a half decade as assistant pastor, he had seen about a hundred deliverances over the course of his career.

Still despite the high frequency of demonic attack encountered by ritual experts, there is a sense that these sorts of events are occurring with less and less frequency. This may be an effect of how these experiences are now stage managed. I was told these sessions used to be handled in a quite different way in the Vineyard. When a manifestation of demonization like the one that occurred in the small group broke out in a public space like a training session, an evening workshop service, a prayer meeting, or even at Sunday worship, it would become the center of attention. The confrontation with the demon or demons would occur right in that semipublic space, serving as a distraction from the planned activities or sometimes bringing the planned event to a halt. I was told of whole rows of folding chairs being taken out by the patient's thrashing about during a deliverance. Today, however, there is a sense that "best practice" would be to move the demonized individual away from the center of attention to some space away from everyone's gaze; occluding these outbreaks lessens their profile, creating a sense that they happen with less frequency or do not happen at all.

The sense that demonic possession occurs less frequently is partly because the people who make this sort of claim belong to an aging Vineyard demographic. For a claim that florid demonic deliverances are on the wane, to be intelligible or to have any degree of credibility, the speaker must have belonged to the Vineyard or to a similar moment for a while, which means they are less likely to be surrounded by the sort of young men who end up being demonized.[12] Another bar to perceived frequency is that speaking in the first person about being demonized can be awkward. On the one hand, there is something about having gone through this level of demonic attack that implies a high level of charismatic experience. Many pastors or other charismatically oriented people often mention some early moment of demonization (though they often also recode it in other accounts as a psychological disorder or substance abuse habit that has been cured through prayer, in effect making it less about combat with an entity and more about the overcoming of a condition). So there is some push for people to reveal their personal experiences of these sorts of events. On the other hand, the commonly understood etiology of demonic attacks hints at aspects of personal and family histories that are usually kept private even in the intimate confines of a church community. There is also something just unnerving about these experiences. I heard people start to talk about these experiences only to stop the discussion abruptly with a comment along the lines of "I'm freaking you guys out."

The decreasing frequency of deliverances in combination with the constant change in church membership that results from greater mobility and a tendency for some members to "church shop" (also known as the "circulation of the saints") tend to dilute the belief in demons.[13] Much like church members who claim to have never heard tongues, even though they have sat next to someone speaking in tongues, some members of Vineyard churches are unsure that demons exist in the modern world; people have sincerely asked in private discussions and in Vineyard small groups whether evil spirits still exist as the Bible says and, if so, what has happened to them?

There is little time for this question among older Vineyard veterans. Even if they have a sense that confrontations with demons are less prevalent, the existence of demons is in no way vitiated. To these older Vineyard members, modernity is not a special time with a particularly limited and circumscribed set of supernatural actors but is just another moment between the Incarnation and the Parousia. As one pastor said with a certain amount of annoyance, it is ridiculous to think that just because there are now airplanes, all the demons have gone away. Still, absent demonstrations, such as what occurred with the prophet, new members, particularly those who are entering from a prior evangelical or "secular" mode of a/religiosity, often question whether demons are active in the contemporary world.

DEMONIC ETIOLOGIES

While it is not uncommon to hear secondhand about women being demonized to the point of a deliverance, I think it's significant I've only seen men demonized firsthand and only men have talked to me about their experiences of being demonized. This does not mean women are not beset by demons; a great many charismatically active Vineyard believers, both male and female, are. This issue is complicated by the fact that there is a sliding scale of demonization, and the low-end-of-the-scale demonic attacks are a common explanatory trope among both men and women. I heard people say they had been "attacked by the enemy" when they had a run of events that someone else may classify as "bad luck." Family squabbles, mechanical difficulties, minor health problems, and even a general irritability can be signs one is being harassed by demons, especially if these troubles interfere with religious or ethical obligations. The husband and wife who ran the small group, for instance, each told me independently that an uptick in such minor inconveniences regularly occurred over the course of a week, hitting its peak on the afternoon of the day the small group was scheduled; obviously the enemy wished to interfere with what the couple saw as their ministerial obligations.

This claim can be given too much weight; not everyone in the Vineyard resorted to the language of demonic attack when explaining mounting frustrations. Furthermore, those who did rely on demonic accounts were fully capable of "code switching," producing demon-free, quotidian secular narratives of the same events. My sense is this is not a case of people having learned to adopt secular language but an indication there are multiple causal models available. This is not about a tiered causality; we are not dealing with Azande apologists, who demand to know not why the grain silo collapsed and killed a man but why the collapse occurred at the particular time when this particular man was underneath it.[14] Rather, these accounts are context dependent; a person who has received a shock from the electric coffeemaker may reference it as a demonic attack but still be sure that the appliance is electrically grounded the next time it is used.[15] And despite their effective copresence, both accounts are complete on their own.

These instances of low-level demonic harassment fall short of requiring the sort of deliverances seen above. Demonic attack and demonization fall along a continuum stretching from mere bad luck to the discontinuities and irregularities of behavior on display the night the prophet attended the small group. What allows for the differential positing in the continuum is how deeply demons can strike their blows.

Demons gain the sort of purchase that can only be undone through deliverance as a result of two things: trauma and sin. Just as demons point to an outside force that has effects on someone's internal constitution and capacities for self-management, the loci of the sins that allow for demonization are not necessarily "within" the demonized subject. Traffic with the occult by either the subject or the subject's parents (or earlier ancestors) is a common vector for demonization, though occult can refer to something as anodyne to secular eyes as playing with tarot cards or Ouija boards. While the occult is the paradigmatic causal factor in demonization, it by no means exhausts the various ethical faults that can be demonically leveraged as grounds for a sustained attack. One partial enumeration by John Wimber reads like a laundry list of failures of the evangelical will: "Unrighteous anger, self-hatred and hatred of others, revenge, unforgiveness, lust, pornography, sexual wrongdoings, various sexual perversions (like transvestism, homosexuality, bestiality, sodomy), and drug and alcohol abuse commonly open the doors to demonic influence."[16]

These sins are all moments of willfulness or being unwilling, failures of self-control, or instances of inappropriate appetites carried out to disproportionate extremes. What is striking is that almost all these activities could be understood to be joyless mechanistic compulsions as well. Whenever I heard Vineyard believers discuss these sorts of behaviors, they were with one or two exceptions never discussed as desires in the way one would discuss an attraction to something pleasurable or beautiful. Rather, they were discussed as ruts, inabilities, repetitions, and traps. More interesting is the fact that this language was also relied on when believers dealt with compulsions, such as pornography, alcohol, or illicit substances, that they credibly claimed to have dealt with firsthand. These sins are surprisingly frequent touchstones for some (but certainly not all or most) members of the Vineyard. There are reasons having to do with speech genres and the performative requirements of some roles that may encourage believers, and particularly male believers, not just to own these topics but to own them in a particular manner; they are ways of celebrating a certain type of sexuality or masculinity even as one simultaneously foreswears it.[17] These caveats aside, there is little reason to think that the framing of these acts as joyless is disingenuous or an instance of phantasmatic countercathexes that serves to push back against the temptations awakened by the jouissance of the other. Rather, these are reactions to ego-dystonic compulsions that cannot be controlled—the sense is of something in the self that is rejected as not the self—and thus can readily be seen as being the exercise of an alien agency, a foreign will.

This explanation may seem to be a crass psychologization of sin, an imposition of an inappropriate mode of analysis; in effect, this may come across as a category mistake. This is not the case, however, because in the Vineyard both sin and the demonic are already heavily psychologized. Recall that the other etiological vector for demonization is trauma. Trauma is understood in almost exactly the same sense as it is understood by most other Americans as an experience, or a set of experiences, so laden with a painful affective charge that it becomes at once inassimilable and unforgettable: charred aspects of the self that preclude growth and warp behavior, creating either phobic counter-reactions or odd compulsions to repeat the experience in a way that appears to lack self-control. There is a like-for-like edge here; the assumption is that someone sexually abused as a child will be likely to act out sexually as a teenager or a young adult, and the children of alcoholics are considered particularly vulnerable to alcoholism. There is also a sense that trauma creates compulsive behaviors that anesthetize the subject from the original psychic injury.

Many people also see these traumas as demeno-genetic. The language used varies: I heard people talking about demons "latching onto the hurt" or even entering "through the wounds." This language depicts the demonic and psychological as cocatalysts, or even as two different expressions of the same phenomenon. When they are seen as cocatalysts, there is an idea that when dealing with serious demonic attack that involves long-running behavioral problems, such as cutting, substance abuse, or forms of painful sexual behavior, the casting out of a demon is an important but not a final step. Pastors often will continue to counsel people after an episode, or at the least encourage (or sometimes bring) them to meet with either a Christian or secular therapist. The sense that these two states are connected is not seen just when people discuss "aftercare" but also when they imagine demonization itself. As an example, I heard a person described as having a narcissistic attachment to the attention that comes both with bouts of demonization and with attempts at deliverance. I also heard Vineyard members seamlessly transition to implicit theories of psychological causation when discussing demonic attacks. For instance, a few days after the interchange between Justin and the prophet, a small group member stated that she was really affected by the thought that human beings had "inflicted" that kind of hurt on Justin and Justin was tormented as a result of another's "relational malfunction." Unlike other explanatory models, here spirituality and psychology do not require much "code switching": the borders between them are porous.

There is a continuum between quotidian harassment by demons and the sort of full demonization that requires a deliverance, as well as a continuum between demonic and psychological accounts of what may be generously called "maladaptive behavior." There is also no sharp break between deliverances and healing. In fact, the two are so closely connected that one Vineyard observer may see a prayer interaction as a healing, whereas another may see it as a particularly tame deliverance.[18] This indeterminacy is sometimes purposefully made use of. People in pastoral roles, whether in name or in effect, sometimes claim to sense the presence of the demonic in church members or small group participants. I heard someone say they felt a "darkness" in some people, while someone else referred to feeling the ambient temperature become colder when they were in the proximity of someone; people also sometimes talk about hairs standing up on the back of the neck or malodorous aromas. These are taken as suggestions though not guarantees of demonization; short of the kind of full-blown manifestation that occurred at the small group, it is hard to know for certain when demons actually are present. But there are ways to work around this lack of certainty. A small group leader told me she had used the following tactic when certain members of her group continually struggled with the same sin or problem: When she prayed over these individuals, she sometimes used the "cast out in Jesus's name" formulation. If the force were demonic, this formulation could function as a prophylactic deliverance, a simultaneous personification and removal of an entity all at once without the disturbance of a major showdown, or the raising of awkward lingering questions about which sins or weaknesses might lie behind it. And because of the indeterminacies of the language, the person at the center of the procedure may not even realize this may be read as a deliverance, albeit a "quiet" one.[19]

Hence ambiguity can be used to facilitate low-conflict interventions. However, deliverance's position at the nexus of several crosscutting continuums can be as much an engine of discord as a way of preventing it. One of the interesting things about the sort of demonic attacks that trigger deliverances is they seem to always occur in charismatically intense settings. The one time I heard about someone who was considered to be "demonized" being brought to the hospital for a psychiatric complaint it did not go well. The person (again, a young, college age man) had a history of cutting himself and other forms of self-harm. He was brought to the emergency room by some close charismatic evangelical friends. They had been making attempts at deliverance off and on for almost a week; each one would seem to be successful for a day or two, but another manifestation would bubble up again. At this point, they were more concerned about his capacity for bodily rather than spiritual injury because his threats of self-harm during these incidents were becoming increasingly common and were sounding increasingly serious. With his permission, they brought him to the emergency room, probably hoping he would receive short-turn psychiatric care and oversight. During the visit, however, he acted perfectly normal, displaying none of the behaviors that had given rise to his friends' concerns. He was shortly released.

This case is interesting because other than the prophet, I never heard of anyone who claimed to have encountered a full demonic manifestation "in the wild," that is, outside a charismatic service or a collective session of charismatic prayer. There are of course reasons why this might be the case, ranging from a sense of the situational appropriateness of charismatic behavior to the fact that in different settings demonic manifestations have different ontological framings; these different framings, in turn, invoke different diagnostic practices and different conceptions of what may be possible. These ontic presumptions certainly have some explanatory power, but they treat the outbreak itself as an independent variable, assuming that the phenomena classified as demonic manifestations sometimes appear in religiously inflected spaces and sometimes in spaces where biomedical or psychiatric nosological logic is in control. But they also assume that the logic, characteristics, or timing of these appearances have nothing to do with the kinds of religious or medicalized spaces that they occur in and merely affect the degree to which they unfold and how they are classified. In short, these presumptions avoid acknowledging the possibility that charismatic modes of religiosity and the creation of religious spaces may actually be *a necessary prerequisite* of these sorts of manifestations.

These demonological incidents are most likely causally overdetermined: There are without doubt autonomous psychiatric, biomedical, depth-psychological, and biographical forces at work, which is to say other diagrammatic relations are also in effect and are being expressed. But there is also something about the vagaries of the charismatic diagram itself that is expressed in these incidents. Consider the indifference with which the charismatic diagram freely traverses the boundaries of the person. The effect of the diagram is to flatten and to some degree laminate the elements that are normally considered "interior" with all the external elements that are captured by the senses; the salience of the outside/inside distinction recedes, occluded by the relationship between crosscutting wills and the miraculous sign. But at the same time that this is a simultaneous operation, it is not an instantaneous or crystalline one; as we will immediately discuss, while some elements in the situation are reconstituted as surprise, as being willing, willful, or unwilling, two *other* processes unfold simultaneously.

First, as the various aspects catalyze each other, they effectively create zones of indistinction that abut. Reconstituting the internal and external borders through their redistribution of will, willfulness, and surprise, the mutual interactions between forces blur their borders even as they allow the forces to retain their natures. They become "clear but indistinct."[20] This allows some of the ethical charge of one force to commingle with others, even as the realization of the diagram is making each segment—the willing, the unwilling, the miraculous sign, and the quotidian ground—"more of what it is."

Second, the diagram's actualization also opens the way for more occurrences that come in the actualization's immediate wake. Sometimes occurrences spark some other diagram, some other state of affairs; these differences either become imbricated with the charismatic diagram as it continues to unfold or short circuit the charismatic diagram, giving birth to a new event that overrides the previous set of relations. This other diagram forces the entirety of the situation into, for example, the realm of medical emergency, the clash of personalities, the problem of denominational or church governance, or theological crisis.

But sometimes a new occurrence falls into the already-existing diagram to become a further moment in the unfolding of the miraculous. We have already seen examples of this in how speaking in tongues at times catalyzes healing or prophecy as the affective charge spills over and the miraculous sign transforms or interrupts itself. In other moments, an element crosses various zones of indistinction as a moment of willfulness becomes willing; this can occur in a manner that is so striking in its speed or intensity that in itself it becomes miraculous, another expression of a partially occluded divine assemblage; think of the barely audible divine glossolalic speech discussed earlier in this chapter, or of the way an account of a prophetic word can touch someone to such an extent that they respond to it as they would a miraculous sign in itself. In events like these, the strength and color of being willing are so striking that willing becomes itself a miraculous sign, a transformation in character that can only be credited to God. All the while, as the charismatic diagram shifts in how it expresses itself, becoming enchained with other diagrams, or even just enduring, the affects that constitute it complement each other and blend together, with layers of texture building and combining. This is the reason why sensations, such as joy and sorrow, submission and triumph, that seem incommensurable to some secular sensibilities can often occur simultaneously in these charismatically loaded moments.

This is not a linear process. We have seen that over the unfolding of the diagram, there is a certain shape to these things; we can talk roughly about how praise music affects how a worship session unfolds and about the perceptible sequence—an opening prayer followed by church members taking turns praying and finally a closing prayer—of collective prayer. But the overlaying of affect and the multiple bodily reactions and freewheeling mental associations mean there is a core lack of predictability. This lack of predictability includes the way bleeding across the zones of indistinction occurs. What happens when a new form of unwillingness occurs, one that expresses itself immediately? And what happens when this expression of unwillingness occurs not just immediately but with a force similar to that found in those appearances of willingness that are so striking they themselves can gain the element of surprise necessary to become miraculous? In short, what happens when the miraculous and the unwilling become for a brief instance conjoined?

These interplays and shifts are visible when we look at the prophet's visit to the small group. When he began his talk, his language was at first centripetal, providing a discursive monologue in which it was clear he was not just the animator but the author as well. This was speech in a recognizable genre, even if it was a genre in which, at least that evening, he had limited facility. The topic of his monologue pivoted when he outlined the capacities he would present during "ministry time." He started to diminish as the guarantor of meaning: while he suggested he was more right than wrong statistically speaking, he also presented himself as having neither power nor agency over whether he produced "true" speech or whether his statements corresponded to an actual or imminent state of affairs. Further, the model he presented for the production of truth was not formed on the basis of any kind of rationalized epistemology or propositionally inductive or deductive process. Rather, building from his "guitar string" analogy, truth is a contagion; that is, the truth of one statement brings about the truth of the following statement in a way that is apparently indifferent to whether these statements are linked beyond their having been presented at this specific time and in this particular space.

And then that evening truly began. This was not a complete break with what went before. As the prophet circulated giving people their truths, he maintained the same speaking persona. Further, as evidenced by the way the coleader's own prophetic intervention was brushed aside by the prophet, this was when a certain monological edge to the evening began in earnest. However, even as he took center stage, questions of attribution, address, and validation became more difficult. The prophet stated that words "are meant for you" (and hence were presumably true for the person as well, especially if he or she initially *rejected* their truthfulness). Further the prophet as animator did not even know whom he was specifically addressing, though he was certain he *was* addressing specific individuals. In addition, when he did discover which individual he was addressing, he had no evidential basis for his statements. He also sometimes claimed not to understand the meaning of his statements.

In what way were truth effects produced during this evening-long prophetic encounter? To some degree, the truth of prophecy is performative, that is, made true simply by its being proclaimed. The woman who was told that she was not "just some accessory for [her] husband" was a successful and notably assertive academic. While her husband was beginning a successful career as a parachurch minister and the author of Christian books, his career was only in its initial stages and whether he would attain a degree of success was not yet evident. Now it may be that (whether by dint of his own lights or through some other force) the prophet had managed to intuit a core concern or insecurity in that woman. It is just as likely, however, that this statement was just one of many that could have been made and that would have become her truth by virtue of their being presented to her in that space.

Even discounting performativity entirely, the formal structure of these communications is the presentation of a truth, a miraculous sign of something of which the recipient is unaware and that he or she may find startling. This makes these speech acts doubly ex-centric: a truth about oneself that one has no access to that is presented by a stranger, who is relaying it from some other horizon and has no insight into its meaning. This means that receiving a prophetic word is not simply an instance of recognition, or at least is not one in the sense of identifying an already known and assimilated proposition. It is an opening up and a crisis of origins and personhood.

Relatively early in the prophet's performance and well before the evening of prophecy had turned into an evening of deliverance, the prophet had some words for me. He claimed that he had heard "drudgery oh-no" transformed to "Heigh-ho, heigh-ho, it's off to work we go," from Disney's *Snow White and the Seven Dwarfs;* he said "God finds favor" with me and I "don't have to feel [like] an outsider." Out of context, these words may sound anodyne and perhaps even a bit generic. But in that space and during that moment, they triggered a swarm of concerns, anxieties, and hopes that were worked through in parallel as I sought to determine their import. What did these statements say about me and what aspects of the will did they summon up? All this occurred despite my ethnographic role and my skepticism regarding the underlying ontological presumptions that animated the exercise. The effect was an odd one because the affective lode of the situation, the too-muchness of the event, locked me into the moment with a kind of sharp insistence that has been rare in my life, while at the same time a welter of possible associations bubbled at the edge of my consciousness. It had no single emotional "tone" but was a stinging, bittersweet sensation set in seemingly autonomous and contradictory keys of sorrow and joy.

That evening, I experienced merely a strange frisson; my role as an ethnographer, emblematized by the notebook and pen in my hand, kept me from becoming as carried away as some of the other people had been when prophecy was given to them. Absent the role and supporting props, however, I could have had a different experience. Of course, there is no guarantee even for those who are conversant in the form and have been habituated to instances like these for years that the process will take. One participant, who was famous in the group for his dedication to nongovernmental organization work involving human trafficking, was particularly nonplussed when the prophet told him "there are such things as 'white Martin Luther Kings,'" he would "be given a microphone soon," and he was "feisty" (the image the prophet reported receiving was of a frog being placed in a specimen jar, the force of the frog's hopping causing the whole specimen jar to jump around). Days later, when asked why he was indifferent to the prophet's seemingly on-the-nose words, he dryly remarked that he and the prophet had met each other earlier at a wedding. The obvious implication was that no supernatural agency was necessarily present (the political clumsiness of the phrase "white Martin Luther King" probably did not help). Others managed to maintain a critical attitude not because of their skepticism but because of their excitement about the possibility of the prophecies' validity. Through subsequent small group discussion and interviews, I learned three people that night were "testing" the prophet, saying there were specific things they wanted to hear from God. Only one of them felt that her question had been answered, another said his or her question did not get addressed, and the third had to leave before the meeting was over and thus never found out whether the prophet was able to answer his or her question.

It would, therefore, be a mistake to say the prophecies were automatic or the truths were manufactured and circulated. However, some participants said they were profoundly affected that night. It takes little imagination then to understand how in the alchemy of the moment willingness and surprise may bleed together and some believers may end up crying. But that is not the only possible blending. During peak events like receiving personally directed prophecy in a charged setting, the subject is thrown into an ethically valued language privileging exterior supernatural casual forces. This collision with ex-centric supernatural language occurs during a moment when the person's boundaries are radically dilated and when the task of deciphering the content of the prophecy opens up expanding associative horizons. While surprise and willingness is one possible conflation of forces, in a moment as fluid as this, it is also possible that other forces might partially fuse. A supernaturally tinged surprise and a forceful unwillingness could bleed into each other. At this strange moment when surprise is sutured to willfulness, the thoughts, sensations, and desires of the believer that run counter to the willing would be given a supernatural valence. This is how demons are actualized.

Therefore, demons' manifesting only during charismatic practices makes sense, since it is *the explosion of potential*—the person's *purposeful openness to a validated and supernaturally understood but essentially stochastic process* and the *crisis of what is self and what is other*—that not only controls and de-escalates manifestations of the demonic but *also* creates the circumstances in which the demonic might be made manifest. This is not to say that demonic manifestations are the telos of the diagram or of any larger ethical processes of self-formation that rely on or have incorporated the diagram. But they are certainly *expressions* of the charismatic diagram, albeit ones with particular features. Demonic manifestations are what Gilles Deleuze would call a "line of flight" from the diagram; if the circumstances are not recaptured by the agentive language and contacted sense of self that are also valued by the Vineyard, then there is the very real potential that the situation could rush ahead of itself, pushing things forward into the unknown and letting both the situation and the subject decohere.

Demons have been called the dark faces of the Vineyard's style of producing God.[21] It is certainly easy to see them as an interest, perhaps even at times an obsession that could be considered unhealthy, especially if charismatic activity is viewed as ultimately a therapeutic process (and therapeutic processes are undoubtedly a core element of contemporary American religion).[22] But it should also be thought of as a continuing escape, even if it is a mode of escape that outsiders do not find inviting. Demonization and deliverance are possible turns that suggest even if these charismatic processes can be considered part of the larger work of ethical self-making and therapeutic self-transformation, the charismatic diagram itself is indifferent to these other long-term ethical concerns and can work toward self-erasure as self-development.

During my fieldwork, my appointments, group meetings, and church services were more than once disrupted by wildfires, which if not unique to are certainly emblematic of Southern California. Usually in the fall, in the parched wastes that sit to the immediate east of the latest expanses of commercially developed, faux-adobe, suburban tract housing, the dry, brown chaparral hills catch fire. Ironically, these incredibly destructive and life-threatening fires are often caused by controlled burns intended to avert the very harms they cause. These fires take a terrible toll on wildlife. A person driving through the blackened moonscape left in their wake may see as many as a hundred thousand acres that are effectively devoid of life. At the same time, these fires are essential to the germination and growth of some plant life and play an important role in the regulation of the chaparral. Without previous cycles of wildfire, the terrain destroyed by any current wildfire would not be.

Immediately after one of these wildfires, I talked to a suburban Riverside county pastor about evil. I asked him what the difference was between the way the Vineyard approaches the devil and the way the devil was approached by classical Pentecostal sects. He used the recent fires as an example. Grinning, he said that classical Pentecostal sects would have seen the wildfires as evil, while members of the Vineyard may wait to see if they were a bad thing. The diagram for fire is not unlike the wildfires. It heals, but it also brings demons. It can be creative, rearranging the will and giving the people who accidentally or intentionally invoke it different purposes and capacities. At the same time it can be destructive. Even when it seems poised to build a believer up by granting fresh hope or a new direction, the diagram for fire might turn, burning out of control and eating away at the person. But just like fires in Southern California's wider ecology, that is only one moment in a wider cycle. In the wake of a fire that becomes wild, there is also the possibility for new growth.

7. Collapses, Traversals, and Intensifications of the Part-Culture

As argued in the previous four chapters, the charismatic diagram is a lamination of ethical, linguistic, sensorial, affective, habitual, and biological strata, a series of relations that are undetermined at the level of potential and therefore have a certain mutability and motility at the level of the actual. While many other processes have these characteristics (and perhaps at a general level all processes have them to a degree), the prizing of novelty and surprise as indexes of divinity, along with the adoption of a way of speaking that is (though only temporarily) corrosive of the classical self-possessed sense of what constitutes an idealized individual, means that these polymorphic attributes are particularly well developed, despite the continuing drag of various forms of typification and elaboration.

This said, though, the charismatic diagram is partial in two senses. First, though it is central to charismatic evangelical Christianity—it is hard to imagine the Vineyard in the movement's current or previous forms without it—it does not constitute the whole. We have seen other mechanisms that are important: ideas of church organization, both ideal ecclesiological structures and the pragmatics of how a church is best configured to be sustainable and, hopefully, worthwhile; ideas about aesthetics; ideas about the will's responsibility to fulfill obligations to the divine and ideas about eschatology and temporality, all of which have resonances with the charismatic diagram but can also be independent of it, appearing on their own or even embedded in different assemblages. Finally, there is the idea of Protestant self-possessed sincerity, which plays an important role in contracting and typifying the range and rate of charismatic expressions and slowing down the proliferation of independent forms. But again, Protestant self-possessed sincerity is not in any way dependent on the charismatic diagram and can be found in Christianities that reject Pentecostal-style modes of religiosity entirely.

Beyond that, the diagram shares space with other arrangements that are concerned with economic and political formations. Simon Coleman has noted that because of its capacity to be carried over into numerous different milieus, Pentecostal and charismatic Christianity should be thought of, not as a whole, complete, and autonomous culture (if such a thing ever existed), but as a "part-culture." As a "part-culture," an iterable set of relations, charismatic evangelical Christianity—including the Vineyard—is embedded in wider sociocultural horizons that do as much to shape these forms of Christianities as these Christianities work to shape them in turn.[1] Either directly, or conjoined with other "religious" constellations, the diagram shapes how these other fields are played out. But as we shall see in this chapter, at times the diagram, rather than merely affecting these other diagrams through the creation of specific expressions that these other diagrams take up in turn, actually makes an appearance in the literal and metaphorical spaces that are set aside for these other diagrams, thus shaping their contours. This results in these other fields' being immanently, though sometimes only temporarily, organized along the lines of a charismatic/Pentecostal diagrammatic logic.

DIAGRAMMATIC COLLAPSES

The diagram is also partial in another way. It is a manifold of intensities and differences that, while having their own characteristics, sit in a certain relationship to each other. But some forces and occasions, such as attempts to look behind the miracle in the sense of either theological speculation or skeptical scientific inquiry reconfigure the diagram so much that they cause it to collapse into something else entirely. And at other moments the diagram collapses of its own weight, simply from chance variations of the constituent intensities, so that it falls apart without any apparent outside labor. Both these forms of partiality are not limitations, however; rather, they are capacities of the diagram that not only create particular situations but also enable the intensities and forces that both constitute and are expressed by the diagram to traverse larger fields, concerns, and times.

How does the diagram collapse? There are two ways. The first is a rapid collapse, in which one element of the diagram suddenly fails. These are moments in which the charismata either do not take or fail to hold. We saw an example during the evening with the prophet, when seemingly prescient words about one member's commitment to social justice were deflated by a simple observation that the prophet actually had met the antislavery activist before. It is usually these small things that trigger a collapse. The collapse does not have to indicate a complete failure or the invalidity of the entire project. I remember talking at a Vineyard-sponsored conference to a rather committed Ivy League undergraduate who was in good spirits but not quite taken with the evening of worship and ministry. The evening's speaker was working through a line of people threading through the central aisle of the church, waiting to be prayed for. Prayer seemed to be going well, with people slain in the spirit (falling down prone) as the speaker prayed for them. While the speaker did not do this for every person he prayed for, and not every person prayed for in this manner was slain, he would often put his hands on the head of the person he was praying for, and the person would start to crumple to the ground, having to be quickly caught by someone else before hitting the floor. All this was going on against the usual sort of confusing babble that constitutes the background noise at these sorts of affairs; in addition to the line of people waiting for the speaker, small prayer circles of two to four people had spontaneously formed and filled the rest of the room, as a keyboardist filled in the sonic landscape with minor-key riffs off familiar worship music. The Ivy League student, though, seemed nonplussed. Later on he told me that he greatly admired the speaker and had had a very powerful experience with him in an earlier encounter, during which he had been slain in the spirit himself when the speaker had prayed over him. From my vantage point, this time he seemed to have had a similarly powerful encounter, having been slain in the spirit yet again when he was prayed over. However, the student said it really wasn't the case. He explained the difference wryly this way: "The first time, I fell. This time, I was pushed."

There are other ways for the diagram to decohere. It is possible for some variations of the diagram to so constrain and naturalize the element of surprise that the diagram gently disaggregates, mutating into some other manifold of differences. One pastor of a Vineyard house church in a slightly rough-around-the-edges beach community had an example of how this flattening could occur. House church congregations are small enough to meet in a single residence; they have long been a favorite form for young churches that are just starting up, for those suspicious of larger human institutions such as church denominations, and for those seeking to capture a certain intimacy in community that they feel is lacking in larger-scale congregations. This pastor, heavily influenced by the Emergent Church movement, in particular wanted to foster closer relationships with and among church members and a certain kind of nondogmatic authenticity.[2] While still members of the Vineyard, and while having strong ties with the largest Vineyard church in the region, he and his wife were so concerned with being down to earth that they had shed most of the evangelical trappings associated with Vineyard churches.

Their down-to-earth style included a different attitude toward prophecy. The pastor explained his approach, one that he particularly relied on when church members who came to him for advice or support when distressed. During a meeting he and his wife would follow the Vineyard model and listen for promptings from the spirit but would do so without the typical invocatory prayer. However, they did not frame their responses as language from God, and their responses did not have the imagistic aspect that was important to so much of Vineyard prophecy; it was the language of questions and suggestions rather than the language of divine imperatives and foresight. In fact, the pastor mentioned that often he suspected the people he was counseling (to the degree that it occurred to them to consider it at all) understood what was occurring as merely *intuition*. Given his laser-like focus on building a tightly knit community, he was more than comfortable with this, but he did see that it was something quite different from what was occurring at some of the other, larger Vineyard churches he was partnered with.

This tendency to shift to constituent framings and let the diagram collapse is at times linked to how Vineyard believers must live in a secular world infused with countless other religious possibilities, including the possibility of there being no religion and no transcendence at all; the knowledge of other possible attitudes toward religion does a certain relativizing work, undermining the sense of sureness of one's particular position.[3] Such awareness, however, is not just an abstract cognitive frame, a simulation or model of the beliefs of other people; it is an embodied and unconscious sense of how one can maneuver in the consensual world created by this cohabited plurality. It is not surprising at all that when a more openly charismatic diagram decoheres, the next stable state that it collapses into should be a set of immanent relations in which the miraculous and God are not immediate forces.

This being said, though, there is something particularly Vineyard about the ease with which members cope with these moments of collapse. The Vineyard is open to seeing God in unexpected places, which means there is a pervasive expectation of the unexpected. But increasing the range of events in which divine agency might be seen also means less certainty about the role of the divine hand in those events. For instance, I have only rarely heard Vineyard believers say with complete unwavering certainty that something specific they experienced "was God." Usually when pressed, they are more likely to say they do not know for sure. Often when recounting an experience they will volunteer, even before the question has been raised, that they do not know if an event had an immediate supernatural divine cause; and they say so not just when they are speaking to an anthropologist but when they are testifying in a small group or speaking from the front of the church. Such statements are so common that they even have a clichéd mode of expression: believers will say that particular prophecies could be from "God" or from last night's undigested pizza (for some reason, they often jokingly attribute fallacious prophecies to colorful but not too distasteful digestive difficulties, perhaps because this was a trope that John Wimber used). They express such qualifications both prospectively, about words of knowledge that they are about to give, and retrospectively, about words they have already given or received from God. This means not only that one should be on guard about words one is to receive but also that in a certain sense one can never be entirely sure about the provenance of past prophecy either. The same goes with healing. There is a certain rhetorical edge to this, in which professions of ignorance about causation serve to underscore how much the event goes against the natural order. A statement regarding a long-running back injury like "I don't know what happened, but the next morning I was able to pick up my infant son for the first time" is a claim that one does not know the exact mechanism but also a suggestion that the exact mechanism is, at least in the realm of day-to-day experience, *unknowable*. And in moments of unknowability, the divine has as much purchase as any other analytic.[4]

This should not be taken to indicate a *constitutive* or *foundational* lack of belief. It is not that Vineyard believers profess to not know whether God works in the world; they are certain that he does. Rather, there is almost always a lack of absolute certainty about any *particular* miraculous act. In one sense, the Vineyard has such confidence in the potential for God to act in the world that actual instances of it, while interesting and affirming, are in some vague way secondary. This stands in sharp difference to other cognate actualizations of the charismatic diagram. I remember standing in a church parking lot one evening during a Vineyard conference, having a discussion with some Vineyard members and a visiting Pentecostal public intellectual. Somehow, the conversation had turned in such a way that the Pentecostal public intellectual was talking about absolute certainty regarding particular instances of miracles, which caused a slight bit of confusion when the Vineyard interlocutors did not quite follow what he was saying. After some back and forth, it became clear to the Pentecostal public intellectual that certainty was not a big part of a Vineyard believer's orientation toward specific miraculous moments; this struck him as a surprising difference from his own Pentecostal approach (though apparently not a particularly troubling theological problem, as his amazement was short-lived and the conversation drifted in some other direction). The difference can best be expressed as one not in the relation that constitutes the diagram but rather in the speed, strength, and reliance with which the relations common to both classical Pentecostalism and to the Vineyard are brought into being. Again, the diagram is the same, but the quality of affect and the forms of habitation that are fed into it or that sustain it in various strata differ, and thus the "structural integrity" of the truth effects differs as well.

Given this, to think of instances of diagrammatic decoherence as always indicating a failure might be a mistake; or to be more exact, failure and mutation can have its own utility. These diagrammatic warps and collapses can serve as a way of creating new forms, such as the supernaturally tinged empathic counseling that the pastor of the beach community house church used, or as a way of dismissing and thus containing inadequate outcomes, as in the case of the student who fell the first time but was pushed the second, or in the case of the Vineyard's refrain that the recipient is the ultimate judge as to whether a word of prophecy is actually correctly interpreted or is actually intended for the person. This devolvement of responsibility for affirming a prophecy is a purposeful culturing of doubt that creates an effect much like the crumple zone of a car: an area where the diagram can be allowed to fail so as to not put the larger project at risk.

OUTWARD TRAJECTORIES AND CHARISMATIC MUTATIONS

The "crumple zone" is often an attraction to those who were raised in more Pentecostal environs. But that does not mean they stay with the Vineyard. Some sojourners from Pentecostalism remain in the Vineyard, but others leave the Vineyard for even less charismatic churches and sometimes for no church at all. Longitudinally, over more than a decade, several of my informants who started out in much more strict renewal-type churches appear in retrospect to have used the Vineyard as a way station on a route that leads outside the Christian faith to agnosticism or atheism.

Overweening authority is a common reason informants give for leaving similar charismatic groups, though it is rare for this to be a Vineyard problem. For the Vineyard, there are other reasons, such as a certain kind of political friction and social exhaustion. Some of those leaving mention hypocrisy, a sense of people not fully living up to implicit ethical claims regarding their behavior or of being in effect "no different" from the secular world. A different commonly given reason for leaving is resentment against the perceived prohibition of wider contact with the world (even though in most voluntaristic churches there is very little way in which any sort of extrachurch activity can be policed—or any real desire at the pastoral level to engage in that sort of policing). This is a perceived and not an actual distance, in which church members feel alienated from the larger world rather than rescued from it.

What is striking is that these statements often come enchained. At one moment in the justification the church is too controlling, and at the next fellow believers' individual behavior too lax; at one moment the church does not have sufficient distance from "the culture," and at the next church membership is a barrier to somehow exploring what "the culture" has to offer. There still may be, for a lack of a better word, a "cascade hierarchy" in how people discuss reasons. Young white men usually begin with a claim that the idea of God "doesn't make sense." Rather than relying on ontological or epistemological grounds regarding the concept of the deity, however, the claim turns on the fact that the nature of the world itself—usually the amount of suffering that is presented as being hardwired into the world through forms of social injustice—is incompatible with the positive, affirming picture of God usually championed by churches like the Vineyards. Quickly, however, the conversation can take another turn. The various infelicities in the church itself are presented as evidence to the same effect, but at the same time there is a scale jump downward: much as a broken universe proves the nonexistence of God, behaviors by constituent church members, and often very specific constituent church members, are given as evidence of the dysfunctional nature of the entirety of the church. Surprisingly, it is rare for the pastor to be the central figure in these narratives. People take and leave pastors, and pastors can be the engine of church splits or of people leaving a particular church, but absent some sort of abuse, specific pastors do not seem to drive people out of Christianity; rather, interactions with fellow Christians are the impetus that often drives people away from churches like the Vineyard into nonbelief.

Obviously numerous factors are involved when someone leaves the faith, and each of these instances of taking leave has its own particular constellation of forces. But generally, it seems that in most cases what disembeds people from religious networks like the Vineyard is not merely a kind of abstract intellectual doubt, the corrosive effects of education, or the allurements of a secular world. Nor is it solely an effect of shifting political commitment (about which we will have more to say shortly). All these forces can make religion an impossible commitment for some people. But they have to find resonance and expression in specific social interactions that go wrong, that become poisonous. It is the specific negative event that turns these disagreements with the church from being merely a potential mode of intellectual difference, or a driver of behavior that occurs in discrete places isolated from the church, like the bedroom or the ballot box, and transforms these doubts or minor illegalities into a revulsion against actual social institutions. It is not so much that particularly bad social encounters catalyze a shift in religious commitment; rather, these shifts are inseparable from particular social encounters in which they are manifested, and they are actualized through such small, negatively charged social events.

INTENSIFICATIONS

Other paths leading outside the Vineyard are the effect, not of an abandonment or retrenchment of charismatic religion or Christianity, but of an intensification of it. While John Wimber was building the Vineyard after MC510, his sponsor at Fuller Seminary, C. Peter Wagner, was not being idle himself. Over the course of his post-Fuller life, Wimber was interested in democratizing the charismata and perfecting church growth as a practical art, all while retaining an identifiable evangelical theological edge. C. Peter Wagner seemed to take away a different lesson, however. His mission as he saw it was to canvass both domestic and global Pentecostal and charismatic Christianity for new models of organizing the church. The goal was to facilitate not just numerical growth but also the discovery of forms of authority that were understood as being based on the Holy Spirit, on "what God is doing now," rather than on human institutions. This search by Wagner and people who agreed with Wagner reached a tipping point in 1994 when a Toronto, Canada, Vineyard church, located felicitously close to an international airport, started a rolling prophetic and healing revival that, for a period of years, became in effect an international Pentecostal and charismatic pilgrimage site. Often visitors brought this revival back to their home church, where "Toronto-style" worship, prayer, and miracles would take place. All this was embraced at first by Wimber, who was always happy to see what developed (as he put it, "Don't cut back the bush until you know what you've got").[5] Not everyone was as accepting, though, especially as reports began to trickle out concerning novel forms of charismatic activity, including bouts of "laughing" or being "drunk" in the spirit and even of pantomiming animals alluded to in the Bible, such as lambs or lions. Soon the "Toronto Blessing," as this continuing revival was dubbed, became the object of intense antagonism in the wider evangelical world; it was not uncommon for people to suggest that what was coming out of the Toronto Blessing were purposefully misleading teachings and works of the devil. Even worse, this had become divisive in the Vineyard, with many believers feeling that it was a continuation and expansion of the radically experimental charismatic direction that the Vineyard had helped chart, and others seeing it as theologically and biblically unsound enthusiasm. In 1995 John Wimber asked this Toronto church to disaffiliate itself from the Vineyard. Some said he did this because he viewed its practices as questionable, while others said he was too weak from fighting the cancer that would shortly kill him to summon up the energy and willpower to deal with the dissension Toronto was causing in the Vineyard.[6]

This split ended up mirroring another divide. Wimber and C. Peter Wagner had broken earlier over the question of territorial spiritual warfare or "spiritual mapping," names for a charismatic technique that, rather than simply seeking deliverance from demons, would have believers instead seek out and expel demonic "powers and principalities" who supposedly had sway over buildings, neighborhoods, cities, or occasionally entire countries.[7] For Wagner, who did a great deal of work to promulgate this approach, spiritual mapping was a novel technique that opened up new possibilities for the church. In contrast, Wimber, despite some early interest, in the end decided not only that spiritual mapping was too dangerous but also that it drew believers away from what he saw as the Vineyard's core evangelical work of church planting and conversion by way of signs and wonders.

Wagner had further innovations. He promulgated a tripartite schema of teachers, apostles, and prophets, with apostles being further divided into "vertical" and "horizontal" subtypes. Vertical apostles were centers of ministerial authority, usually standing at the core of a megachurch or a tightly controlled network of megachurches, and often seeming to accrue a great deal of responsibility with a relative lack of institutional governing mechanisms. Horizontal apostles served as coordinators between the various sets of vertical apostles, transmitting new concepts, organizational practices, and charismata from the social space of one vertical apostle (and one vertical apostle's center of power) to the social space of another.

Organizationally, this was a break from the Vineyard. These groups, sometimes collectively referred to as the New Apostolic Reformation (NAR), are no longer affiliated with the Vineyard officially (as in the case of the Toronto Airport Vineyard, which changed its name to Toronto Airport Fellowship and now goes by the moniker Catch the Fire Toronto) or unofficially (as in the case of C. Peter Wagner). Several of these nodes have never even had any sort of well-developed ties with the Vineyard (such as Bill Johnson's nondenominational Bethel Church megachurch in Redding, California, which has been associated with Toronto Airport–style spiritual charismatic practices and claims of revival). More telling than the observation that these churches are no longer affiliated with the Vineyard is that they are not structured governmentally like the Vineyard. At the level of church-to-church relations, they are acephalous, nodular, rhizomatic; but on the local level the official and continuing endorsement of teacher, apostle, and prophet as divine offices creates internal differentiations in sorts of leadership, and given the importance of apostles, a leadership structure that is organized much more autocratically. This new organizational scheme in effect was a break with the Vineyard's maxim that "everybody gets to play." There was no longer just some variation in distribution of gifting. There were now particular strongly gifted individuals whose gifting could not necessarily be used as a template or model for the gifting of others because the level and form of gifts were particular to these authoritative figures alone.[8]

Wimber's refusal to adopt techniques like spiritual mapping and organizational schemes like the teacher/prophet/apostle triad marked a developmental fork in the American Charismatic movement. There was now a separate stream of neocharismatic practice that would produce innovations in actualization of the diagram, innovations that might not necessarily be adopted by the Vineyard. The Toronto Blessing in particular accelerated this. Practices such as being "drunk in the spirit" and "holy laughter" declined in the Vineyard; in other circles, though, these practices were embraced and elaborated, and combinatory variants were experimented with (there were even small sets of Evangelists who tried to popularize odd miracles such as being "stoned in the spirit," which included at times taking pantomimed bong hits off copies of the Bible).[9] Other forms of charismatic practice were produced in this network as well, many of them centered on working with the materiality of the miraculous. Waves of people claimed that their fillings had been transformed to gold by the Holy Spirit, or that gold dust ("glory dust") or angel wing feathers ("glory feathers") had appeared over crowds worshiping together. Almost all cases that are circulated are said to have occurred in large, church- or conference-sized gatherings, but I also have heard from people who claimed to have witnessed instances occurring in more intimate settings, such as house churches or regular prayer groups.[10] There are even newer, though less accepted, charismata: leaders of Bethel Church are rumored to engage in *grave soaking*, which has been described as "a means of absorbing the spiritual anointing of deceased Christians by lying atop their graves."[11]

Collectively, this may be a separate stream of charismata, but it would be incorrect to say that it has no influence on the Vineyard at all. In an increasingly postdenominational media landscape, especially one with access to forms of distribution like cable or the Internet that can reach widely dispersed audiences with low start-up costs, it is easy for people to hear of other charismatic practices like these and to adopt them. And a certain subset of Vineyard churches is much more aware of what is occurring in these other networks, either because of pastoral connections or their location in a spot where this kind of revival church is more common.

Another parallel charismatic line of development that has traction in some Vineyard communities is the Prosperity Gospel, which holds that part of what God wants for believing Christians is high levels of health and financial prosperity.[12] Healing is a common practice in the Vineyard, and while I have not heard people in the Vineyard pray for wealth, I have heard believers ask for prayers when they are experiencing financial difficulty. A large difference between what occurs in much of the Vineyard and what occurs in Prosperity Gospel churches, however, is that the discourse in the latter churches is predicated on a language of rights, creating a sense that God is obliged to provide health and wealth for believers as long as believers are steadfast in their reliance on the inevitability of this bequeathing. During group prayer, this allows for moments when some Vineyard believers, familiar with this form of prayer from media or from previous experience with other charismatic churches, will make what is called "positive confession"—that is, prayer as specific statements about what God will deliver, presented as if that outcome is in effect already certain.

Neither the forms of charismata associated with the NAR nor the Prosperity Gospel is well regarded among Vineyard leadership, though of course particular leaders vary. Older Vineyard pastors who have had firsthand experience with Toronto often have mixed feelings about what occurred there and are less likely to be critical of the forms of charismatic practice that it gave rise to, as long as these practices are not too disruptive. For instance, I have never heard the Toronto Blessing spiritual sign of "becoming" a biblical animal defended, nor have I heard any Vineyard members claim to have undergone this peculiar charism themselves when they recount their experiences during the time of the Toronto Blessing (though I did once see the pastor of a small, rural Southern California Vineyard church manifest this gift, shaking his head and roaring like a lion at the top of his lungs in the middle of a large spontaneous prayer circle that erupted at the end of a one-evening citywide Vineyard conference). At the same time, there is often a claim that Toronto was an "authentic work of the Holy Spirit." This reluctance does not protect all of Toronto from criticism, though. Later Toronto miracles such as glory dust or gold tooth fillings run counter to the Vineyard's more evangelical sensibilities in their materiality and in their iconicity of financial value and hence are again more likely to be criticized by pastors, though more often in conversation than from the pulpit.

The effect of this wider extra-Vineyard context is that non–Vineyard-originated practices and concepts faintly but continuously percolate through the Vineyard in recognizable forms but are not given a great deal of attention from the front of the church. To engage with them would mean crossing the permeable barrier between the Vineyard and movements like the NAR and entering another mediascape, other realms of authority, and other networks, all of which are corrosive of the evangelical sensibilities that are an important aesthetic of what remains of the Vineyard. The people who do cross these barriers end up tracking online rumors of revival, wanting to know "what God is doing right now," taking the element of surprise and transmuting it into a drive for novelty: they fall into a warren of warring ministries, each of which is concerned with creating a sense of a "hot" Christian temporality that is particular to itself. Ministries achieve this effect by creating novel charismatic activity but also by revivifying apocalyptic narratives that most churches in the Vineyard do not emphasize and that some even purposefully back away from or reject. Temporally hot ministries constantly produce prophetic statements about imminent events at the national level, full of eschatological claims about topics such as Israel and the American electoral cycle. They double down on the rhetoric of demons, making everyday life a continuing exercise in spiritual warfare, and they often combine healing as a concern with other New Age bodily disciplines involving dietary restrictions, anxieties about imagined environmental hazards, and self-medication with unusual dietary supplements.[13]

Just as important, though, temporally hot groups feature a different relation to the commodity. As argued earlier, in an age of capitalism, the quality of the commodities the Vineyard produces is viewed as the measure of the church's care for members and potential converts, as well as for the resources that God has given them stewardship over; hence there is a drive to standardize Vineyard-produced media in such a way that they bear the imprint of the community's aesthetic. Movements like the NAR share an interest in the commodity, but there the commodity is doing different work. While some may be interested in the wealth that can be garnered through the production and circulation of commodities (it is hard to observe from the outside, and as an anthropologist I do not have the sort of relations with ministers in the

NAR that would enable me to measure the degree to which they personally profit from their exercise of religion), there is certainly an interest in the *temporality* of the disposable consumer commodity, the idea of the commodity not as a standardized product but as an item that has a certain transience linked to its consumption, meaning that new forms must continually be produced. One good example is instructional and edifying literature. Established authors in the NAR write at an astonishing pace. While I have been unable to find a full bibliography for the works of C. Peter Wagner, for instance, he appears to have authored over *seventy* monographs; Wagner's own biographical material simply states that he is the author of "over fifty" books. The production of new literature is not warranted by a need to address complexity: the theology of the NAR has a certain minimalism necessitated by an openness that precludes rigorous doctrinal consistency, an effect of the movement's being a network of similar but still varying churches. Rather, the warrant for the continual production of new literature is the promulgation of new techniques: new ways to engage in spiritual warfare, new tactics to use against territorial spirits, new ways to identify your spiritual gifts, new ways to grow your church, new ways to have God transform your mind, new ways to pray with power, new ways to produce prayer shields, new ways to exercise dominion over the secular segments of society. While there is certainly a redundancy in these topics, the continual production of new material not only presents the idea that there is a set of "best practices" for engaging in this sort of charismatic campaign but also claims that this set is a body of knowledge that is continually advancing. Hence the presumption that the underlying goal of this knowledge, God's immanent work in the world, is continually transforming his church as well.

The Vineyard expresses a sense of "hot" temporality as well in that it also presents God as being continually engaged in new projects in this world. The speed, form, and loci of these novel projects are different, however. There is a tendency to see God at work in the lives of unlikely people: it is a language of God changing lives in distant mission sites, at homeless shelters, and with people who have been saved from psychological illness, substance abuse, or financial woes. Of course such language is in one way not particular to the Vineyard. Many American forms of evangelical Christianity privilege similar narratives, and many evangelical groups underscore how such processes are supposedly being carried out in the present. What is particular to the Vineyard is that it uses the same language of surprise and outlandishness to describe God's projects in the world that is seen in their discussions of charismatic miraculous events. A certain kind of typification of language occurs with these narratives. As soon as you hear a testimony concerning someone struggling with problems of this order, you can be certain of the narrative arc that this figure is about to travel. Even if this gang member, street person, human trafficking victim, or addict is not completely made whole, he or she is going to have God work in a way that cannot have been expected in advance, given these abject conditions, and that cannot be explained through normal human causal factors. In the language heard both from the pulpit and in conversation, such unexplainable moments of kindness, mercy, or grace are manifestations of divinity. This process can be scaled. A person saved can be a successful ministry, a homeless person given dignity can be a homeless outreach program. While this jump in scale may make a difference in institutional logistics, it makes only a small change in the discourse. Even if a discussion presents statistics on roughly how many people have been assisted through food drives, shelters, or outreach programs, these numbers are almost always presented as decontextualized signs of extraordinary change, and come in tandem with a particular narrative about some specific sex worker or prison inmate who has been changed by what can only be God.

It is hard to gauge which demographic subgroups are most affected by such narratives of social transformation; as anyone who has read an opening ethnographic vignette can attest, both anthropologists and evangelists are prone to think in terms of the anecdotal and the exemplary. My sense, however, is that these accounts of social transformation are more appealing to younger believers, in their thirties or earlier, and particularly to believers who have not had children yet. Narratives of charitable social engagement can still speak meaningfully to older believers, and, even in its most charismatically oriented days in the eighties, many Vineyards had sizable food drive programs and homeless outreach. However, my sense is that a greater percentage of older members are more interested in questions of new charismata, such as those introduced by the NAR, than in new social outreach exemplified by the Vineyard's work toward what is sometimes presented as social justice. Conversely, some young people are interested in the "hottest" form of charismatic experimentation, but they look more to places like Bethel Church than to the Vineyard. For those already in the Vineyard, the lure of the spiritual pyrotechnics that brought many Baby Boomers and Generation Xers to the Vineyard may fade over time, though not necessarily to the point of extinction: it may simply become less intense and perhaps more sustainable. All the same, though, a steady number of older believers drifts away in the direction of more spiritually extravagant churches that think in terms of novel instantiations of the charismatic diagram.

Both of these religious trajectories leading out toward either atheism or a more baroque neo-Pentecostalism are in sharp contrast to yet another trajectory: people who come to the Vineyard from other churches because they desire an intensification of the charismata. Now, the Vineyard originally stressed "evangelizing," and in fact the evangelical effect of the miraculous was the stated warrant for the exercise of charismata. Thus in its early days the Vineyard often used the term *power evangelism* to refer to these activities. And while it is difficult to know how great the numbers were, some people did join the church without having any serious prior history with Christianity as a religious practice. However, most early recruits to the Vineyard were already practicing some other form of Christianity. The Vineyard even developed a bit of a reputation with other churches for "stealing sheep" and was classified as a "transfer growth" rather than a conversion movement in some sociological work.[14] The early prototypical Vineyard recruit was often talked about by older members of the church as someone already attending, but also deeply dissatisfied with, a mainline church where the idea of an experiential connection with God is not countenanced; such a person then would come across the Vineyard and discover that a whole new mode of engagement with God was possible.

But with the demographic explosion of "born again" Christian believers in America since the late middle of the twentieth century, there are fewer and fewer "liberal" Christians to poach from. A reserve of various charism-denying modes of fundamentalism can still be relied on as a pool of possible converts. But many of the sort of Southern California fundamentalists who categorically reject the idea of charismata have a well-developed epistemology that places into doubt any form of experiential knowledge, and in fact dependence on the Bible as the only source of reliable religious knowledge is as much a function of the push factor of a radical skepticism as it is a function of the pull factor of a form of Biblicism. Finally, the Vineyard approach to worship music, which was for years their other major distinctive feature, has now been adopted by many other churches. It is now not uncommon to step into a strictly evangelical church on a Southern California Sunday morning and hear the worship band play a Vineyard song, performed in a Vineyard style. In what may be the final twist of the knife, Vineyard songs can now even be heard in Protestant churches that decades earlier fired pastors for having an informal association with John Wimber.

Apparently the days of power evangelism and a unique Vineyard worship style are over for good; and while this does not mean the death of the miracle as a sign that organizes the willful and the willing, the miracle may have to be actualized in different arenas, in different ways, if it is to assist in the Vineyard's continual challenge to re-create itself. And so this brings us to this chapter's concluding discussion, an account of how the charismatic diagram works to reorder monetary exchange and the political imaginary.

MONEY, THE ACTUARIAL DIAGRAM, BROKEN SYMMETRIES, AND THE TEXT AS MIRACLE

The importance of money was one of the first things I noticed just a few weeks into attending small prayer group meetings. One night, after the usual intense half hour of communally sung worship songs accompanied by acoustic guitar, and an icebreaker to introduce the two or three new people who had dropped in on the then fourteen-person group, the woman who was running the group that evening asked if there was anything "weighing on [anyone's] hearts" that could be prayed over so the burdened people could "be present" during the rest of the prayer meeting. A little hesitantly, another women in her late twenties volunteered that she was stressed, to the point of being physically ill, about a multi-million-dollar budget that she was putting together for her new job at a (nonreligious) charitable institution; she had never worked with sums of money this large before, and the stress was turning her stomach against itself. Emma, the group's youngest member, stated that the day had been "tear filled" for her—a statement that came across as all the more unsettling because of the brave smile she was wearing as she said it. She had just received the bill for a recent root canal treatment, which at over a thousand dollars she could not afford, and the same day was told that what she had thought was simply a pulled muscle in her back was actually what she described as a "broken vertebrae" (a doctor in the group, asking some clarifying questions, saw that what she actually meant was that one of the protrusions that grew out of the vertebrae had a hairline fracture). For someone like her, fresh out of college and without health insurance, this was an economically crushing combination. What made the situation even more bleak was the fact that she was afraid it would mean her missing a series of important auditions that were vital for advancing her career as a professional dancer.

The soft drink- and snack-covered table in the center of the circle of chairs was lifted up and carried to the side; the two women kneeled down where the table had been, and one by one they were prayed over. Hands, either resting on the head or the back of the women being prayed over, or held out in their direction with the palms facing them, ringed them all around. A moment or two of silence would be punctuated by spontaneous prayers, centering first on one of the women, then on the other. Praying over the woman with the budget woes, someone pleaded to God that this would be the moment she would prove herself, that she would take this challenge as an opportunity to show the talents that God had given her. This statement was punctuated by a barely audible "Yes, yes!" from the person on whose behalf these prayers were offered. For the woman with the dental bill and the back trouble, though, the prayers had a different, slightly more resigned cast, as if there was an edge of doubt about what could be done for her. People prayed that she would heal quickly, that she would "enjoy the rest" created by this gap, that her last performance before this news would "not fade from the mind" of her business connections in the dance world, and even that "in the name of Jesus" "the back pain [would] be gone." No prayer, however, was offered about her debt.

A few days later, an e-mail from a young doctor in the group who was just beginning her pediatric practice (and the small group member who had identified the injury as a hairline fracture) was sent out to everyone in the group: that is, everyone excluding the dancer. It read:

> Hi fellow small group people [...]
> I don't usually do this very often, actually. . . . I don't think i've ever done anything like this before . . . but anyway . . . Last tuesday at small group when we were all praying for each other, I really felt that God put a burden on my heart to help out [the dancer] with her root canal situation. . . . (For those of you who may not know, her job doesn't offer dental or health insurance, and recently, she had a bad tooth problem that needed a root canal which now has caused her to be $1000 in debt) And when i talked with [my husband] after we left, it was kind of weird cuz God put a similar burden on his heart (though slightly different) . . . so we decided that God was probably asking us to help her out. . . . I was reminded of the early church as an example in Acts 2:42–47[:]
>
> "They devoted themselves to the apostles' teaching and to the fellowship, to the breaking of bread and to prayer. Everyone was filled with awe, and many wonders and miraculous signs were done by the apostles. All the believers were together and had everything in common. Selling their possessions and goods, they gave to anyone as he had need. Every day they continued to meet together in the temple courts. They broke bread in their homes and ate together with glad and sincere hearts, praising God and enjoying the favor of all the people. And the Lord added to their number daily those who were being saved."
>
> It really impresses upon me how the early members of the church shared everything with each other and helped those who were in

need. . . . So anyway, [my husband] and I decided that we would contribute some money to a little fund to help [the dancer] with her current financial need. . . . So if any of you guys feel any desire or burden to contribute anything as well, please let one of us know. . . . and it could be anything . . . $1, $10 or whatever . . . (we'll be there on tuesday night karaoke. . . . We'll try to remember to bring a little card to sign if you want to write any words of encouragement. . . . Just pull one of us aside from all the chaos of singing!) And if you don't, please don't feel obligated. . . . Just ignore this email. . . . That's why i'm just emailing you guys instead of asking or calling . . .

anyway, i hope you are all having a good week!

The doctor's request was answered, and during that group's night out, among the fourteen or so group members, the entire amount was raised. The envelope was slipped to the dancer without any ceremony, though certainly not without comment the next week, when the small group opened with the dancer's ebullient testimony. She reported how she had been giddy all week. She also reported how those around her (particularly "unbelievers") had been taken back, not only by her joy, but by her good fortune as well: not only had she received the amount of money necessary to straighten out her dental debt, but despite her injury she had also received a coveted dancing position and had been given a long-term housesitting gig located at the beach in one of the most exclusive communities in the region. "What?" she squawked in faux surprise, her tone mimicking an unbeliever's lack of faith, "The Lord gave you all that?" Even two years later, long after the dancer left the small group, what had occurred would still be remembered by many of the group members, but not as an instance of anyone's particular generosity. Rather, it was recalled as a "move of God."

This was not the only instance I saw in the small group where money changed hands. A year later, the soft-spoken pediatrician's husband took over the reins of the small group when David and April left; his wife was reluctantly brought into a leadership position as well, unsteadily playing worship music for a while on an untuned guitar. (Eventually the group transitioned to the much less emotionally engaging practice of singing along with recorded worship music at the beginning of the small group sessions.) One evening, after a somewhat truncated worship session, he started the main part of the meeting by whipping out his wallet and handing each person a twenty-dollar bill. The purpose, we were told, was to see "what we did with it."

About a month later, the evening program ran as usual, with first worship and then a series of short announcements (there was an evening of worship through creative art and spoken word performances on an upcoming Saturday night; the pastor's birthday was approaching, an announcement that led someone to mention helpfully that he "liked books," causing another person to add that the pastor had probably already read everything you could think of, so maybe just a nice e-card instead). Then we were held to account for what we had done with the twenty dollars we had been given.

What was of note was that everyone was capable of giving an exact account: ten dollars spent to purchase food for a struggling graduate student, twenty dollars given to a Christian housing project, another twenty given to a relief group in the wake of a tidal wave in Sri Lanka. The new leader quickly shifted the topic. Now we were to turn to a sign-up sheet that had a list of charitable endeavors we were "encouraged" to volunteer for; the small group stalled in chitchat as in groups of two or three people looked over the sheet, deciding where to spend their time.

Discussions related to money were not always in this key, however. A few members were dutiful about informing the group about bargains such as clothing sales, and one evening the small group was derailed by an extended debate regarding how long after the fact you could reasonably return a piece of defective clothing to the store (one woman stated with a surprising amount of conviction that it was all right to do this well over a year after purchase); on another evening the same woman openly chided a fellow group member for being wasteful when he mentioned in passing that he kept the water faucet running the entire time he brushed his teeth. Not all discussion necessarily framed economizing as a positive. During this stage of fieldwork, Southern California was a superheated real estate market, and people often expressed a fear that they were on the verge of being permanently priced out of the market. One member who worked in a campus ministry had an opportunity to purchase a subsidized condominium downtown but was torn because the housing development was part of a redevelopment plan that was displacing many of the very homeless people he had spent time volunteering to help; he got a good laugh out of someone sarcastically commenting that "it gets easier and easier to follow Jesus" (he eventually declined to purchase the condominium). This was part of a wider pattern in the small group; taken altogether, though money never eclipsed other subjects, discussion of it, and prayer requests about issues related to money or career, occurred virtually every evening and often dominated the discussion.

Money as a concern was not limited to small groups. One guest pastor started his sermon by quoting Notorious B.I.G., saying "More Money, More Problems." The sermon transitioned seamlessly to the next big citational callout, Matthew 6:21: "For where your treasure is, there your heart will be also." The idea was that money was simultaneously given too much importance and too little. People were at once too concerned with it, letting it dominate their lives, and yet not concerned with it enough to bother to record and control their spending habits, something that would give them much-needed balance. Toward the end of the sermon, specific spending and budgeting software was referenced by name. Other sermons worked in the opposite direction, challenging people not to exercise more restraint but to abandon it and to donate money in what was sometimes called "love offerings." On a somewhat regular basis, believers were asked to spontaneously give to a host of church initiatives, parachurch operations, and foreign mission endeavors, sometimes from the front of the church, when people were asked to donate for the church's homeless ministry (sometimes solemnly referred to as the ministry for "our friends who live outside"), at other times from someone in small group who "had a heart" for a particular project, such as sending disadvantaged youth to a Christian camp on Santa Catalina Island. E-mail chains were another way requests could find their way to believers. They almost always asked message recipients to respond to an exigent circumstance or to fund a specific initiative (as opposed to supporting the general operation of long-standing charities or parachurch organizations). This was even the case for requests that seemed to be pinned to some sort of regular cycle, such as winter housing for the homeless; their immediacy was always the warrant for the request. Such contributions were completely distinct from tithing, which was also encouraged. Tithing a fixed percentage of income was spoken of as a *discipline,* and while it was certainly understood to be doing important work in the church, it was also understood to be an ethical good in and of itself. The moral value of tithing did not mean that the church wasn't accountable for what it did with the funds. While it did not trumpet the fact, the church's budget was open and available to those who wanted to see it (though I was unaware of anyone who was concerned enough to take a look at those books). There was a general feeling, at least at that church, that the church's thriftiness was self-evident; when asked what people should make of the church's habit of meeting in a school auditorium that was rented on the weekends instead of in a church-owned building, one believer said confidently that it showed the church put people and not money first.

All this affected people's day-to-day habits, though in different ways and to different degrees. The chief mode was as a kind of smoldering resistance to and resentment of consumer culture. I heard one believer admit during a prayer group that she "struggled" with judging some fellow believers when she walked past their high-end cars in the church parking lot. Another church worker spoke with what was at once open desire for and resentful condemnation of Apple products, being obviously attracted, yet unable to see them as anything other than a self-indulgent sign of consumer culture. In other instances, this concern was expressed in a more supernaturalized key, as when I called one informant on his cell phone only to find him praying in front of the dairy case, trying to determine what milk he should purchase. At times this mix of dutifulness and generosity worked against the force of consumer desire in ways that seemed to be saturated with unconscious irony. When I mentioned a particular homeless man who went about my neighborhood collecting cans, one group member took out several bags of crushed aluminum cans for me to personally give to the man; they were all being held in plastic shopping bags from Brooks Brothers.

Such diverse and countervailing practices and instances are not as disordered as they may appear at first glance. They can be placed on a continuum from a sort of careful, almost actuarial ethical constraint to an unrestrained, spontaneous giving. This continuum is crosscut by another axis, in which transactions range from being seen as entirely quantifiable and material to being seen as involving only qualitative forces such as love and care that are understood as ultimately immaterial. This is the ideational terrain that these charitable and pecuniary transactions transect. The presence of money in transactions, as an instrumental, anonymous, and quantitative medium, tends to be associated with an evaluative, actuarial sense of the ethical, and conversely its absence in emotive-immaterial transactions tends to be associated with an ethics of self-abandonment. This is not absolute, of course. At times an ethics of obligation and constraint appears alongside the immaterial and emotional, as can be seen in the example of the small group where members were somewhat coercively "invited" to sign up for volunteer work. Further, moments of seemingly unconstrained affective generosity (such as the twenty dollars that the small group leader gave to every person present) can turn into moments of fiscal obligation, in which a gift suddenly turns into a responsibility to discharge an unexpected bounty in a responsible manner that can be publicly accounted for.[15] This does not exhaust the possibilities, for these modes of exchange are variously implicated with consumerism—another way of engaging with the world that Vineyard believers are familiar with, as despite their ambivalence they have no greater immunity to the pressures and enticements of the larger consumer society than anyone else. Together, this consumerist outside, the fiscal/constrained, and the affective/unrestrained make three broad bands, and gifts and exchanges often cut across the borders between these bands.

Every topography, with its bends and folds, is an expression of a topology, and every topology is alternately capable of being formulated as a problem. The problem for us here is how to bring together two separate topographies that we have already worked with and see if they have some subsisting diagrammatic relation. The first concerns the space of possibilities made by the fiduciary duty one has toward a God whose needs can only speculatively be met through an obligation of care (that is, the ethical responsibility to use the worldly wealth that ultimately belongs to God in a faithful and responsible manner). In this framing, this set of flexible and substitutable relations presumes that God is always, if not occluded, then hidden behind some other mediator: a spokesman, a text, an authoritative ecclesiology, or a constellation of statements constituting what Foucault called a moral code.[16] The mediator does as much to mystify as it does to transmit, which in turn means that this figure, text, institution, or code must be constantly interrogated, not just to see if it is applicable to the current situation, but also to determine what applicability means in such a moment. The result is continual recourse to the law and, at the same time, a chronic uneasiness, since the law raises as many issues as it assuages.

We have seen this pattern before in an approach toward the Bible, not as a form of *personal communication*, but rather as the public presentation of *general legislation*. We have also seen it in another form: the idea that the church must aspire to make the commodities it produces adequate to the standards of excellence in the modern age, which is the impulse behind the controlling aesthetics of the Vineyard. It may seem strange to think of Helvetica and Leviticus as related, but they are both the fruit of a logic that sees proper action as a result of a prior one-way communication where one must retrospectively hypothesize the animating intent. There may be differences in the complexity of the coding, and the various levels of complexity are associated with correspondent differences in the swath of potential that can be brought into being through variously situated interpretive labor. This means that there are greater or lesser degrees of freedom, in the mathematical sense of the term of degrees of play, in this set of relations. But despite the various degrees of freedom, the same set of relations form the contours of the textual forms that generate all of the possibility states.

This textual/juridical diagrammatic creates a faux or fictive transcendence. It is a transcendence because it suggests some kind of universal obligation or code; but this transcendence is fictive because it has effects only to the degree, and in the form, that it is immanently actualized, and actualizations are always context dependent because they crystallize the specific forces in play in that interpretive moment.[17]

A distinctive element in the judicial context is the play of will: within this framing, the role of will is to bend itself to the rule. The exercise of the will and the responsibility for the will are with the subject, however that subject scales (person, small group, church, denomination, religion). Everything is about exertion of the will or failure of the will; you are either disciplined enough to restrain spending, or to make regular tithes, or you are not. The same responsibility is invoked in relation to moral and ethical codes, and even aesthetic standards for church-produced commodities: How much work has been done on a flyer, an advertising campaign, or for that matter a sermon? Will is not necessarily equally distributed, it can wax or wane over time, thresholds for what constitutes sufficient will can vary, an individual can have a particular strength (or weakness) of will that is characteristic of him or her as a person. But it is always the will working on itself to its own end.

The second topography is the one we have traced throughout this book: the charismatic diagram, the diagram for fire. The presumption that can be drawn from the series of relations and transformations that this diagram enables is that God is capable of manifestations in the world with a situatedness and an immediacy that break with the absences identifiable in the biblical text and the occluding gaps that come with the mediation of institutions. Interpretation is still an element, but here what is more important is the response and the transformation. The response and transformation in turn are a function of something that, in terms of either an unexpected intensity or an unlikely probability, indexes an immanent agency that is not that of the natural order. In the other, textual/juridical diagram, where obligations are known even as they present interpretive challenges, the question is whether the will is adequate to the task. In the charismatic diagram, however, strength of will is not an issue, since the miraculous supplements, transforms, or ratifies the believer's will. What is unknown is whether, and in what form, the surprise will manifest. Even when will "precedes" the miracle, the unnaturalness and the element of a surprise that is beyond the natural order of things work against the miracle ever being completely typified in its expression, and against surprise being absolutely domesticated. Unnaturalness and surprise can be overstressed. Typification can contain surprise to a degree, and the relative nature of the break can be managed to prevent wills and affects from being too extreme and miraculous signs from being too bizarre. But this just points to the fact that the topological variation allows for actualizations that take the form, not just of a radical disjuncture between human will and divine grace, but of minor shades of differentiation as well.

The various charismata—healing, prophecy, tongues, and deliverance—may seem to have a certain kind of consistency in themselves, with each one forming a class or kind, and we have discussed them as if that were the case. But their classifiability is only a function of typification; they are simply actualizations marked by a broken symmetry as the primary effect, the primary *force*, of a moment of surprise that happens to fall more on the body, the imagination, the linguistic, or the subjective. And that does not exhaust the forms that are out there—Providence provides endless opportunities, and typification and elaboration can work in new directions. New miracles can occur, miracles that do not map onto any of these preexisting categories, yet are also shaped by surprise and a redistribution of the willing and the unwilling. We have seen this already in the production of new miracles by alternate streams of charismatic Christianity. But it can happen even among Vineyard believers. For example, a Christian academic told me that while he was giving an important paper at a conference a known and influential opponent of his paper's positions was in the audience; during the question-and-answer period, the opponent was gesticulating wildly to catch the chair's attention so that he could ask a (presumably hostile) question, but the chair did not see him. That failure of the chair to see and thus recognize the opponent, the academic told me, was without doubt an act of God.

The gift to the injured dancer was seen as an act of God as well; a "move of God" is a quite handy definition of a miracle. These moments of generosity are seen as being at odds with the economic natural order of a self-interested eudemonic consumer capitalism. Giving that breaks with this order is just another instance of the miraculous, only in this case during actualization the order being broken with is not bodily, imaginative, linguistic, or subjective but economic. Unlike the general reciprocity that was the presumed mode of human interactions in the sort of societies that were the object of classical anthropological attention, generosity here cannot be human.[18]

How can these two different topographies be seen as a single topology? By being contained in what might be called a metaproblem, though this phrasing unfortunately suggests some kind of hierarchy. It might be better to say that this is instead an interstitial or subsisting problem situated between the problem that animates the charismatic diagram (how to accord the will with an immanent God, without accidentally merely according the will to an order of immanence) and the problem that animates the textual/juridical diagram (how to accord the will with a God present only in the form of a trace). Even this framing of an interstitial or subsisting problem is not quite correct, as these two problems are instances or variations of the *same problem* in a more underdetermined form. In the textual/juridical diagram, the miracle itself is hidden behind the screen that normally obscures what produces and sustains the miracle as an active agent, leaving just a play of will, the unwilling, a ground, and a textual/ethical trace. The miracle is expressed as a text or a law, so the contours of the miracle are restricted to what the medium of law or text allows, even as the fixed form of the miracle as law or as text allows for a greater circulation. What we have in effect is a fold in immanence in which the miracle is present on the ground but is then made distant by having the series of linkages that run between the miracle and the text, and the text to the present event, pinched off by those folds. This obscuring of the immediacy of the text and the linkages between the sign and present circumstances decelerate time to the point at which time appears to be arrested. One does not rush through an event but encounters a (seemingly) perduring and transcendent sign. By contrast, the contemporary miraculous is the sign made fully immanent, with its ties to the present not obscured but highlighted, so that one becomes hyperaware of how the present actualization of the diagram is changing both in how it is being expressed and in how it is relating to the other assemblages that are imbricated with it; this gives one a sense of time speeding up, since attention turns to the sign not as an emblem of the past (for it is not past, it is obviously in the here and now) but as a contemporary event and an index of the future. And since the future is readable only by being counterpoised with a differently arranged past, this means transformation and not fidelity.

POLITICS

And so we finally come to the problem of the political.

Some readers may say that this section, rather than being one of the shortest discussions, should be the longest and that rather than being at the end, it should have been at the beginning. This privileging of the political in ordinality and importance has certainly been the trending social science approach to "theologically conservative" American religion ever since speculative social science started to talk about another "great awakening" in the second half of the twentieth century.[19] Some would even say that the existence of an anthropology of Christianity, or at least an American-centered anthropology of Christianity, is a function of the academic confusion following the rise the "Religious Right." I am not faulting these approaches; people will naturally place emphasis on what they find to be important for them. But we should note the placement of the operative words "for them."

In stressing the political, social scientists may have foregrounded the aspects of the demographic and cultural shifts inside theologically conservative religious America that threatened to have the most effect on their lives. However, this focus has done three things. In presenting the political as the core object of inquiry, it suggests that there is a unity to a theologically conservative Christian politics, an autonomy to a theologically conservative Christian politics, and finally a primacy to politics in the lives of theologically conservative adherents.

The best books, of course, did not fall into this trap, and pointed to a plurality of emergent or fully constituted theologically conservative political positions, or at least to the possibility of the emergence of such a plurality.[20] These books are also notable for following the classical anthropological dictate of being interested in what your informants are interested in. Although this book is interested in political variation as well, its argument is that the same *événementiel* relations that are expressed in the charismatic practices are also expressed in actualizations of the political imaginary and that variation and differentiation therefore exists in charismatic politics too.[21]

Is it possible to think of the political as yet another instance of a broken symmetry in the actualizations of some problem that result in a clash between two diagrammatic modes of organization, as we did with the pecuniary and donative frameworks we see in the Vineyard? The answer to this question depends on what is understood as constituting politics. There is a tendency in the discipline of anthropology to consider almost all forms of collective sociality and of identity formation as political, especially if they can be seen as a form of resistance to some other more dominant group. The reasoning here is that since these practices transform the social landscape, they have effects on the fields of power that constitute social life. The problem with this approach is that opening up what is meant by *political* to such an extent leaves us with an awkward question: What do we do with the particular set of practices that the people in question themselves denote with the word *politics*? If everything is politics, what do we do with things like ballot boxes, political parties, and voting guides?[22]

This problem is particularly salient with regard to the Vineyard. No one political label or orientation can be safely said to be common to the Vineyard as a whole. Regional differences, class differences, and generational differences cut across the Vineyard in ways that make any such totalization, except in the most superficial statistical sense, worthless. Many older Vineyard members were closely associated with the Promise Keepers movement, an organization known for a series of stadium-sized rallies celebrating a conservative view of the rights and responsibilities of fathers, and of conservative gender roles more broadly as well.[23] This would seem to classify the Vineyard as another exemplar of the Christian Right. But at the same time some Vineyard members and some charismatic Christians who are closely affiliated with the Vineyard are a part of an evangelical Left concerned with combating racism and anti-immigrant sentiments, criticizing American military overreach, and exposing the deleterious effects of unhampered capitalism; some in the Vineyard have even argued for a more open and affirming attitude toward gay, lesbian, and transgender people.[24] Rather than adopt a common Christian Right view of a civilizational and eschatological war between Christianity and Islam, many in the Vineyard have asked, "What does it mean to love our Muslim neighbors?" and through a series of meetings, picnics, and even soccer games have built ties to mosques in their communities. Though it would be an error to say that this line of thought is representative of the Vineyard as a whole, I would argue that it is alive and vigorous, particularly with post–Generation X Vineyard adherents. This leftward trend is undoubtedly a reaction against the "Christian Right" and part of a wider trend in Protestantism to break with previous generations in an attempt to realize a more perfected vision of the good; it certainly is in line with trends among other young, well-educated theologically conservative Protestants. But some older Vineyard members see themselves as political "progressives," and some younger members still deeply identify with the political program that is put forward by the American Right (particularly young Asian American members—a sizable presence in some Southern California Vineyard churches—though again this group as well is far from politically homogeneous).

The difficulty of charting a single political imaginary of the Vineyard is further complicated by the fact that it is possible to suppose one commonality when it comes to politics, albeit one that is formal and not substantive: the fact that even while the members acknowledge the existence of a special domain called politics, at the same time they think in ways similar to much of contemporary anthropology, and often talk as if there was something about their membership in the Vineyard, and about their status as Christians, which is in and of itself "political" as well.

There are two ways of reading this. One is to see it as an indication of the centrality of politics: the political casts such a shadow that other ethical and religious practices can be given importance only by being given a political warrant. This seems odd, though. While politics was important to many of the Vineyard members I knew, it was an all-consuming passion only for a certain set, and many paid no mind. It certainly was not for John Wimber, who (according to the lore that has been handed down to me) answered that Christians should challenge issues like abortion not by engaging in direct political action but by "making more Christians." Furthermore, the importance of the political would not square well with the diversity of political positions I found not just in different Vineyard churches but at times in the same Vineyard church. At the church where I spent the most time during fieldwork, some believers would regularly place local Christian Right newsletters on the free literature table, while others would surreptitiously throw these publications away, or lay down alongside them back copies of *Sojourners*, the Christian progressive magazine dedicated to "social justice." I heard pastors celebrate America's wars in the Middle East, and I heard pastors mourn them. There is no totalizing summary.

This may seem to be an unstable mix, and it is. Several years after I ended continual extended fieldwork, there was almost a split in the church where I had spent most of my time. It was driven in part by the kind of personality clashes that so often are the engine in these sorts of affairs, but also by discontent with the pastor's allowing women to preach, as well as his refusal to endorse Proposition 8, the ballot initiative that (temporarily) revoked the California constitutional right to same-sex marriage. Some of the older, more established families left, a blow to the church since they had brought in proportionately a greater amount of tithes. But the church in the end managed to keep itself together and was still marked by political diversity.

There is another way of seeing the problem of the "political" nature of seemingly nonpolitical activity. By this understanding, various spiritual and ethical activities that we would not normally classify as political have a political cast because ethics, charismata, and the political imaginary are all expressions of the charismatic diagram. The key to this is the concept of the already/not-yet. In a fallen order, one would not expect the sort of justice and mercy that Vineyard believers see as a part of the Kingdom of God to come from quotidian social processes. They are rather *breaks in the order of things*, a *foretaste of what is to come*. For this reason, the specific mechanisms bringing about justice cannot be anticipated: even when they are worked for, their appearance is a scandal, as it overcomes the "powers and principalities" of this world. For this reason, the progressive wing of the Vineyard, instead of calling for incremental social activism through coalition politics, is drawn toward hopeful anticipation of large transformative events.[25]

This approach to politics is illustrated by an emotional sermon by the pastor of the Vineyard Christian fellowship where I did my fieldwork. Its argument was that politics and religion are indissociable—a faith that does not change how one acts, not just as a person but also as a citizen, is not faith at all. In its final moments, the sermon shifted from a discussion of the general necessity of using Jesus's radical, otherworldly, and moral message as an organizing imperative to the question of how Bible-believing Christians might carry out this imperative in the political realm. Arriving at the issue of gay marriage, he invoked an evangelical truism: "I think marriage is between a man and a woman because the Bible says it is." But his next turn might have surprised those familiar with the rhetoric of theologically conservative Southern California Christians. With pain audible in the timbre of his voice and tears starting to stream down his cheeks, the pastor stated,

> I thought a long hard time on this issue of equal protection under the law. Should I as a pastor, should we all . . . as believers, make an argument that there isn't protection? . . . I really believe gay civil rights are important—it's hard to say from up here. I feel I have to say that there are other Bible-believing people who believe it. . . . I think civil unions, something that gives you equal protection—Genesis 1 constrains my definition of marriage, but the reason that I think that civil rights are important for gay people is that I believe that it is important for me. My life is sexually broken, it is broken in all kinds of ways, it's getting wholer and wholer, praise the Lord—ought one kind of people be denied civil rights because of what's in their hearts, because of their brand of brokenness? That cannot be the way forward.

This was a dizzying inversion of the normal theologically conservative parsing of this subject. The pastor took homosexuality's status within proper evangelical sexuality as, at best, another type of sin and relabeled it "brokenness," the evangelical term for the sinful weakness that leads a person to God. This move gave homosexuality an affective charge that transformed it into an identity rooted in the most sacred space in charismatic folk biology—the heart—and put forward a basis of rights derived not from righteousness but, instead, from one's fallen nature.

The pastor's call was for more than the mere extension of rights to others as a way of protecting one's own, for he advocated not merely an extension of legal liberties but a sustained commitment to what he called "the gay community": "I believe that if we're to advocate, we've got a lot to say. I believe that we've got to love the gay community. I believe . . . if we don't speak the language, don't know the customs, don't want to hear the brokenness, don't want to hear the stories, we don't have a right to say anything about it. If we want to have credibility, we've got to have some buy-in—I'm still growing, this is a tough question."

His subsequent statements gained a certain momentum, calling for aid for the poor, both private and governmental; for an end to abortion, not through legal means, but through the creation of support structures for pregnant mothers so that neither woman nor child would go uncared for; and, finally, for an end to "killing children" in the war in Iraq. At the end of the sermon, rather than invite people to the front of the church for prayer or healing, as he usually did, he had people break up into small groups to pray for the leadership of the nation. Afterward, the congregation was startled but electrified; some people milled excitedly in the parking lot outside the grade school auditorium that the church rented on Sundays, while others stayed inside, going to the front of the auditorium to pray some more. Although no one had expected this moment, I did not hear a single word of protest or complaint that day.

This is the politics of gestures, and grand gestures, which proved shocking enough in context even for those familiar with the pastor's politics and personality. In the manner of its presentation, and in the sweep of what it called for, the sermon followed the logic of surprise, and the surprise reordered what was in the key of willing, and what were wills that went contrary to the sign. At the same time, the necessity for surprise hampers the capacity to work through the usual political institutions, since doing so would let the sign that is the miracle fall back into the familiar political order of things. The pastor illustrated such reluctance in a later lunchtime conversation that I had with him in the spring after my major fieldwork was completed. During the meal, he recounted a recent occasion when some longer-term church members left in response to a prayer he uttered at the end of a service; the prayer had started as a request to remove racial divisions within the church and had expanded outward in its scope until it ended in a call to literally tear down the fence that separates California from Mexico. The pastor, who in earlier years had been quite concerned with allowing space for differences of opinion within his congregation, seemed untroubled by the departing members. His attitude shifted significantly, though, when I asked him if the sentiments he had voiced meant that he would be participating in what was expected to be a rather large (and well-publicized) march for immigrant rights that was to coincide with the Great American Boycott of May 1, 2006. He demurred, saying that although as a Christian he stood with those who were strangers in a strange land (echoing the words of the biblical exile narrative) he was not comfortable participating; he was uncertain what the politics of the situation were, although he was conversant with the issue. Other people from the church would be there, he was certain, particularly the "younger" members (a forecast that turned out not to be as true as he imagined; only a few people from that church participated, according to others I talked to). But because he was uncertain of the provenance of coalition members and what their desired goals were, he would not be marching with them. This inability to participate, to engage in political actions, despite strong ethical convictions had precedents in other moments. Earlier, after a hazardous mission trip to a Burmese Christian Karen refugee camp located in a no-man's-land on the Burmese-Thai border (there were credible reports of shelling in the vicinity by the Burmese military during the visit to the site), the mission group came back with "a heart for the Karen people" and an appreciation for their suffering; but when I asked the pastor if he would consider working with Burmese democracy activists he demurred, although he admitted that it was probably the only way the Christian Karen could end their refugee status and be set free from the camps in which they had been sequestered for years.

The examples discussed here are drawn from the Vineyard's progressive wing, but this logic is not peculiar to them alone. The Christian Right speaks a language of what can be willed through identifiable political mechanisms.[26] But by the same light, they use the language of revival, an outbreak of religious fervor seen as a result, not of human endeavors, but of God's will. Even more to the point, the evangelical Christian Right's common tendency to bring together its political and eschatological narratives shows that this is a politics of the miraculous as well.[27] The miraculous nature of the Christian Right's vision of the perfected order is tempered by supplementation with signs of a realized perfected order in the past, during the early days of America as a "Christian Nation."

This should be no surprise. Both the Christian Left and the Christian Right are interested in change. The Christian Left is uninterested in the technocratic perfection of the contemporary order, and the conservatism of the Christian Right is not a Burkean conservatism but one that wishes to tear down the whole facade of social and political liberal modernity. And change is what the charismatic diagram, the diagram for fire, achieves. It captures surprise—which by its nature always escapes expectations, either in its substance, its speed, or its force, and makes a sign of it, thereby reordering the play of various wills. The miraculous sign is indifferent to the barrier that normally separates the subject from the exterior world, just as it is indifferent to whether it is identifying wills that are internal to, are external to, or cut across the subject. It does not operate completely unhampered, of course. We have seen that at moments the miraculous immanent sign is transformed into a universal text. We have also seen that at times, through language and through the habituation of bodies, the expressions of the diagrammatic are typified and elaborated in a way that controls its force or torques its unfolding. And the diagrammatic is itself unstable, prone to collapse or to shifting in such a way that it becomes something else. But that does not take away the fact that the diagram for fire is a divinization of change, an openness to the event that people rely on not just to change their politic circumstances, or to reorder their quotidian lives, but to make themselves and others anew as well. Signs and wonders, indeed.

Conclusion

*On the Problem of Religion
and on Religion as a Problem*

This book has taken up the question of what is distinctive about the Vineyard. More broadly, it has asked whether we can speak of the Vineyard's distinctive features in a way that allows us to simultaneously say something about the Vineyard as an expression of a broader Pentecostal and charismatic Christianity and of the larger set of Christian religiosities. For while the Vineyard has its own history, and its own individualized approaches that differ from much of larger Pentecostal, charismatic, and Christian practice and thought, it is still recognizable as having some close kinship to these other domains.

While acknowledging the importance of institutional practices at the levels of both individual churches and the larger movement, and while appreciating the influence of larger socioeconomic forces, this book has argued that these frameworks are by themselves insufficient for understanding the Vineyard. Rather, a discussion of the various timescales and time-scapes involved in the Vineyard suggests that institutional and socioeconomic factors are crosscut by other modes of becoming. Some of these modes are practices that hone bodies and minds through repetition, with each iteration leaving a mark. Others are purely cyclic, consisting of the buildup and release of affective energies. Some are disjunctive, lurches in which the subject and the subject's relation to the larger world shift. And then there is a becoming in cosmological time, an already/not-yet eschatological kingdom temporality that is also disjunctive, in that this temporality always divides the present into tokens of either a fading damaged past or a redeemed and perfect future.

In a sense, all these time-scapes and scales are disjunctive, as they do not mesh with one another. Yet they are all layered onto each other and therefore should be thought of as working in (atonal, arrhythmic) concert. This book sees the key to harmonizing these temporally and ontologically various processes as the charismatic diagram. Borrowed from the work of Gilles Deleuze, *diagram* is a term for a repeatable set of relations between forces. In diagrammatic thought, the specific nature of the constituting forces in relation to one another in any particular instantiation is left open; this openness, as well as openness to the possibility of diminishing or intensifying the various forces once they are set in relation to one another, allows diagrams to be expressed as different phenomena. On top of the natural variability in any one diagram, there are multiple, and possibly endless, diagrams for all sorts of processes that constitute both the "social" and the "natural" worlds (and for processes that run orthogonal to that divide, too). For the Vineyard, though, the argument is that the charismatic diagram is the most vital diagram. It animates the sort of Pentecostal and charismatic miracles/charismata that have been such a large part of both the Vineyard and the larger Pentecostal/Charismatic religious movement over the twentieth and twenty-first centuries: speaking in tongues, healing, prophecy, and deliverance from demons, to name just a few (the set is broader than that, and potentially open ended). The diagram is invoked when an event crosses a saliency threshold and an aspect of it works as a sign or act of God; this saliency is associated with an unnaturalness of some kind and is marked by surprise. At the time that the miraculous sign registers, the space relevant to the miracle is reorganized. Various forces on the ground are not reorganized according to whether they are internal or external to the person, persons, or institutions; the diagram is indifferent both to organizational charts and to the conventional middle-class American boundaries of the self. Rather, this reorganization asks only whether forces, in their relation to the miraculous sign, are willing, unwilling/willful, or mere backdrop.

Affects and precepts are the primary forces threaded through this diagram, and as intensities they are transformed as they are set in new relations to one another. Further, both the language used to speak about the miraculous and the pedagogy of the miraculous also shape the expressions of the diagram. Pedagogy and language typify and elaborate the expressions of the charismatic diagram and in large part distinguish Vineyard miracles from other Pentecostal and charismatic miracles; the other miracles in different Pentecostalisms and charismatic Christianities, in addition to containing different affects and other forces, are typified and elaborated in different ways.

The charismatic diagram is not expressed merely through the classic Pentecostal and charismatic charismata, however. Reading, if it becomes saturated by the requisite divine-indexing surprise, can be an expression of the charismatic diagram as well.[1] In the same way, abstract terrain usually populated by other diagrams, such as the economic and political, can become sites where the charismatic diagram can express itself. Here, economic and political material and events are given a different valence, as aspects of them are colored by surprise and hence alterity, and as the constitutive materials of economic and political life are changed and placed in different relations to one another. Economic and political spaces become locales for the kind of becoming that is understood to be effectively supernatural, as events in those spaces that are perceived to be unlikely seem to not be a part of the natural order of this secular world.

The charismatic diagram is not the only pattern found in the religiosity of the Vineyard. A different pattern can be found in (among other places) approaches to scripture as a public authoritative text and in attempts to establish a religiously informed fiscal practice based on a model of stewardship. In this other pattern, rather than being reorganized by the miraculous sign, the will struggles to interpret and accord itself with the sign, which comes in the form of revealed truth. This sign appears to be "transcendent," unlike the immanent miraculous sign, but only because the linkages of the sign to the present moment in which it is actualized are obscured and because a seeming deceleration of transformations in the revealed sign gives the revealed transcendent sign an appearance of permanence. However, the revealed truth both acts and is acted on through interpretation in the immediate world and is therefore just as immanent as the miraculous sign. What appears to be transcendent is actually just perduring, as the text has a different temporality than the miraculous sign. And this suggests that we can view the charismatic diagram for fire and the diagram for revealed truth as permutations of each other, different attempts to grapple with the same problem of the temporality and placement of the miraculous/revealed sign.

THE PROBLEM OF DEFINING RELIGION

The Promethean capacity for change that comes with charismatic diagrammatic expressions brings us to our final question: Is the study of this mode of religiosity valuable for reasons that exceed a topical interest in this particular object? Does it tell us something about, say, religious change and permutation itself?

Before answering, we should note that there are two challenges in asking this question. The first is that an answer to it can only be framed in a speculative, as opposed to an empirical, anthropology.[2] This means thinking in a different key, in a way that must always breathlessly outrun its evidence. But that may be all right. This is an intellectual moment in which academics in fields like philosophy are starting to embrace exactly the kind of speculative thought that we would have to engage in if we were to fully take this question up.[3] And while the claims they make are not without controversy, and while I would not want to see this current work as another instance (or another rejection) of their project, we have seen similar speculative thought in much of the current anthropological discussion of ontology.[4] Finally, anthropologists, particularly anthropologists taking up the issue of ethics, are returning to the kind of broad, comparative anthropological thinking that would be an important facet of our own question here.[5] But we must acknowledge the provisional and vulnerable nature of speculative and comparative thought as well. So perhaps it is best to be brave and humble at the same time. We are not claiming to conclusively answer questions or rebut other positions: we are simply testing the borders of the current academic conversation regarding religion.

The second challenge is that it is not obvious that we can differentiate the conceptual apparatuses deployed here in a way that makes the Vineyard, charismatic Christianity, Christianity itself, or for that matter even religion anything other than historically contingent categories particular to a certain moment in the West. This challenge is exacerbated because this book has framed things in a way that makes the miraculous hard to distinguish from other phenomena. It has gifted the charismatic diagram with a capacity for change, but it has also assumed a wider Heraclitian world, of shifting intensities and clashing wills, that would seem to make change a general feature of existence. If flux and a capacity to engage in change are universal and if much of social life can be thought of as in some way diagrammatic, there seems to be no reason to privilege any one instantiation of change as an object of study, or even to distinguish that instantiation as being in opposition to or exemplary of anything else.

But change has its differentials not only in how it may be realized in any particular moment but also in the way that differing changes create further future capacities to engender or constrain further specific change. The production of difference comes in different forms, and by definition differently differentiated material is not fungible. Even if all religion implies change, that does not mean that all change is the type of change that is found in religion. For this reason an identification of what may be particular to the forms of change wrought by "religion" as a category is important, even if we see that category as a fuzzy one, bleeding into other poorly bounded spaces such as magic, philosophy, politics, ethics, and aesthetics. It is hard to know exactly what existed "before" religion, and what "became" religion as well: perhaps it was a certain kind of perduring social hierarchy suggesting an ontic plane beyond that of the biological individual, a continuity of office lasting beyond the person holding it, a capacity for the production of causal theories in the absent of visible agents.[6] It may be that religion has been invented more than once, with each place summoning up religion independent of each other. These issues, while impossible to fully answer, are important because they suggest we can have religion (as a phenomenon, not an analytic category) only as a historical process that came from some other site, some other mode. In short, the specificities and the degrees of freedom afforded to religion are a function of previous sets of topologies and transformations that were traversed by what would later become religion, and therefore also by the fields and effects these other sets created. And for this reason religion in its specificity matters; whatever it was before, when the predecessor form or forms became "religion," it was bequeathed a very specific set of degrees of freedom (again, in the mathematical sense of the word).[7]

These varying capacities of religion, though, which include a power to determine not only its own constitution but also its borders with other social institutions, are so historically specific that it has been suggested that even proposing a universal definition of "religion" is an error, a failure to acknowledge that each thing called religion itself produces the local category of "religion" that makes it recognizable. Furthermore, many things that we now call religion, usually in spaces that are outside of or prior to the modern "West," often become labeled as "religion" only retroactively, when they become ensnarled with metadiscourses that emanate from a colonial or postcolonial academic or administrative authority.[8] Often these cultures and societies historically lacked any lexeme that could be translated into English as "religion," or at least any that could be so translated without a great deal of hermeneutic violence.[9]

GIVING RELIGION (VIRTUAL) CONTENT

Extrapolating from what this book argues, though, it is possible to create a productive, albeit contingent, definition of religion. Further, it is possible to do so, not despite the problem of historical specificity and variation, but because of that specificity and variation. In short, we need not be held down by the problem that the category of religion is either of local origination (and thus not conducive to comparative work) or imported and alien (and thus more of an exemplar of discursive co-option or intellectual violence than a guide for any meaningful typology). Genealogies after all presume change, and also presume a refusal to identify any particular actualization or set of actualizations as either a historic prototype or a contemporary telos. But as the name implies, they presume kinship as well, lines of virtual continuity that look like a set of objects bearing an underdetermining family resemblance only when viewed from the angle of the actual.[10] It would be fair to say, then, that what we are proposing is not a discussion of religion per se, with its historical baggage that occludes a full understanding of its potentialities, but a discussion of "system r" or better yet, "diagram r," which is expressed in different organized assemblages that themselves concatenate, envelope, or are encompassed by other assemblages that are the expression of other diagrams.[11] The term *system/diagram r* may in some ways be more parsimonious than religion, as many elements often associated with the common use of the word *religion* may not be essential to it (though this is not to say that system/diagram r is always the most important aspect of any religion). It also is more expansive, as it includes things normally excluded by the term, such as "spirituality" or "magic." And there will always be the hard cases, such as Confucianism and some ascetic and conceptual modes of Buddhism.[12] But still, system/diagram r has a shape, recurring again and again.

Furthermore, discussing this "diagram r" or "religion" (and let's continue to call this thing religion, "because it's nice to talk like everybody else, to say the sun rises, when everybody knows it's only a manner of speaking") gives us something useful.[13] We can discuss this in a way that underscores the idea that religiosity, while not being *the* privileged site to think through the characteristics and scope of all change, plasticity, and transformation, is *a* privileged site to think of these things. The reason for what may seem to be a rather strong claim is the common features of the miraculous sign and the revealed truth. Both of these can be thought of as contingent attempts to resolve the "problem of presence," the struggle either to make divinity an immanent force that one grapples with or at least to make divinity's absence a productive lacuna and not merely a sterile void.

As we will see, this "problem of presence" is just one variant of a much more protean phenomenon. But the problem of presence, a problem that is solved by both charismatic and biblical diagrams, is where we start. To see why, it is best to start with another, older definition of religion and see what happens when we hybridize it with some of the thinking and problems that animated our discussion of charismatic Christianity. One of the most longstanding social science definitions we have for religion is that of the

Victorian anthropologist Edward Tylor, who saw it as "the belief in Spiritual Beings."[14] While it is far from the only definition of religion that anthropology has offered up, it is at least distinctive in that it is one of the longest-running formulations. Unfortunately, there are (at least) two difficulties with its terminology. First, there is reason to be a little wary of the word *spiritual*. It summons up a material/immaterial divide; a similarly structured nature/supernatural division seems to also ominously lurk in the space opened up by the implicit divide in the world that the word creates. This is unfortunate because these categories, while relevant for the Vineyard, are not universal.[15] There are plenty of spaces where what we call spiritual may be conceived of by others as having a material instead of an ethereal substrate, or where the holy is conceived, not as a function of a supervention of a natural order, but rather as a wider range or greater intensity of potential than is found in the immediate human world. Far better to use a term like *more than human*, which simply notes this presumed difference in capacity, rather than *spiritual*, which presumes an ontology (even if our use of the category "human" is probably far from innocent).[16]

Belief is another troublesome word. For much the same reason that "religion" has been critiqued as a universal category, "belief" has been critiqued as a category, too.[17] Making belief central to religion is an anachronistic global projection of a relatively recent, relatively local post-Reformation Western way of framing religion as intellectual adherence. Belief can be as much a reliance on (a "belief in") as a catechistic affirmation (a "belief that").[18] It might seem, then, to frame religion as some kind of *relation with* or *orientation toward* beings that are in some ways strikingly more than human; such a frame encompasses intellectual, affective, and ritual forms, from the most pious to the most instrumental.

But how does one relate with or interpret such beings? This is where we come to the problem of presence. We have already observed that there are at least two potentialities in literate Western Christianity with regard to having some kind of relation with or trace of the divine; the austere text and the immanent event. This is not an exhaustive list by any means—some modes of Christianity privilege the iconic as well. Then there are the Weberian categories. We could consider religion as something facilitated by the charismatic figure—*charisma* meaning here the classical figure as exceptional case.[19] Conversely, there are modes of religion as bureaucratized reason, social forms and governances the realization of which is seen as a religious good in and of itself.[20] And again, we should remember that none of these modes is necessarily exclusive; given that even charismatic religion is shot through with a textual element, it is likely that for other forms of religion a hybridity in expression is the norm. This raises the question of why there are so many differing modes of religion, and how separate modes can coexist.

An answer is that religious modes of being share one characteristic. As suggested by the phrase "the problem of presence," they address, mask, or mark an absence. This does not mean that absence is the most thematized aspect; hypercognition of absence is a particularly (though not uniquely) Christian concern, and other religious forms, even other Christian forms, may not view this absence with such existential dread, or be as chronically dissatisfied as Protestantism is with whatever technical fix is used to deal with absence. Nor should this be thought of as absolute and as *necessarily* demanding an atheism. There is a problematic aspect to any encounter with divinity; even a theist can acknowledge that contact with the divine is in no way guaranteed. As something predicated on a void—an empty space caused by a divine total withdrawal from the world, a divine immediate absence, a divine incomprehensibility, or merely a divine imperceptibility or fickleness—attempts to mitigate the problem of presence can rely on any object or method that allows one to engage with or position oneself with respect to this void. This is made clear in a passage by the anthropologist Webb Keane addressing the variety of language practices associated with the full panoply of human religiosity; his question is whether, set against such a broad comparative horizon, anything can be considered distinctive of these forms of speech when viewed across the board. Keane states that "to the extent that participants consider religious language different from everyday speech, this distinctiveness seems to respond to some of the common semiotic and pragmatic questions they face: By what means can we, and in what manner ought we, talk with invisible interlocutors? How can we get them to respond? How should we talk about them? By what marks do we know that some words originate from divine sources? Are these words true, fitting, efficacious, or compelling in some special way?"[21]

Keane's issue here is with the pragmatics of communication and semiosis in the widest possible sense, and hence encompasses effectively all extra-linguistic practices that interact with or facilitate a transformation through contact with more-than-human entities as well. In short, this is a problem that language will encounter when it takes this challenge up, but the problem is not particular to language.

THE IMMATERIALITY OF MATERIAL RELIGION

The effective invisibility or inscrutability of the divine, its obdurate absence of presence or easily decodable meaning, has "special effects."[22] Most other practices have as their object things that have visible presences or materially sensible instantiations. In short, almost all other practices are directed at specific things or materials that have a resistance of their own because of that materiality. Agriculture, production, exchange, even the meting out of socially sanctioned violence, are processes that are semiotically rich but also have a recalcitrant material substrate and constrained affordances that fix the range of potential variation. For example, agriculture can change, but only to the degree that the crops can be coaxed into adapting new measures and the climate can be either worked with or overcome through technologies. Speaking generally, for most human practices meaning exceeds bare materiality, which is to say that physical features of the immediate signifying agent or object alone are not sufficient to decode the message, or alternately to receive the intended pragmatic work of the communicative act. Materiality, semiotically, is not everything. Still, materiality is an ineluctable aspect of the process and sets both the horizon of what is possible and the speed at which possible change can be realized. There is a plasticity, but not an infinite plasticity, to most things, with the plasticity both coming from and constrained by their form and arrangements, which are themselves shaped by whatever project the process is supposed to effectuate.

All this is in contrast to the religious entities that Keane refers to above. These entities, because they have no *particular* known visible or material form, can in potential have *any* form. As long as two or three people are gathered together and can agree on what constitutes a means of hailing, an instantiation, or a sign of one of these more-than-human entities, or can alternately agree regarding a mode of relating to, conceiving of, commemorating, or anticipating one of these beings or forces, then the work of religion, in its purely formal sense, can be said to be done. Kitchen rituals, private prayers, grand cathedrals and temples, visions and possessions, and a Deism's abandonment of any hope of a rapprochement with God are all possible responses. This is the most puissant aspect of religion: since nothing is special to religion, nothing is excluded at all.

There are of course apparent counterfactuals, forms of religiosity in which specific material objects are themselves held to be sacred, or in which aspects of a present human being are the object of religion. Examples of these might be some variants of what anthropology occasionally calls totemism, in which a plant or animal species, or sometimes even a specific animal or natural phenomenon, has a privileged relationship with a group of people, often imagined as one of kinship. This relationship can be generative (the animal or plant as genitor of humanity, or usually merely genitor of a specific politico-kinship delineated set of humans), processual (human ancestors transform into animals on passing), or based on an identity (plants and/or animals share sufficient features with a particular human population to be enumerated as a part of it, at least in that population's understanding of the world). There are similar cases in which material objects themselves are thought to have potencies; ritual practices around human remains, which are often understood as being both agentive and dangerous, are another example, though there are probably few objects that cannot possibly be imagined as having some supplement, energy, or aura. Their stubborn presence, the way these divinized objects stand for themselves and do not act as a sign or index for some other divinity, may appear to place in question the problem of presence (since in one way the object is already present), as well as a freedom to cast the divine in a multitude of ways (since we begin with something that already has a fixed form of materiality).[23]

We will return to this problem later on. For now, though, we should note that it is predicated on a mistaken presumption that this selection of an instantiation or placeholder is a conscious, voluntaristic act in which each stage in the process is carried out sequentially and purposefully. Better to think of the process in four ways. First, we can see it as a simultaneous and nonconscious arrangement: a suturing of the more than human, an unfixed category locatable potentially everywhere and therefore effectively seated nowhere at all, to a specific and immediately present personage, creature, or relic. Second, we can lean on the sense of "problem" in "the problem of presence" as an immanent, exigent crisis. The driving problem in all cases is not necessarily a speculative question of how to summon the divine back; it can be about how to keep a sense of present but communicatively problematic surplus from escaping in the first place, how to tether this non- or extrahuman potency in such a way as to prevent its loss or redirect its expressions. Also, the attitude toward presence need not be celebratory; it can invoke the dread that leads to protective prohibitions or a sense of the ordinary that can be found in some exercises of magic. Presence may be manipulated as much to situate, localize, and contain a threat as to hang on to a resource; the presumption of either the beneficence or the omnipresence of the divine is not universal. Third, we should recognize that problems never come alone. Either structurally or logically, they are occasioned by the solution of some other problem and give rise to their own problems. The problem of presence is invoked by effects resulting from some other crisis in health, authority, exchange, or some other domain, and the actualizations that temporarily obscure and partially resolve the underlying problem of presence in turn unsettle some other assemblage that is an expression of a different underlying problem. These problems may be so entwined at times that they join to form a "total social fact," with all the actualizations of a set of problems so tightly locked in a self-referential network that these actualizations effectively constitute a single object, thought, or practice.[24] Finally, these conjoined problems, for all their exigence and immanence, can seem to disappear when a certain solution is employed—at least to disappear for as long as circumstances permit the solution's insistent and continued transmission.[25] But given a shift in circumstances, the problem may become live again, and multiple approaches (ritual or sincerity? icons or iconoclasm?) can begin to proliferate, disturbing a consensus. And that is when the unchecked potential can return.

The flexibility that comes from the lack of a particular material substrate for religion does not mean a total lack of limits. There are the restrictions that come with the biological limitations on human cognition, of course. However, human cognition displays a high degree of plasticity. And although at least some involvement of human cognition is necessary in any assemblage that is an expression of the problem of presence, human cognition is a necessary aspect in any human endeavor, so it no more limits religious discussion than it would any other discussion. But with religiosity, *that limit is the only limit.* This does not mean that all forms of religiosity are equally significant, or that any form will be as successful as any other in a specific milieu. Some forms may be unable to become autopoietic and to construct their own modes of self-continuity to capture other already established modes, or to join with other assemblages. But even here, we should remember that unlike other technical-material practices that fail to thrive, a mode of religiosity can thrive when it is upheld by (or, to reverse agency and subject, when it has captured) just a single individual.[26] Finally, unlike failed forms of production or social coordination, modes of religiosity that end in death do not necessarily die themselves but lie latent for as long as memory of them subsists. They are always ready to come to the surface again when they are summoned up by human imagination. After all, there are self-fashioned Gnostics in the suburbs of Southern California, and Druids dwell in the flats of London.

We should also note that the absent object makes religiosity more protean than other human acts of creative aesthetic production that are often engaged in for reasons that are arguably nonutilitarian. Of course, not everything aesthetically pleasing is categorized as "art" in the spaces where it is crafted; often the utilitarian aspects of the object will fix form and have certain material entailments. And in spaces where art is a category, modes of production that are judged primarily on aesthetic criteria are vulnerable to limitations of genre. But in comparisons of art and religiosity, the limitations of genre in art are not important. Like religion, which can posit new modes of relating to or being educated by absent supernatural others, aesthetically oriented production can challenge genre. However, art is still vulnerable to specific material regimes of production and circulation; the strictures of human memory and language control the manner in which epic poetry unfolds, and the set of techniques and equipment for painting is large but has limits intrinsic to their materiality. Switching from one mode to another to escape the limitations of a specific means of creation is possible, but doing so is more about breaking into an entirely new set of strictures and powers than about expanding one's territory into a continuous field of potential. Still, at times there appears to be a kinship between art and religion. And while art and religion do not always necessitate each other, perhaps their shared plasticity is the reason why people imagine a resonance between them in places where both are marked and salient categories. (Similarly, a religious and aesthetic strain is found in certain kinds of nationalism, probably because both are centered on impossible, communicatively challenging, and perhaps nonexistent objects.) This is also why religion and mediation seem to be so ineluctably locked together, both in practice and in contemporary critical and anthropological reflection.[27] Expansions and mutations of media are just another moment in the capacious shape-shifting of the capacities of religion, offering yet another material form. And each new medium, arriving with different material entailments, is just one more extension of how, and in what way, religion can imbricate itself with the world.

To sum up, religion, while unavoidably material, is less tied than other human endeavors to *specific* material practices, and is less vulnerable to strictures acting on its capacity to reproduce itself (though religious forms with similar capacities to self-reproduce may share features and forms). Again, religion's characteristic as a human phenomenon means that it cannot be anything or everything at all, but there is still an infinite set comprising what it could be, and because of the comparatively negligible set of material constraints on this set, it is a *larger infinity* than the set comprising other human modes of being.[28]

THE POSSIBILITY SPACES OF RELIGION

We have addressed the abstract range of potential implicit in religion. The question is whether some pattern or sense emerges in or from particular modes of religiosity. If religion can be anything that points to a possible transhuman actor or supplement, is there any shape to the field at all? The answer, it would seem, is "Sometimes." Not all instances of religiosity will form a stable but malleable system; and other forms of religiosity may be stable but borderless, gliding from one constellation of religious thought and action to another without trauma, or perhaps even without registering the change. But of course other instances of religiosity will be locked into specific sets of problems that cause definite recurrent patterning. I would suggest that while this range of possibilities does not exhaust the field, a "visualization" of what is allowed in particular religiosities as an abstract possibility space would portray various attractors or mathematical singularities, at the level of statistical distribution, at least, marking tendencies that not only are more common but even exert a pull. These pulls can be thought of as the result of the elaborations, purifications, or rationalizations of concepts, language, practices, and techniques involving these personages, objects, and surpluses, or even the sort of retrenchment that comes with iteration. But speaking of attractors allows us to think of variation in specific modes of religion without presuming chaos.

We have seen the work of attractors already in Vineyard churches and believers who oscillate between an immanent event and a universal but distant law; we could see these two extremes as attractors, and the believers and institution as caught up in the pull between these attractors. But while the specificities may be different for other religious forms, the effect of being suspended between multiple attractors most likely is not. In almost all cases where there is variation, we are most likely dealing with multiple attractors, and furthermore attractors that are distributed in several different dimensions (*dimensions* meaning here continua between attractors that implicate one another). There is no reason why we should limit ourselves to the more ready-to-hand two or three dimensions just because there are conventions for easily representing them. Nor is there any reason to think that attractors, like poles, always come in opposed pairs (though often they do). It is perfectly possible for a particular expression of a mode of religiosity to be suspended between multiple attractors, changing its location in the space between them in stochastic jitters, curves or loops, or nonlinear jumps.

I will not claim to exhaust all the issues here; this is no claim of completeness. But it is possible to think of the abstract, formal features that are exhibited to a greater and more precise degree as practice moves toward particular poles. At one extreme, there might be absence itself: a purposeful cultivation of a cognitive and affective subjectivity, and even sensorially apprehensible architectural features, as void, with this void paradoxically taken as a sign for or expression of presence; while this may seem perverse, it can be seen in phenomena like Christian apophatic prayer[29] and the high-Buddhist Zen concept of *Mushin,* or "no mind." At another extreme, the icon can stand as a recapitulation of and link to some other privileged original, which serves as a reminder and bridge to another scene and is therefore capable of producing effects. This would be a pole of pure simulacra, the endless proliferation of concrete signs and objects.[30]

Pure transcendence—not as a philosophical truth, but as an aspect of or tendency within actual practice, could function as another pole. Thought of this way, practices that glide toward transcendence would show an increasing propensity to fold space and time, bringing two imaginary points together through means other than a linking metonymic slide.

Two more poles—or perhaps a single axis that bisects these two poles—are probably also both relevant and certain enough to be posited. They concern the degree of closure or openness that marks each group. At one end of a continuum we have the hermetically sealed group; at the other, a group with unpoliced borders, characterized by an absolute universalism.[31] This feature concerns degrees of tension about inclusion and not a group's actual size; a small group, essentially a closed community, can be marked by a virtual openness, while a numerically far larger and encompassing group can comparatively mount higher levels of resistance to attempts to enter—and perhaps exit—it.

One more characteristic is particularly relevant for discussing issues of boundedness, though it could also apply to any of the poles/attractors that we have previously addressed: a pressure to move toward or away from a pole or set of poles. Other forces internal or external to the system may be preventing any actual movement, but this sense of not just a *position* in this abstract space but a *direction* as well is essential to understanding the tensions and possibilities of groups. It is particularly important for thinking through the resistances that in their actualization shape the borders of these groups—membership in a closed community that always feels to be on the cusp of opening may afford a much different experience than membership in a closed group that does not appear to be opening, or in an open group that seems to be constantly militating for closure.

These poles are not preexisting Platonic forms but rather asymptotic limits that are emergent in the way that various forms of religiosity unfold. Pure self-erasure is an impossibility, as is ultimate transcendence, or a fully realized infinite proliferation of signs and objects, or a hermetically sealed or a completely open group. These attractors just mark the possibilities that religion can work toward, potentials that are exhibited to greater or lesser degrees of intensity, and at a faster or a slower pace. This is not a system of interlocking oppositions, expressible only in a digital form or through a specific quantum of meaning. Rather, it is a possibility space, a nonmetric, abstract range of potential transformations that modes of religiosity explore.[32]

This is important because while some modes of religiosity will unproblematically dash to some of these limit points, for the most part religiosities will drift between them, at some moments tacking one way and at other moments tacking another, and doing so with different velocities and intensities. Some will discover in the spaces between these abstract attractors patterns or planes that have a particular (although not total) stability.

These planes, and the patterns that religiosities trace on them, constitute the space proper to *specific modes* of religiosity. This is the link to the previous discussion of Christianity as an abstract, plastic form, a kind of typology that can be realized in multiple ways. A particular "religion" writ large is a pattern, a set of resonances, that sketches out *sections* of a possibility map and the degrees of freedom that allow for the traversal of the possibility space; it is also the technical measures—including ideational ones—that are used to allow this space to be created in the first place, and (in most instances) to autopoietically sustain itself. Other social practices that are organized by problematics or informed by some iterable mode of production have their own possibility spaces, and it is important to remember that not every human practice is capable of fully peregrinating across a possibility space (some are fixed, and others are "linear" in that, once begun, they necessarily transform into something else or decohere completely). Furthermore, it is important to remember that the possibility space of a religion can overlap with other possibility spaces; they may (temporally, but perhaps in some cases permanently) resonate with or map onto specific political or economic assemblages.[33]

All this is to say that despite the seeming similarity to other practices that are implicit in the concept of an abstract "possibility space," differences matter, and every so often something unique, a "religion," is forged, which is to say that at times something will be assembled that has a relatively high likelihood of successful autopoiesis, a high ability to affect different matters and materials, and high (though not unlimited) malleability in its self-expression. "Christianity" was such an invention. As millennial expectations, metaphysical speculation, philosophical exercises (in the classical sense), and Hebrew text and ritual came together an object cohered. This object had numerous joints with free play in them and a capacity for reorganization. Consequently Christianity had a higher degree of freedom, and a greater range of abstract capacity and abstract utility, than many other competing Greco-Roman Mediterranean modes of religiosity. Thanks to these features (and a large amount of contingent historical accident) it has variations ranging from Arianism to Unitarianism to the Latter Day Saints. Its wide field of possibility also ensured space for further articulations and rearrangements if and when circumstances allowed—as they did in the late nineteenth and early twentieth centuries, when European Christianities became world Christianities and started to deploy expanded transportation networks, media technology, and modes of national and colonial government; this allowed first Methodism and other "enthusiastic" Christianities, then Pentecostalism and its daughter charismatic movements, to sweep across the globe. This is not to say that Christianity is unique, but it is particular. Other religions have other possibility spaces, results of the historical accidents that gave rise to them as sustaining though mutable autopoietic structures. And there is no rule saying that religions cannot filch from one another, or, at spaces where they come into contact, interact in ways that may themselves become self-sustaining, with autopoietic powers of their own. But particular problems in the sorts of entities or forces they give credence to, and the implicit range of potential modes of relating to them, will give each mode of religion its specific grain.

ETERNITY AND REVOLUTION

If we are to speak about Christianity (or any other mode of religiosity) as having more abstract capacity and abstract utility, and being able to overwrite or envelop other religious systems, then we need to be able to say what this utility, this capacity, is for. This brings us back to the question of sensually palpable, immediately present sacred items, the ones that put the concept of "problem of presence" into doubt—devices that are not representations of an absent sacred other but rather what earlier generations of anthropologists would call mana-saturated presences, sacred in their own right. When discussing that phenomenon, we said that the simultaneity of positing of an extrahuman power (either explicitly, through discursive statements, or implicitly, through practice directed toward it) and a material instantiation is just another example of the fecundity of the religious imagination.

What was not discussed was the way that very simultaneity changes the problem of presence and how we understand the problem's implicit narrative. Without underscoring the simultaneity of the operation, we have a narrative reducible to reaching for a being that is otherwise inaccessible without specific techniques, a way to make up for either a constitutive limitation on our human senses or a mythological or historical wound incurred when we were separated from that entity. It is a story of incapacity or loss.

But this process appears to be very different if we do not frame our account sequentially. Viewed with a different sense of temporality, the crisis stemming from absence or inscrutability occurs at the same time that this crisis is overcome through a reorganization of relevant forces. It is no longer a story of some foundational injury that is only partially restored. In a narrative in which the entity is summoned up and lost at the same moment that the immanent manner of reaching the more-than-human appears, we have something else: *the sense of a capacity to reach an absent more-than-human entity or force that is the actual presence of a more-than-human capacity for change; this absence or withdrawal actually is a plentitude.* Through reaching out for God, or through struggling to control or placate the demonic, or even a supplementary or constitutive invisible plenum, we create the sacred object even as at the same time, the creation, because it must be given a material instantiation, has its own autonomy. It is like the story of the classical Greek painter Parrhasius: challenged to create a painting that would best trick the eye, he painted a veil, a flat illustration that gained depths by implying a phantasmatic space behind it.[34] With religion, the noumenal follows from the phenomenal, and not the reverse. Thus all religion is about immanent forces, even when they seem to be pointing to transcendent spaces.

This is not to say that religion is an illusion, or entirely a "fictive" form, a bit of humanity's alienated creative potential that works back on us in the form of a fetish. While religion can be sewn together from anything at all, the set of objects that it is made from have their own capacities, and to the degree that change in the abstract is housed in particular items, it will be expressed through the potential of these items. (This includes the potentialities inherent in ideational aspects of religion, which should be thought of as operating in the same plane as the material and as further having specific material infrastructure necessary for their instantiation.) Indeed, this is why one can speak of patterning and abstract forms of specific religiosities in the first place. To this extent, actualized forms of religiosity are agents in the same way that anything else in the material world is an agent, something that has its own emergent characteristics, insists on its own ways, and most importantly has its own specific effects, whether or not those effects are foreseen or desired. Even *if* they are in some ways the product of human beings, gods and spirits are still independent actors on the stage.[35]

This production of some sort of beyond by way of a right-here is neither unique nor original to Christianity. It is arguably a trait found, in various manners, in all modes of magic and religion; and it is found in an iterative and easily disseminatable form (often congealed as the sort of iterable organized problems of self-formation and self-critique that has been so important in the anthropology of ethics) in the "Axial Age religions," the world religions that were invented in the period running roughly from 800 BCE to 200 BCE.[36] The presence of an easily transmitted and overtly pedagogical system of multiple specific delocalized assemblages, with components that interlocked but not in a fixed way, and had flexibly differing levels of priority and degrees of proximity to each other, was arguably specific to this shift. It was, in short, a series of transposable and transportable folds in immanence.[37] This is not a supercessionist or Darwinian argument (or at least not a Darwinist argument that imagines evolution having a telos and makes fitness a function of anything other than contingent circumstances). The adoption of one set of capacities inevitably means the loss of others, and different "non-Axial" modes of religiosity may do well in other spaces, or even in overlapping spaces, forming parallel niches where religiosities are doing different work for different people (and where different people are being worked on by different religiosities in different ways).[38] Further, the term *Axial Age* is more useful to describe a typology of a certain set of relations than a historical moment, so one should expect non-Axial modes of religion to follow the Axial Age, and Axial Age modes of religion to be produced without any historical ties to the Axial Age as a historic event.[39] But this acknowledgment of the particular capacities of a broader set of "Axial" religions is also an acknowledgment that Christianity and other "traveling" modes of religion each have specific transportable capacities to realize wide swaths of the abstract possibility space of religiosity.

This still leaves open the question of what religiosities do and how they endure. Why are these abstract mechanisms, realizable in so many different ways, so hardy? The ability of a religiosity to recreate itself is a matter of chance, most likely, but there is a specific genius (in all senses of the word) to this abstract mechanism's organization. Part of it is that this interlocking variability allows the mechanism to respond differently to different circumstances, giving it enough freedom to conform to new needs while not necessarily being so complex as to become cumbersome in all its instantiations. But the specific adaptability of religion is its differing entities allow for *greater regulation in the flow of change across multiple material and ideational domains*—with some aspects acting to exacerbate and shift change and others acting to retard it. Inserting itself into specific political, economic, aesthetic, scientific and even cognitive and neurological assemblages, religion changes the nature and the timing of the unfolding.[40]

And is this not the work of religion, to act as a way to control change not only slowing it to preserve ancient orders, but also at times accelerating it to birth new ones?[41] Whether working for good or for ill in any particular circumstance, religion is nothing but change and its antonym, slowed down to eternity or accelerated to revolution, and envisioned as more than human both because change precedes humanity as it goes into the future and because the deceleration of change grounds and conserves the past. The value in this is not just that religion and modes of religiosity express and explore the variabilities of change as an abstraction. Earlier, we discussed the limitations on the state of play found in human activities other than religion. In their materiality and in their technical limitations, their capacity for change—for acceleration and even for a sort of stasis—is (comparatively) lacking.

Religion, however, as variations in the abstract of particular forms of possible change, can serve a regulatory function when combined with other, nonreligious assemblages. Religion is a flywheel for social assemblages. We have already seen this at work in the way that religious change intersects with and assists in the effectuation of intraindividual, individual, and transindividual change, working simultaneously at different scales and across various domains. This process, which Gilbert Simondon referred to as transduction, is not specific to religious change, but the capacities of religion as change in the abstract make it invaluable in affecting the actual speed and degree of change.[42] And a capacity to affect rates of change in variable ways is also a capacity to shape and mold, as it enables some features to be hyperdeveloped and other capacities to be minimized, allowing all manners of variations, mutations, and sports to be cultivated.

That does not mean religion always works. In addition to breakdown and overpriming, there is the danger that resonances can play out in a nonlinear fashion, so that change comes about faster than can be intended or assimilated, or the pace of change decelerates too abruptly. There is also the possibility that rather than engage with the veil, to work on it and be worked on by it, humans can engage in an impossible attempt to rely directly on what lies beyond the veil; there is a difference between relying on the capacities of religion to effectuate or retard change in critical moments, and waiting for providence or fate to rescue everyone in the moment of existential crisis for a people or a species. To those who are not theists, such an attempt is at best a haphazard throw of the dice.

But if religion is change as change, if Christianity is a particularly (though not uniquely) mutable but quasi-structured mode of effecting or retarding change, and if new techniques have produced new Christianities capable of more rapid and more intense change, then their study becomes particularly pressing if we wish to understand the work done by religiosity in the contemporary world. We would do well to attend to these forms, and especially to forms that are central nodes in global Christian networks. They are important not only for what they tell us about the specific changes that we are experiencing in an age where secularism seems brittle but also for what they teach us about human powers to change, or to resist change, as such.

Notes

PROLOGUE

1. At that time, the Vineyard had received little social science attention, and no anthropological attention, despite the speed with which it was growing and the vibrancy of its membership's worship. The most complete discussion then extant was a book-length sociological work by Donald Miller (1997). Here, the Vineyard was just one of three exemplars of a "postmodern" turn in American Protestantism.

Since that time, Tanya Luhrmann, an eminent psychological anthropologist, has come to study the Vineyard. Her beautifully written book *When God Talks Back: Understanding the American Evangelical Relationship with God* (2012b) presents a very clear-eyed ethnographic portrait of the aspects of the Vineyard that she is interested in. However, her questions are not my questions, so unsurprisingly, her book is quite different from mine. There are moments when our discussions overlap; in my book, chapters 4 and 5 are where my work comes closest to hers. But that does not mean what she describes and what I describe will necessarily look the same. Nothing here impeaches her data or her arguments. Because of the differences in what animates our interests, however, and because of some differences in our starting assumptions, the aspects of the Vineyard that come to the fore are not the same, and where we do discuss the same material, the tones we hit are not the same.

2. Bialecki, Haynes, and Robbins 2008; Cannell 2006; Coleman 2006b; Engelke and Tomlinson 2006; Hann 2007; Lampe 2010; Robbins 2003a, 2004a, 2008.

3. The claim to commonality lies in the mutual citation of authors engaged in these issue. On exchange patterns, see Bialecki (2008), Elisha (2008, 2011), Haynes (2012, 2013), Scherz (2013), and Schram (2010). On semiotics and speech, see Bauman (1983), Bialecki and Hoenes (2011), Bielo (2009a, 2009b), Coleman (2006a), Csordas (1997a), Engelke (2007), Handman (2015), Keane (2007), Robbins (2001a), Shoaps (2002), Stromberg (1993), and Tomlinson (2009, 2014b). Issues of temporality generally touch on whether the adoption

of Christianity in milieus that were until recently non-Christian is understood locally as constituting a major break, and whether it actually demarcates a major break from an external vantage point. These two issues are usually collapsed into the single term *rupture*. On temporality, see Bialecki (2009b), Chua (2012), Engelke (2010b), Meyer (1998), Rafael (1988), and Robbins (2007a). Discussions of subjectivity tend to come in three different varieties: one relating to the phenomenological, psychological, and experiential; one concerning Foucaultian and Aristotelian ethics and techniques of self-formation; and one focusing on the architectonic structure of the subject. The dividing line between them is quite blurry, however. For the phenomenological/psychological/experiential, see Csordas (1994) and Luhrmann (2012b). On ethics and techniques of subjectification, see Brahinsky (2012), Daswani (2013, 2015), Faubion (2001a), Reinhardt (2014), Robbins (2004a), and Zigon (2010a). On the architectonic structure of the subject, see Bialecki and Daswani (2015), Mosko (2010), Vilaça (2011), and Werbner (2011). Finally, each of these issues tends to have implications for the other, with the possibility of historical breaks having resonances with the question of the architectonic structure of the subject, or with exchange being imbricated with moral and ethical subjectivity.

4. On privileging Pentecostal forms of Protestantism, see Hann (2007) and Howell (2003). For material that starts to attend to non-Protestant modes of Christianity, see Bandak and Boylston (2014), Boylston (2013b), Hann and Goltz (2010), Mayblin (2010), and Norget, Napolitano, and Mayblin (forthcoming).

5. For discussions that caution against defining Christianity as an overarching institutional, social, and cultural form, or at times militate against having "an" anthropology of Christianity, see Cannell (2005, 2006), Comaroff (2010), Engelke and Tomlinson (2006), Hann (2007), and Lampe (2010). For a general discussion, see Bialecki 2012.

6. The subject of social differentiation among Christian groups has not received much anthropological attention. But there has been some. While neither centers their concerns on these issues, both Chua (2012) and Webster (2013a) discuss milieus where denominational differences matter. Courtney Handman's (2015) ethnography of Protestant Christianity as it is practiced in the Waria Valley of Papua New Guinea takes this issue by the horns, though. The engine driving denominational difference there is an admixture of linguistic plurality and ethical anxiety. Language matters not just because of the necessity of using language in worship but also because of the values that are indexed by the available language choices. And choice of values matters because Protestantism is seen as a critique of the indigenous, pre-Christian society. Finally, these choices have to be threaded through institutions, which causes these differences to be expressed as a limited range of sharp contrast and not as a plane of subtle and gradually shifting distinctions (which is not the contemporary American case, where denominational borders are more fluid and denominational structures increasingly disaggregated and decentralized: compare Bialecki 2014a). Handman's book is strongly argued, and had I read it earlier in the writing process, it would have left quite a mark on this book. But

this book would still have been different. In contrast with Handman's ethnography, the focus here is on variation in charismatic practice within a denomination, or even variation between different instances of the same charismatic practice when it occurs with the same person or set of people. Further, it is a certain underdetermination in the issues of authority and presence as located within these charismatic acts that is the engine of differentiation for the larger church and denomination-like levels.

7. There is also a rich body of literature that makes understandable certain religious phenomena as exercises in ethical self-formation (Brahinsky 2012; Daswani 2013, 2015; Fader 2009; Faubion 2001a; Laidlaw 1995; Lester 2005; Mahmood 2005; O'Neill 2010; Reinhardt 2014; Robbins 2004a; Rudnyckyi 2010; Simon 2009). These works see the production of a certain kind of religious subject as the implicit or explicit telos of these exercises, though the subject formed of course differs with the different exercises conducted. This body of work has had the salutary effect of reconfiguring issues of agency and structure in religious practice. While the arguments in this book are positively informed by much of this thought, they differ in two ways. The first is in an emphasis on the plasticity of the set of arrangements that "produce" religious subjects. These subjects produce shifts and mutations as the forces and perceptions threaded through each exercise change, even if the set of relations between each aspect of the exercise remains the same (see Bialecki 2014b). Second, this work differs in that it has a more ambivalent reading of these ethical exercises. Those other works tend to see these exercises as the production of capacities, which is accurate. But this work also shows that these exercises constrict potential and result in a loss of other possible ways of being (an observation that was independently made by Anna Strhan [2015] in her discussion of upper-class London evangelicals). My articulation of this point owes a great deal to an extended series of conversations on the anthropology of ethics with Adam Reed.

The points made here are also informed by recent social science and critical theoretical interest in affects, and more specifically in the role of affects in religious practice. On affects, see Hardt (1999), Massumi (2002), Mozzarella (2009), Navaro-Yashin (2012), Richards and Rudnyckyj (2009), and Stewart (2007). On the place of affect in religion, see Muehlebach (2012), O'Neill (2013), Pfiel (2011), Rudnyckyj (2010), Schaefer (2015), and Whitehouse (1995, 2004)). To be more precise, it might be better to say that this work *presupposes* the establishment of affect as a legitimate object of anthropological inquiry; despite the fact that affect has been the object of critique (see Leys 2011; Rutherford 2013), affect is not really interrogated as a category here. There are two differences from the standard anthropological account of affects, however. First, one particular affective tonality, surprise, is given a certain privilege in many of the events discussed. Other than that exception, I have endeavored as much as possible to depsychologize affect and see it as another force that is in play. The second difference is that I have endeavored to be technically rigorous with affects. Most uses and theorizations of affect have an impressionistic edge to them and often bleed into discussions of subjectivity and emotion. There is nothing wrong with this when it is productive, and it is most often quite productive. However, when handled this way, affect sometimes becomes synonymous with emotions and subjectivity. Here, I have endeavored to stay close to a vision of affect as presubjective, following the understanding of affect that informs the work of Gilles Deleuze (1978, 1990a, 1992, 1993, 1998). See also Deleuze and Guattari (1994). Affect is another qualitative force, or *intensity* (a term commonly employed by Deleuze), that is actualized in ways that are more immediately perceived. See Bialecki (forthcoming-a).

Ontology has also been at the center of debate in anthropology. Many have called for a renewed attention to ontology as both the primary object of anthropological analysis and the primary means of analysis (in short, both the *explanandum* and the *explanans*). I am thinking here of works by Course (2010), Descola (2013), Henare, Holbraad, and Wastell (2007), Holbraad (2012), Kohn (2012), Pedersen (2007, 2011), Scott (2007, 2013), Viveiros de Castro (2014), and Willerslev (2007). This interest in ontology has also had its critics. One common criticism is that much of this "ontological" category carves the world into separate incompatible worlds, making interactions that bridge ontologies unthinkable (see, for example, Keane 2009, 2013). The other major complaint is that the multiplicity of ontologies suggests that they are all subservient to some "metaontology," an idea that is treated as aesthetically distasteful and intellectually untenable (Heywood 2012; Laidlaw and Heywood 2013). My book intervenes in this debate by suggesting that it would be better to think of what is referred to as an ontology as the effect or appearance of an expression of one assemblage into another assemblage. By way of a concrete example, "miracles" are what happen when the expression of some other assemblage (for instance, one that is psychological, neurological, physiological, literary, or, for that matter, supernatural, if one presupposes the existence of supernatural actors) enters into the specific miraculous diagram discussed here. This specific example may not help now, as it probably seems to be abstract to the point of being indecipherable. But what is being described in the example should (hopefully) be comprehensible by the end of the book.

8. While it is not emphasized, this work does make an implicit contribution to and provide a critique of the recent spate of research that has focused on the will as a category (see Ahmed 2014; Murphy and Throop 2010; O'Neill and Matza 2014; Povinelli 2012). The approach here is distinguishable from that literature in that the will is understood as a response to stimuli by a passive subject and not as a loci of agency and action initiated or unleashed by an active subject. The will is a force, but it is a force moved by other forces.

By way of contrast with the literature on the will, there has been a great deal of anthropological interest in Deleuze (see, for example, Hamilton and Placas 2011), though there is not a crosscutting anthropological *discussion* of Deleuze or Deleuze's thoughts in the same way that there was of Foucault a generation ago or of Marx in the 1970s. While there are some very important exceptions, it seems safe to say that Markus and Saka's (2006, 103) observation that most anthropologist's innovations in Deleuzian concepts lack "a technical and formal analysis of how this concept functions in their writing" is true. It is more common for anthropologists to take their choice of Deleuzian concepts, deterritorialize them from Deleuze's larger project, and reterritorialize them in their own. This is not a knock on most anthropological uses of Deleuze—such combinatory freedom is something Deleuze himself would most likely approve of. But still, most anthropological evocations constitute something other than a sustained engagement with Deleuze. Examples of anthropological interest in Deleuze can be seen in writings on the assemblage (Collier and Ong 2004; Rudnyckyi 2010; Zigon 2010a, 2010b, 2015), in work on affect (Stewart 2007), in discussions of "becoming" (Biehl and Locke 2010; Khan 2012), and in not unrelated issues of temporality (Hodges 2008; Pandian 2012). There is also an anthropological conversation taking place regarding virtuality, another concept closely associated with Gilles Deleuze (Goldman 2007; Holbraad 2007, 2012; Kapferer 1997, 2004, 2007, 2013; Pedersen 2007, 2011; Viveiros de Castro 2007, 2014; Willerslev 2011).

Virtuality is worth attending to in slightly more detail. While one doesn't need an understanding of the virtual to follow the argument of this book, the concept of the virtual was an important part of this book's genesis, so it is worth expanding on. Virtuality is not meant here in the sense of virtual worlds created through information technology. Rather, it refers to fields of potential given some ontic weight. This is different from a more sober approach that would dismiss potential objects as phantasms that would bloat reality with unrealized possibilities (see Heywood 2012; Quine 1948). Instead, the virtual is understood as the "real but not actual" (Deleuze and Guattari 1994, 156) aspects of phenomena, expressed in (but not solely constituting) concrete individual actualizations (Deleuze 2002; see also Deleuze 1988a, 1993, 2001). Every actual object would have a virtual "double" or, better, the actual and the virtual are the obverse and reverse faces of a coin. But in another way the reaction between the actual and the virtual is closer than the one between two sides of the same coin. The actual opens up the virtual, just as disparate elements are continually threaded through the virtual to become actual. This virtuality can be thought of as the qualitative expression of potential inherent in physical objects (see DeLanda 2002), but it is also clear that it can be ideational, in that the virtual can give rise to concepts and be addressed (though not quite directly experienced in the psychological sense of the word) through aesthetic means (Deleuze 2001; Deleuze and Guattari 1994).

Virtual objects are not essences. Rather, they are made of disparate heterogeneous aspects: "a multiplicity constituted of differential elements, differential relations between those elements, and singularities corresponding to those relations" (Deleuze 1994, 278). These relations and elements are open. This means that in different environments, or with different material, as objects become actualized, they can be quite different, despite their being expressions of a similar virtual field. Since this actualization is in a sense a process of determination, a function of how elements in a certain relation will be expressed at a particular time, it is possible to think of the virtual as a *problem* as well. There is no one problem to the virtual; rather, as different forces come into being, withdraw, or substantially shift their relations, different virtual fields open up, different problems arise, and different objects are actualized.

9. The Pentecostal and Charismatic miracle has been written about as an anthropological or ethnographic object before; see Goldstone 2011; Marshall 2009, 2010. While there is some similarity to the way that miracles are conceptualized in this book, the reliance on sovereignty as a Carl Schmitt–derived category of thought found in these works makes their approaches analytically distinct. Pelkmans (2015), in his discussion of Kyrgz converts to Christianity, has an ethnographic description of the Pentecostal and Charismatic miracle that is very similar to the one in this book. However, Pelkmans's article came to my attention too late to give it the attention it deserved.

INTRODUCTION

1. This would make the speaker, in Goffman's (1981) terms, a mere animator.
2. Wimber and Springer 1986. This narrative was also recounted (in ways that vary slightly) by Wimber in several sermons, lectures, and classes.
3. While I ultimately draw my use of mode from Spinoza (even if my reading of Spinoza is strongly influenced by Deleuze 1990a), the concept of modes as I use it could be said to "rhyme" with Whitehouse's (2004) use of the term. It is different from Whitehouse, though, in that I do not necessarily presuppose a cognitive basis for modes, nor do I in any way restrict modes to a simple binary.
4. Engelke 2007.
5. Meyer 1998; Robbins 2007a.
6. Similarly, there are Protestant and post-Protestant anthropological narratives that stress religious continuity over religious break; see, for example, Chua (2012) and Scott (2005).
7. Agamben 2005; Handman 2014, 2015.
8. Garriott and O'Neill 2008.
9. See King (2012).
10. Bialecki 2008: 114; Robbins and Engelke 2010: 626.
11. Foucault 1990.
12. Deleuze 1993.
13. Deleuze 1993.
14. Intensity has a technical meaning in the work of Deleuze; it refers to the qualitative aspects unaffected by division: temperature is a perfect example of the qualitative, in that if you divide something with a temperature of 100 degrees in half you do not get two objects that are each 50 degrees but two objects that are still at 100 degrees. This suggests that in some ways intensities could be ranked against one another, and sometimes it makes sense to talk that way. But often intensities resist quantification. As Deleuze (1990a, 196) says, expounding on the medieval philosopher Scotus, "whiteness . . . has various intensities; they are not added to whiteness as one thing to another thing, like a shape added to the wall on which it is drawn; its degrees of intensity are

intrinsic determinations, intrinsic modes, of a whiteness that remains univocally the same under whichever modality it is considered."

15. On Sheilaisms, see Bellah et al. (1985); for an argument that conservative forms of Christianity may be in demographic decline in America, see Jones (2016) and Merritt (2015).

16. Acts 2:7, 9, 13 (NRSV).

17. 1 Cor. 12:8–31 (NRSV).

18. On nineteenth-century Methodism, see Kent 2002; on Mormons and glossolalia, see Copeland 1991.

19. Robbins 2004b.

20. On Pentecostalism as a break with Protestantism, see Meyer (2010).

21. Csordas 1997a.

22. On the domestication of Pentecostal religious practices in charismatic Catholic communities, see Csordas (1994, 168–80).

23. See Marsden (1987).

24. See Kraft (2005).

25. For a full discussion of how this occurred, see Bialecki (2015c); for a history of the Vineyard before its association with John Wimber, see Higgins (2012).

26. Jackson 1999.

27. Bloch 2012; Simondon 1992.

28. 2 Cor. 5:17; Rakow 2013.

29. It is unsurprising that it has been argued there is a modern strain of self-improvement in at least some strains of early Pentecostalism (see Robins 2004).

30. Graeber 2001, 49–90.

31. Faubion 2011.

32. "Opposites . . . are things alike in all significant respects but one" (Sahlins 1994, 424).

33. Deleuze 1988b; see also Bialecki 2012, 2014b; DeLanda 2006; and Zdebik 2012.

CHAPTER ONE: VINEYARD TIME

1. The ubiquity of these stickers increased exponentially during my time in the field.

2. Nongbri 2013.

3. This problem happens in other Pentecostal forms as well. See Haynes (forthcoming).

4. Without suggesting that it is something on the order of a prototype or a complete or exhaustive instance, this example is meant as something at once indicative of and participatory in what is being put forward (Agamben 2009; Bandak, forthcoming).

5. It should also be mentioned that many figures in Christian rock began as members of worship bands. On the very off chance that a band becomes a

recognized name in Christian music and the members find themselves with viable careers, it is not unusual for them either to continue to participate as a worship band for a specific church, though perhaps at a reduced frequency, or to play frequently at denominational conferences or other special events.

6. Bodily transformations through repeated ethical exercise have been a recurrent thematic in the anthropology of Pentecostal-influenced movements (Brahinsky 2012; Luhrmann 2004; Reinhardt 2004); something similar can be seen in Csordas's (1994) reliance on the concept of *habitus*.

7. Luhrmann 2004, 2012b; Poloma 2003.
8. Geertz 1973, 360–411.
9. Bateson 1972.
10. Caleb Maskell, personal communication.
11. Rauschenbush 1917, 131.
12. I would like to thank participants in the Society of Vineyard Scholars for their assistance in helping identify the pre-Vineyard, pre-Ladd history of kingdom theology and the already/not-yet.
13. D'Elia 2008.
14. Harding 2000, 228–46. See generally Boyer (1992). For an ethnographic depiction of one way in which this can play out on the ground, see Webster (2013a).
15. Ladd 1959, 18.
16. Ladd 1959, 19.
17. Ladd 1959, 28.
18. Ladd 1959, 42, 44.
19. Ladd 1959, 38, 41.
20. D'Elia 2008.
21. Ladd 1959, 76, 77.
22. Ladd 1959, 78.
23. Ladd 1974, 211.
24. Wimber and Springer 1986, 24.
25. Wimber and Springer 1986, 29.
26. Wimber and Springer 1986, 28.
27. Cullmann 1962, 84.
28. Agamben 2005, 70.

CHAPTER TWO: INSTITUTIONS AND GOD'S AGENTS

1. Coleman 2000.
2. See, for example, Comaroff (2008, 2009).
3. Jackson 1999, 169–70
4. Jackson 1999, 170.
5. Miller 2005, 161.
6. To be more precise, the font that was used in the original graphic design of much of the Vineyard material was Kabel. Kabel is not a Vineyard proprietary font but was developed in Nuremberg in 1927; later, it was part of a broader

wave of sans-serif fonts like Helvetica and Futura that were rediscovered in the 1970s. Michael Stevenson, personal communication.

7. See Engelke 2013; note that while a Vineyard-style kingdom theology is commonly held by the people who make up the group Engelke studies, it is not the group's only theological framework.

8. Bashkow 2010.

9. Matt. 28:19.

10. Specifically, this was an instantiation of the then popular Willow Creek model. For a general discussion, see Sargeant (2000).

11. Jackson 1999, 59–60.

CHAPTER THREE: A DIAGRAM FOR FIRE

1. On centrifugal and centripetal forces, see Bakhtin (1981). For a more expansive reading of the same phenomena, but one that is delineated solely in the spheres of ethics religion, see Bergson (1935); both these positions have resonances with the open/buffered self-opposition in Taylor (2007) (though there copresence somewhat troubles the presecular/secular divide; see Bialecki [2015a]). For an earlier formulation of the centrifugal/centripetal dynamic as a Vineyard phenomenon, see Bialecki (2011a).

2. For the locus classicus of the neoliberal model of a religious free market, see Finke and Stark (2005). Parenthetically, that book's model of church growth and denominational decay was one that was frequently referenced by pastors and other Vineyard leadership.

3. See, for example, Faubion (2001b, 2011); Laidlaw (2002, 2014), and Mahmood (2005).

4. This disjunct between ideal and actual behavior, which necessitates pastoral intervention, is the reason we have to be wary of taking pastoral discourse of proper religion as a description of actual religion; see Timothy Jenkins (2012).

5. This would be, in the words of Graham Harman (2011), a perfect example of social "undermining."

6. At a governing level, the churches in these disparate places are parts of different governing structures. In addition to Vineyard USA, churches include Vineyard Canada, Vineyard UK/Ireland, Vineyard Germany, Vineyard Austria, Vineyard Switzerland, Vineyard South Africa, Vineyard Costa Rica, Vineyard Australia, Vineyard New Zealand, Vineyard BENELUX, and Vineyard Norden. There is also a variety of independent Vineyards outside of these jurisdictions. Despite this dizzying level of decentralization, though, the Vineyard conveys a sense of collectivity. These governing bodies coordinate through Vineyard International, share much of the same media, and circulate many of the same speakers. Pastors from outside the United States tend, with differing degrees of regularity, to participate in Vineyard USA conferences. Finally, pastors and many of the more involved laypersons understand themselves as being "Vineyard."

7. See Bender (2010) and Lofton (2011).

8. See Deleuze (1990a, 94–99).

9. Freud (2010) referred to this phenomenon as *nachträglichkeit* and Lacan (1978) discussed it as the *après-coup* (Laplanche and Pontalis 1988, 111–14).

10. Deleuze 1990b.

11. Bergson 1912, 1960.

12. See the discussion in note 14 to the Introduction.

13. Only during the process of particular instantiations of this abstraction or as Deleuze would put it its actualizations as concrete assemblages would it "break state" and become particular divergent differentiations of the expression and content, the discursive and nondiscursive, the visible and the invisible (Deleuze 1988b, 38).

14. For this reason, it is not quite appropriate to refer to what we are discussing as an element of culture unless one is thinking of culture in the particularly broad sense used by early twentieth-century American anthropologists. These understandings would include material items, practice, and language alongside ideational material, which was considered markedly labile and partial (see Brightman 1995).

15. Deleuze 1988b, 2012; Deleuze and Guattari 1999.

16. Johnson-Laird 2002.

17. Partridge 2014.

18. "The diagrammatic or abstract machine does not function to represent, even something real, but that constructs a real that is yet to come, a new type of reality" (Deleuze and Guattari 1999, 142).

19. See Zdebik (2012, 19).

20. Compare the diagram used here with Stasch (2006).

21. Deleuze and Guattari 1999.

22. Foucault 1977; Deleuze 1988b.

23. On the multiplicity of different diagrams (as opposed to different instantiations of the same diagram), note that "Deleuze writes of a feudal diagram, a Napoleonic diagram, a Greek diagram, or even a pastoral diagram" (Zdebik 2012:6). On diagrams as imbricated maps, see Deleuze (1988b, 44) in which he writes, "a diagram is a map, or rather several superimposed maps. And from one diagram to the next, new maps are drawn."

24. Deleuze (1988b) himself observed this, noting that while it is not the same thing as the Kantian schema, it is a sort of analogue to it; the chief difference between the two is that unlike the schema the diagram is not internal to the subject's perception but an actual set of relations in the world.

25. There are, of course, numerous instances where people have thought through religion (or at times, thought against religion) using Deleuze. See Barber (2011, 2014), Bryden (2001), Clayton (2011), Justaert (2012), Keller (2003), Raschke (2008), Shults (2014), Sherman (2009), and Simpson (2012). These works are either guides to Deleuze for theologians who are otherwise uninitiated, attempts to use Deleuze to forward theological programs that still see themselves as Orthodox (Raschke 2008), or attempts to forge heterodox theologies (Keller 2003), atheistic theologies (Shults 2014), or "anti-" theolo-

gies (Barber 2011). There are also discussions that can be understood as "political theologies" (Crockett 2011). All these approaches are distinguishable from this project—though Barber's works, which I have learned a great deal from, have without doubt atmospherically influenced this entire book.

There are also "secular" thinkers who argue that Deleuze's thought, despite its prizing of immanence and Deleuze's professed atheism, are crypto-religious. Sometimes this is a bug (Hallward 2006) and sometimes this is a feature (Ramey 2012). Hallward's reading of Deleuze is very much against the grain and seems to have been influenced by Alain Badiou's (2000) equally idiosyncratic reading of Deleuze. Given Deleuze's own history of reading philosophers "from behind," it seems wrong to object on those grounds, but it is hard to recognize Hallward's religious Deleuze in Deleuze's own texts. Ramey's (2012) claims seem much more plausible, though not necessarily true, but even granting they are true, they seem more cogent for the work of historians of philosophy than for the present project.

26. Engelke 2007; Keane 1997; Lempert 2015.

27. Bialecki 2009b; James Smith 2010. See comparably Taves (2009) on the religious saliency of "unintentional" events.

28. Geertz 1973, 100. This is not to adopt Geertz's theory of religion but merely to acknowledge that either despite or because of his Protestant baggage (Asad 1993), he has identified the times in the Vineyard in which God is most salient.

29. Wasserman 2008.

30. Williams 2011.

31. Berger 1996.

32. For anthropological alternatives to methodological atheism and reflections on the problem of belief in and experiential contact with supposedly more-than-human others, see Droogers (1996), Ewing (1994), Favret-Saada (1981), Turner (2003), and West (2007); on this issue generally, see Bialecki (2014c).

33. On the autonomy of objects, see Bryant (2011) and Harman (2011); on their heterogeneous constitution, see Delanda (2006).

34. On black boxes, see Latour (1987).

35. Bialecki 2014c.

36. Faubion 2011, 203–66.

37. This is what Deleuze and Guattari (1999) meant (or at least is one of the possible meanings we could attribute to them) when they spoke about politics as the creation of a people that is to come.

CHAPTER FOUR: *TOLLE, LEGE*

1. This also means that we should not consider "Sheilaism" (Bellah et al. 1985) to be private religion to the degree that it is a) capable of being communicated to others; b) draws on intellectual material that preexisted the individual, and c) has social effects, that is, linkages, resonances, and results in the outside world.

230 / Notes to Chapter Five

2. On atmospherics, see Engelke (2013, 37–63).

3. Luhrmann's (2012) instance of Ignatian prayer is an outlier but a productive one. While not representing a commonly shared Vineyard apparatus, it is useful for an understanding of the capacities and scope of the imagination to be trained through prayer.

4. While there are no statistics, like many evangelical and Charismatic movements, the Vineyard tends to have more women than men as members, though men hold a disproportionate number of leadership positions. Add this to the biblical imperative that when it comes to marriage it is better not to be "unevenly yoked" or married to someone who is not or is only nominally Christian, and it is easy to see why there are an inordinate number of prayers about loneliness.

5. On Bible study, individually and collectively, see Bielo (2009a, 2009b).

6. The Scofield Bible is a traditional Bible text, usually a King James or New King James version, that has been supplemented by annotations explaining how the various verses fit into the apocalyptic scheme created by dispensational millennialist thought. This causes interesting spaces of imaginative freedom and practical constraint. See Boyer (1992), Harding (2000), and T. Weber (1979).

7. Benjamin 1968.

8. The following section of this chapter was first published in Bialecki 2009a.

9. This concludes the section that first appeared in Bialecki 2009a.

10. Derrida 1988.

11. This is not to say there are no "secular" reading practices that do not evoke a sense of authorial presence or no reading communities that foster a sense of presence. They do exist (see Reed 2004). But they are exceptions and tend to be informed by a different metaphysics of reading.

12. Bialecki 2009a, 149–150.

13. Simons 1996.

14. Tompkins 1995.

15. Bialecki 2009a.

16. James Smith 2010, 33.

17. James Smith 2010, 33.

18. See also Elisha (2011).

19. This is a reference to Judges 6:36–40, where Gideon puts out a golden fleece to judge the God's intentions. He had stated in advance that if the fleece were wet in the morning, then Gideon would take it as a sign that he should militarily command Israel in its conflict with the Midianites.

20. Ansell-Pearson 1999, 7.

CHAPTER FIVE: THE LIVING ROOM SEMINARS

1. Bialecki 2014b; Brahinsky 2012; Daswani 2013, 2015; Luhrmann 2012b; Reinhardt 2014.

2. Blanton 2012.
3. Bialecki 2015c; Marsden 1987.
4. Bateson 1972.
5. The allure of Messianic Judaism for American evangelical Christians is complicated (see Dulin 2013, 2015; Kaell 2014).
6. Bielo 2011.
7. Willard 1998.
8. Bielo 2011.
9. Cassaniti and Luhrmann 2014.
10. On coincidence as an index of divine activity, see Webster (2013b).
11. See Csordas (1997b).
12. See chapter 6 of this book.
13. Kroskrity 2000; Woolard 1985; Woolard and Schieffelin 1994.
14. Robbins 2001a; Engelke 2007; Keane 2007. See also Bialecki and Hoenes del Pinal (2011).
15. For prior instances of a similar linguistic problematic in Protestantism, see Bauman (1983).
16. On the performance of exterior voices in Pentecostal/charismatic speech, see Shoaps (2002); on the parasitic nature of speech, see Bakhtin (1981).
17. See Lambek (2003a).
18. See Jackson (1999).
19. Urban 1989.
20. While the equivalence could be overstated, this is not unlike secondary revision in Freud's (2010) theory of dreams, where the act of narrating dreams while waking is just as important an aspect of the dreamwork as the original dream event itself.
21. Reed 2004.

CHAPTER SIX: THE BODY, TONGUES, HEALING, AND DELIVERANCE

1. Brahinsky 2012; Csordas 1994; Luhrmann 2008; Reinhard 2014.
2. How to account for my ability to do things such as receive messages from God or pray for healing was apparently not even a problem they noticed, let alone one that was undertheorized by my informants; for many, it was one that they worked through. The closest thing to an explanation I was ever given was since it was the Holy Spirit who was accomplishing these feats and not me my own spiritual status was incidental.
3. On atmosphere, see Engelke (2013).
4. Goffman 1981.
5. Keane 2007.
6. Deleuze 1990b.
7. See Bialecki (2015c).
8. Text for this section of the book chapter appeared in Bialecki (2011a).

9. Conclusion of passage that first appeared in Bialecki (2011a).

10. Wimber and Springer 1986, 109.

11. On the relationship between spirit possession and property, see Johnson (2011).

12. While it is not uncommon to hear secondhand about women being demonized to the point of a deliverance, I think it's significant that the only examples I've seen firsthand are men. With only one exception, men are also the only ones I've had the opportunity to talk to about being demonized (cf. Luhrmann 2012b).

13. Bibby and Brinkerhoff 1973.

14. Evans-Pritchard 1937.

15. On the use of multiple supernatural and natural explanatory frames, see Bialecki (2014c), Coleman (2015), and Luhrmann (2012a).

16. Wimber and Springer 1986, 118.

17. For a fully developed example informed by the culture of machismo, see Thornton (2016).

18. Unsurprisingly some charismatic evangelicals have created forms of psychic healing not unlike the practices found among some charismatic Catholics (see Csordas 1994).

19. Bialecki 2011b.

20. Compare this with Deleuze and Guattari (1994) on zones of indistinction in concepts.

21. Luhrmann 2012b.

22. Rakow 2013.

CHAPTER SEVEN: COLLAPSES, TRAVERSALS, AND INTENSIFICATIONS OF THE PART-CULTURE

1. Coleman 2006b, 2010. While he does not use either Coleman's language of part-culture, or this book's language of diagrams, Kevin O'Neill's (2015) ethnography of neoliberal street gang prevention programs in Guatemala is an excellent depiction of how various seemingly unlikely assemblages such as prisons, call centers, and even television reality programming can become imbricated with and sometimes captured by Pentecostal diagrams.

2. On the Emergent Church movement, see Bielo (2011).

3. This has been argued recently about the Vineyard in Luhrmann (2012b); see also Taylor (2007) on the general effect of multiple imaginable ontological framings in contemporary society.

4. For more on this point, see the discussion of correlationism in Meillassoux (2008).

5. Jackson 1999, 280.

6. Poloma 2003.

7. On spiritual warfare, see Holvast (2009), Jorgensen (2005), McAlister (2012, 2013), O'Neill (2010), and Robbins (2012b).

8. See Bialecki (2016).

9. McManus 2009.
10. For more on the Toronto Blessing, see Brown (2012).
11. Wendall Jones 2016.
12. Coleman 2000, 2004, 2006a, 2006a, 2006b; Haynes 2012, 2013, 2015, n.d.; Wiegele 2005.
13. Brown 2013.
14. Perrin 1989.
15. Elisha 2008, 2011.
16. Foucault 1990.
17. To this degree, I believe that Reinhardt (2016) is correct but with this caveat: I want to stress his point that it is important to attend to anthropological informants' discussion of transcendence but also his point that we must remember that transcendence is effectuated only through immanent forms.
18. See Sahlins (1972); of course, this is a function of broader shifts in the political economy and the regime of truth (Parry 1986).
19. Fogel 2000; McLoughlin 1978.
20. On variation and differentiation in the political imaginary of conservative Christians, see Bielo (2009a), Crapanzano (2000), Connolly (2008), Elisha (2011), and Harding 2000.
21. See similarly Marshall (2009), though Marshall's project can be separated from this one in that its focus exclusively on processes of Foucaultian auto-subjectification is inescapably teleological.
22. Candea 2011; Spencer 2007.
23. Bartkowski 2004.
24. See Bialecki (2014a). It should be noted, however, that this turn was met with more opposition from current Vineyard leadership and the leadership position continues to be divisive.
25. To this degree their thinking is structured like the future-facing politics of hope found in Miyazaki (2004) but also suffers from the limitations described in Crapanzano (2003). See Bialecki (2011a).
26. Harding 2000.
27. Marshall 2009.

CONCLUSION

1. Compare with Robbins (2004a, 132).
2. See Willerslev (2011) on reclaiming speculative thought in anthropology. It should be noted that the argument presented in this chapter cannot be collapsed into Willerslev's argument that animist "high gods" are a mode of thinking through a nonlocalized plane of pure virtuality; however, it would not be going too far to say that these two arguments "rhyme."
3. An example of this is the unlikely success of the anti-Kantian speculative realism in continental philosophy, which is far too broad to fully rehearse here; see Bryant, Harman, and Srnicek (2011). While what we are doing is not a claim to escape the phenomenological/neumenal distinction, we will be stepping

beyond anything our ethnographic evidence can conclusively show, so there is similarity to that other project.

4. See, for example, Course (2010), Descola (2013a), Henare, Holbraad, and Wastell (2007), Holbraad (2012), Kohn (2012), Scott (2007, 2013), Viveiros de Castro (2014), and Willerslev (2007). Again, though this book presents a different picture from that presented by much of the "ontological turn" and the ontological turn's fellow travelers, I would be reluctant to see this book as a rejection of this "ontological turn" for two reasons. The first reason is that this work and much of the ontological turn share an interest in Gilles Deleuze. The second reason is that while I do not go as far as to make it a grounding heuristic, as I discuss in chapter 3, I agree that it is sometimes analytically profitable to at least provisionally not "look behind" a phenomenon being interrogated and instead to take it on its own terms. The expression of other assemblages, once they become part of a new assemblage, obscures the very processes that gave rise to that prior assemblage. Rather than being seen as an expression of some other constellation, they are cogent only within the array of connections and associations that constitute the current assemblage, as a part of the assemblage, which is why physiological or neurological processes are recognizable as psychological processes only when encountered within psychology—or why other processes, when they are recognized within the miraculous assemblage because they carry or trigger an affective charge of surprise, become recognizable as miraculous. This argument, it should be noted, is not too different from systems theory, though without a presumption that this plays out at the level of institutions and with an acknowledgment that a stable mode of self-replication, or autopoiesis, is hard won and often lacking. At the same time, this kinship with the ontological turn also marks where I break with the turn. I differ sharply from the main line of this ontological thought in that I do not carve up the world into different ontological ghettoes. All sorts of framings and systems bleed into each other all the time. After all, the world is, at least from some vantage points, inescapably interconnected.

5. For all their theoretical and stylistic differences, Faubion (2011), Laidlaw (2014), and Keane (2016) are examples of this return to broad comparative thought in the anthropology of ethics.

6. Bloch 2008.

7. See similarly Tweed (2006), which proposes a framing of religion not unlike the one presented in this chapter. Tweed's approach focuses more on the linkages to other systems, and on a typology of work done by religion, than on the process of sketching a generative topology of religion, as this chapter endeavors to do.

8. Asad 1993; Bialecki forthcoming-b; Masuzawa 2005; Nongbri 2013; Saler 1987; Jonathan Smith 1998. Although I appreciate this critique, I see it as a spur not to abandon the word *religion* but to speak about it in new ways, with different degrees of precision (see also, for instance, Lewis 2015; Schilbrack 2014, 85–111).

9. For a full elaboration of this common critique, see Nongbri (2013).

10. Colwell (1997); see also Bialecki (2015b).
11. Bialecki 2014d.
12. See, for example, Sun (2013).
13. Deleuze and Guattari 1999, 3.
14. Tylor 1874, 424.
15. Descola 2013a, 2013b; Latour 1993.
16. Spiro 1966.
17. Asad 1993; Lindquist and Coleman 2008; Needham 1972; Ruel 1997.
18. Robbins 2007a.
19. See Weber (1968), though we should note that a fixation on the charismatic figure alone misconstrues the real conditions of possibility for charismatic leadership. See Bialecki (2014c) and Csordas (1997a).
20. For those who doubt that bureaucracy and governance can constitute a full mode of religiosity, I recommend turning to Holston (1999).
21. Keane 1997, 48.
22. De Vries 2001b.
23. This has certain resonances with Wagner (1986).
24. Mauss 2016, 193.
25. Simondon 1992.
26. For examples, see Engelke (2005) and Faubion (2001a).
27. Blanton 2012, 2015; Boylston 2013a; Engelke 2010a, 2010b, 2011; Hirschkind 2006; Meyer 2010, 2015; Peters 1999.
28. To put it in technical language from Deleuze and Guattari's *A Thousand Plateaus* (1999), the claim being made here is that the heightened capacity for deterritorialization and assemblages found in the "alloplastic" strata reaches its greatest extent in religion, since religion can choose from a more capacious set of imaginable machinic assemblages and assemblages of enunciation.
29. Luhrmann 2012b.
30. This would be an equivalent to the sort of logic we see in early Renaissance hermeticism (Foucault 1971) or in other analogic ontologies (Descola 2013a).
31. See Bergson (1935); this also has some resonance with Mary Douglas's group/grid theory, though the insistence here on a continuum rather than discrete categories should be stressed.
32. See Delanda (2011) and Kauffman (1993). One way of conceiving this space might be as a topological version of Descola's (2013a) four ontologies that is joined by smooth spaces of transitions instead of sharp, quantum borders between ontological kinds (even if this would run against his animating structuralist logic).
33. Connolly 2008.
34. Lacan 1978.
35. See Gell (1998), Latour (2010), and Bialecki (2014c).
36. Eisenstadt 1982; Jaspers 1953; Robbins 2012b.
37. See Massumi (1992), 114.
38. See Bellah (2011).

39. Robbins 2009.

40. Read this way, it appears that cognitive accounts of religion that see religiosity as a result of various neurological and evolutionary spandrels have placed the cart before the horse (and here we are referring to cognitive stories built around different memory systems, overactive agent identification complexes, hardwired neurological assumptions about ontology that have specific effects when violated, or even "God spots" in the architecture of the brain). Such systems, if they do exist, are captured by specific actualizations of various religious diagrams; therefore they are not obligatory to religious practice, and they have no structural causal primacy (for a similar argument regarding ethics, see Keane 2016). Even if religion presumes a brain for its existence, the features of the brain are just other assemblages for religion to work on.

41. The phrase "machines for the suppression of time" is Edmund Leach's (1996, 135) alternate translation of a passage that is originally found in Lévi-Strauss (1964, 26) ("Instruments for the obliteration of time" [Lévi-Strauss 1970, 16] is the way the passage is presented in the standard English translation of the book). On the concept of religion and myth, as well as music, as machines for the suppression of time, see Lévi-Strauss 1970.

42. Simondon 1992. This model has some similarity to Lévi-Strauss's analysis of mana as a "floating signifier" in *Introduction to the Marcel Mauss* (1987); but whereas for Lévi-Strauss signification has a surplus over knowledge and the world that is used to overcome contradiction, I see the diagrammatic aspect of religion as a pure surplus itself, the greatest and freest range of change and stasis that humans are capable of engaging in and undergoing, always entailed with something else but without having any natural or automatic entailment to other specific activities or objects.

Works Cited

Agamben, Giorgio. 2005. *The Time That Remains: A Commentary on the Letter to the Romans.* Stanford, CA: Stanford University Press.
———. 2009. *The Signature of All Things: On Method.* Translated by Luca D'Isanto with Kevin Attell. New York: Zone Books.
Ahmed, Sara. 2014. *Willful Subjects.* Durham, NC: Duke University Press.
Anidjar, Gil. 2009. "The Idea of an Anthropology of Christianity." *Interventions* 11 (3): 367–93.
Ansell-Pearson, Keith. 1999. *Germinal Life: The Difference and Repetition of Deleuze.* London: Routledge.
Asad, Talal. 1993. *Genealogies of Religion: Discipline and Reasons of Power in Christianity and Islam.* Baltimore: Johns Hopkins University Press.
———. 2003. *Formations of the Secular: Christianity, Islam, Modernity.* Stanford, CA: Stanford University Press.
Badiou, Alain. 2000. *Deleuze: The Clamor of Being.* Minneapolis: University of Minnesota Press.
Bakhtin, Mikhail. 1981. *The Dialogic Imagination: Four Essays.* Edited by Michael Holquist. Austin: University of Texas Press.
Bandak, Andreas. Forthcoming. "The Power of Example." *Journal of the Royal Anthropological Institute.*
Bandak, Andreas, and Tom Boylston. 2014. "The 'Orthodoxy' of Orthodoxy: On Moral Imperfection, Correctness, and Deferral in Religious Worlds." *Religion and Society* 5:25–46.
Barber, Daniel Colucciello. 2011. *On Diaspora: Christianity, Religion and Secularity.* Eugene, OR: Cascade Books.
———. 2014. *Deleuze and the Naming of God: Post-secularism and the Future of Immanence.* Edinburgh: Edinburgh University Press.
Bartkowski, John. 2004. *The Promise Keepers: Servants, Soldiers, and Godly Men.* New Brunswick, NJ: Rutgers University Press.
Bashkow, Ira. 2010. *An Anthropological Theory of the Corporation.* Chicago: Prickly Paradigm.

Bateson, Gregory. 1972. *Steps to an Ecology of Mind: Collected Essays in Anthropology, Psychiatry, Evolution, and Epistemology*. San Francisco: Chandler.

Bauman, Richard. 1983. *Let Your Words Be Few: Symbolism of Speaking and Silence among Seventeenth-Century Quakers*. Cambridge: Cambridge University Press.

Bellah, Robert N. 2011. *Religion in Human Evolution from the Paleolithic to the Axial Age*. Cambridge, MA: Belknap Press of Harvard University Press.

Bellah, Robert, Richard Madsen, William M. Sullivan, Ann Swidler, and Steven M. Tipton. 1985. *Habits of the Heart: Individualism and Commitment in American Life*. Berkeley: University of California Press.

Bender, Courtney. 2010. *The New Metaphysicals: Spirituality and the American Religious Imagination*. Chicago: University of Chicago Press.

Benjamin, Walter. 1968. "The Task of the Translator." In *Illuminations*, edited by Hannah Arendt, 69–82. New York: Harcourt, Brace.

Berger, Peter. 1996. *The Sacred Canopy: Elements of a Social Theory of Religion*. New York: Anchor.

Bergson, Henri. 1912. *Matter and Memory*. London: G. Allen.

———. 1935. *The Two Sources of Morality and Religion*. New York: H. Holt.

———. 1960. *Time and Free Will, an Essay on the Immediate Data of Consciousness*. New York: Harper.

Bialecki, Jon. 2008. "Between Stewardship and Sacrifice: Agency and Economy in a Southern California Charismatic Church." *Journal of the Royal Anthropological Institute* 14 (2): 372–90.

———. 2009a. "The Bones Restored to Life: Dialogue and Dissemination in the Vineyard's Dialectic of Text and Presence." In *The Social Life of Scriptures: Cross-Cultural Perspectives on Biblicism*, edited by James Bielo, 136–56. New Brunswick, NJ: Rutgers University Press.

———. 2009b. "Disjuncture, Continental Philosophy's New 'Political Paul,' and the Question of Progressive Christianity in a Southern California Third Wave Church." *American Ethnologist* 36 (1): 110–23.

———. 2011a. "No Caller I.D. for the Soul—Demonization, Charisms, and the Unstable Subject of Protestant Language Ideology." *Anthropological Quarterly* 84 (3): 679–703.

———. 2011b. "Quiet Deliverances." In *Practicing the Faith: The Ritual Life of Pentecostal-Charismatic Christians*, edited by Martin Linderhart, 249–76. Oxford: Berghahn Press.

———. 2012. "Virtual Christianity in an Age of Nominalist Anthropology." *Anthropological Theory* 12 (3): 295–319.

———. 2014a. "After the Denominozoic: Evolution, Differentiation, Denominationalism." *Current Anthropology* 5 (S10): S193–S204.

———. 2014b. "Diagramming the Will: Ethics and Prayer, Text, and Politics." *Ethnos*. doi:10.1080/00141844.2014.986151.

———. 2014c. "Does God Exist in Methodological Atheism? On Tanya Lurhmann's *When God Talks Back* and Bruno Latour." *Anthropology of Consciousness* 25 (1): 32–52.

———. 2014d. "Ending a Conversation with System R." Review of Brent Nongbri, *Before Religion: A History of a Modern Concept*. AnthroCyBib (blog), March 6. www.blogs.hss.ed.ac.uk/anthrocybib/2014/03/06/ending-a-conversation-with-system-r-book-review-of-nongbris-before-religion/.

———. 2015a. "The Judgment of God and the Non-elephantine Zoo: Christian Dividualism, Individualism, and Ethical Freedom after the Mosko-Robbins Debate." *AnthroCyBib* (blog), March 17. www.blogs.hss.ed.ac.uk/anthrocybib/2015/03/17/occasional-paper-bialecki-the-judgment-of-god-and-the-non-elephantine-zoo/.

———. 2015b. "The Problem with Critique, and Critique as a Problem." *Journal of the Royal Anthropological Institute* 21 (1): 202–5.

———. 2015c. "The Third Wave and the Third World: C. Peter Wagner, John Wimber, and the Pedagogy of Global Renewal in the Late Twentieth Century." *Pneuma* 37 (2): 177–200.

———. 2016. "Apostolic Networks in the Third Wave of the Spirit: John Wimber and the Vineyard." *Pneuma* 38 (1): 23–32.

———. Forthcoming-a. "'The Lord Says You Speak as Harlots': Affect, Affectus, and Affectio." In *Religious Language*, edited by Courtney Handman, Chris Lehrich, and Robert Yelle. Berlin: De Gruyter Mouton.

———. Forthcoming-b. "'Religion' after Religion, 'Ritual' after Ritual." In *Companion to Contemporary Anthropology*, edited by Simon Coleman and Sue Hyatt. New York: Routledge.

Bialecki, Jon, and Girish Daswani. 2015. "What Is an Individual: A View from Christianity." *HAU* 5 (1): 271–94.

Bialecki, Jon, Naomi Haynes, and Joel Robbins. 2008. "The Anthropology of Christianity." *Religion Compass* 2 (6): 1139–58.

Bialecki, Jon, and Eric Hoenes del Pinal. 2011. "Introduction: Beyond Logos, Extensions of the Language Ideology Paradigm in the Study of Global Christianity(-ies)." *Anthropological Quarterly* 84 (3): 575–93.

Bibby, Reginald, and Merlin B. Brinkerhoff. 1973. "The Circulation of the Saints: A Study of People Who Join Conservative Churches." *Journal for the Scientific Study of Religion* 12 (3): 273–83.

Biehl, João, and Peter Locke. 2010. "Deleuze and the Anthropology of Becoming." *Current Anthropology* 51 (3): 317–51.

Bielo, James, ed. 2009a. *The Social Life of Scriptures: Cross-Cultural Perspectives on Biblicism*. New Brunswick, NJ: Rutgers University Press.

———. 2009b. *Words upon the Word: An Ethnography of Evangelical Group Bible Study*. New York: New York University Press.

———. 2011. *Emerging Evangelicals: Faith, Modernity, and the Desire for Authenticity*. New York: New York University Press.

Blanton, Anderson. 2012. "Appalachian Radio Prayers: The Prosthesis of the Holy Ghost and the Drive to Tactility." In *Radio Fields: Anthropology and Wireless Sound in the 21st Century*, edited by Lucas Bessire and Daniel Fisher, 215–32. New York: New York University Press.

———. 2015. *Hittin' the Prayer Bones: Materiality of Spirit in the Pentecostal South*. Chapel Hill: University of North Carolina Press.

Bloch, Maurice. 2008. "Why Religion Is Nothing Special but Is Central." *Philosophical Transactions of the Royal Society B* 363 (1499): 2055–61.
———. 2012. *Anthropology and the Cognitive Challenge*. Cambridge: Cambridge University Press.
Boyer, Paul S. 1992. *When Time Shall Be No More: Prophecy Belief in Modern American Culture*. Cambridge, MA: Belknap Press of Harvard University Press.
Boylston, Tom. 2013a. "Food, Life and Material Religion in Ethiopian Orthodox Christianity." In *Companion to the Anthropology of Religion*, edited by Janice Boddy and Michael Lambek, 257–73. Chicago: Wiley-Blackwell.
———. 2013b. "Orienting the East." *Anthrocbybib* (blog), May 26. www.blogs.hss.ed.ac.uk/anthrocybib/2013/05/26/orienting-the-east.
Brahinsky, Josh. 2012. "Pentecostal Body Logics: Cultivating a Modern Sensorium." *Cultural Anthropology* 27 (2): 215–38.
Brightman, Robert. 1995. "Forget Culture: Replacement, Transcendence, Relexification." *Cultural Anthropology* 10 (4): 509–46.
Brouwer, Steve, Paul Gifford, and Susan D. Rose. 1996. *Exporting the American Gospel: Global Christian Fundamentalism*. New York: Routledge.
Brown, Candy Gunther. 2012. *Testing Prayer: Science and Healing*. Cambridge, MA: Harvard University Press.
———. 2013. *The Healing Gods: Complementary and Alternative Medicine in Christian America*. New York: Oxford University Press.
Bryant, Levi. 2011. *The Democracy of Objects*. Ann Arbor, MI: Open Humanities Press.
Bryant, Levi, Graham Harman, and Nick Srnicek, eds. 2011. *The Speculative Turn: Continental Materialism and Realism*. Melbourne: Re-Press.
Bryden, Mary. 2001. *Deleuze and Religion*. London: Routledge.
Candea, Matei. 2011. "'Our Division of the Universe': Making a Space for the Nonpolitical in the Anthropology of Politics." *Current Anthropology* 52 (3): 309–34.
Cannell, Fanella. 2005. "The Christianity of Anthropology." *Journal of the Royal Anthropological Institute* 11 (2): 335–56.
———, ed. 2006. Introduction to *The Anthropology of Christianity*, 1–50. Durham, NC: Duke University Press.
Cassaniti, Julia, and T.M. Luhrmann. 2014. "The Cultural Kindling of Spiritual Experiences." *Current Anthropology* 55 (S10): S333–43.
Chua, Liana. 2012. *The Christianity of Culture: Conversion, Ethnic Citizenship, and the Matter of Religion in Malaysian Borneo*. New York: Palgrave Macmillan.
Coleman, Simon. 2000. *The Word and the World: The Globalisation of Charismatic Christianity*. Cambridge: Cambridge University Press.
———. 2004. "The Charismatic Gift." *Journal of the Royal Anthropological Institute* 10 (2): 421–42.
———. 2006a. "Materialising the Self: Words and Gifts in the Construction of Evangelical Identity." *The Anthropology of Christianity*, edited by F. Cannell, 163–84. Durham, NC: Duke University Press.

———. 2006b. "Studying 'Global' Pentecostalism: Tensions, Representations and Opportunities." *PentecoStudies* 5 (1): 1–17.

———. 2010. "An Anthropological Apologetics." *South Atlantic Quarterly* 109 (4): 791–810.

———. 2015. "Ethics, Ethnography, and 'Repugnant' Christianity." *HAU* 5 (2): 275–300.

Collier, Stephan, and Aihwa Ong, eds. 2004. "Global Assemblages, Anthropological Problems." In *Global Assemblages: Technology, Politics, and Ethics as Anthropological Problems*, edited by Stephan Collier and Aihwa Ong, 3–21. Walden, MA: Blackwell.

Colwell, C. 1997. "Deleuze and Foucault: Series, Event, Genealogy." *Theory and Event* 1 (2).

Comaroff, Jean. 2009. "The Politics of Conviction: Faith on the Neo-liberal Frontier." *Social Analysis* 53 (1): 17–38.

Comaroff, John. 2010. "The End of Anthropology, Again: On the Future of the In/Discipline." *American Anthropologist* 112 (4): 524–38.

Connolly, William. 2008. *Capitalism and Christianity, American Style*. Durham, NC: Duke University Press.

Copeland, Lee. 1991. "Speaking in Tongues in the Restoration Churches." *Dialogue* 24 (Spring): 13–33.

Course, Magnus. 2010. "Of Words and Fog: Linguistic Relativity and Amerindian Ontology." *Anthropological Theory* 10 (3): 247–63.

Crapanzano, Vincent. 2000. *Serving the Word: Literalism in America from the Pulpit to the Bench*. New York: New Press.

———. 2003. "Reflections on Hope as a Category of Social and Psychological Analysis." *Cultural Anthropology* 18 (1): 3–32.

Crockett, Clayton. 2011. *Radical Political Theology: Religion and Politics after Liberalism*. New York: Columbia University Press.

Csordas, Thomas. 1994. *The Sacred Self: A Cultural Phenomenology of Charismatic Healing*. Berkeley: University of California Press.

———. 1997a. *Language, Charisma, and Creativity: The Ritual Life of a Religious Movement*. Berkeley: University of California Press.

———. 1997b. "Prophecy and the Performance of Metaphor." *American Anthropologist* 99 (2): 331–32.

Cullmann, Oscar. 1962. *Christ and Time: The Primitive Christian Conception of Christ and History*. Rev. ed. London: SCM Press.

Daswani, Girish. 2013. "On Christianity and Ethics: Rupture as Ethical Practice in Ghanian Pentecostalism." *American Ethnologist* 40 (3): 467–79.

———. 2015. *Looking Back, Moving Forward: Transformation and Ethical Practice in the Ghanaian Church of Pentecost*. Toronto: University of Toronto Press.

DeLanda, Manuel. 2002. *Intensive Science and Virtual Philosophy*. New York: Continuum.

———. 2006. *A New Philosophy of Society: Assemblage Theory and Social Complexity*. New York: Continuum.

———. 2011. *Philosophy and Simulation: The Emergence of Synthetic Reason*. London: Continuum.
Deleuze, Gilles. 1978. *Lecture Transcripts* on *Spinoza's Concept* of *Affect*. www.gold.ac.uk/media/deleuze_spinoza_affect.pdf.
———. 1988a. *Bergsonism*. New York: Zone Books.
———. 1988b. *Foucault*. Translated by Seán Hand. Minneapolis: University of Minnesota Press.
———. 1990a. *Expressionism in Philosophy: Spinoza*. New York: Zone Books.
———. 1990b. *The Logic of Sense*. New York: Columbia University Press.
———. 1992. "Ethnology: Spinoza and Us." In *Incorporations*, edited by Jonathan Crary and Sanford Kwinter, 625–33. New York: Zone Books.
———. 1993. *Difference and Repetition*. New York: Columbia University Press.
———. 1998. *Spinoza: Practical Philosophy*. San Francisco: City Lights Books.
———. 2001. *Cinema 2: The Time Image*. Minneapolis: University of Minnesota Press.
———. 2002. "The Actual and the Virtual." In *Dialogues II*, rev. ed., translated by Eliot Ross Albert, 148–52. New York: Columbia University Press.
———. 2012. *Francis Bacon: The Logic of Sensation*. London: Continuum.
Deleuze, Gilles, and Félix Guattari. 1994. *What Is Philosophy?* New York: Columbia University Press.
———. 1999. *A Thousand Plateaus: Capitalism and Schizophrenia*. Minneapolis: University of Minnesota Press.
D'Elia, John A. 2008. *A Place at the Table: George Eldon Ladd and the Rehabilitation of Evangelical Scholarship in America*. Oxford: Oxford University Press.
Derrida, Jacques. 1988. "Signature, Event, Context." In *Limited Inc*, 1–23. Evanston, IL: Northwestern University Press.
———. 2001. "Above All, No Journalists!" In *Religion and Media*, edited by Hent de Vries and Samuel Weber, 56–93. Stanford, CA: Stanford University Press.
———. 2002. "Faith and Knowledge: Two Sources of 'Religion' at the Limits of Reason Alone." In *Acts of Religion*, 40–101. New York: Routledge.
Descola, Philippe. 2013a. *Beyond Nature and Culture*. Translated by Janet Lloyd. Chicago: University of Chicago Press
———. 2013b. *The Ecology of Others*. Chicago: Prickly Paradigm Press.
de Vries, Hent. 2001a. "In Media Res: Global Religion, Public Spheres, and the Task of Contemporary Religious Studies." In *Religion and Media*, edited by Hent de Vries and Samuel Weber, 4–42. Stanford, CA: Stanford University Press.
———. 2001b. "Of Miracles and Special Effects." *International Journal for Philosophy of Religion* 50 (1): 41–56.
Droogers, Andre. 1996. "Methodological Ludism: Beyond Religionism and Reductionism." In *Conflicts in Social Science*, edited by Anton van Harskamp, 44–67. London: Routledge.

Dulin, John. 2013. "Messianic Judaism as a Mode of Christian Authenticity: Exploring the Grammar of Authenticity through Ethnography of a Contested Identity." *Anthropos* 108 (1): 33–51.

———. 2015. "Reversing Rupture: Evangelicals' Practice of Jewish Rituals and Processes of Protestant Inclusion." *Anthropological Quarterly* 88 (3): 601–34.

Eisenstadt, S. N. 1982. "The Axial Age: The Emergence of Transcendental Visions and the Rise of the Clerics." *Archives Europeennes de Sociologie* 23 (2): 294–314.

Elisha, Omri. 2008. "Moral Ambitions of Grace: The Paradox of Compassion and Accountability in Evangelical Faith-Based Activism." *Cultural Anthropology* 23 (1): 154–89.

———. 2011. *Moral Ambition: Mobilization and Social Outreach in Evangelical Megachurches*. Berkeley: University of California Press.

Engelke, Matthew. 2005. "The Early Days of Johane Masowe: Self-Doubt, Uncertainty, and Religious Transformation." *Comparative Studies in Society and History* 47 (4): 781–808.

———. 2007. *A Problem of Presence: Beyond Scripture in an African Christian Church*. Berkeley: University of California Press.

Engelke, Matthew. 2010a. "Number and the Imagination of Global Christianity; or, Mediation and Immediacy in the Work of Alain Badiou." *South Atlantic Quarterly* 109 (4): 811–29.

———. 2010b. "Past Pentecostalism: Notes on Rupture, Realignment, and Everyday Life in Pentecostal and African Independent Churches." *Journal of the International African Institute* 80 (2): 177–99.

———. 2010c. "Religion and the Media Turn: A Review Essay." *American Ethnologist* 37 (2): 371–79.

———. 2011. "Response to Charles Hirschkind: Religion and Transduction." *Social Anthropology* 19 (1): 97–102.

———. 2013. *God's Agents: Biblical Publicity in Contemporary England*. Berkeley: University of California Press.

Engelke, Matthew, and Matt Tomlinson. 2006. "Meaning, Anthropology, Christianity." In *The Limits of Meaning: Case Studies in the Anthropology of Christianity*, edited by Matthew Engelke Matthew and Matt Tomlinson, 1–37. New York: Berghahn Books.

Evans-Pritchard, E. E. 1937. *Witchcraft, Oracles and Magic among the Azande*. Oxford: Clarendon Press.

Ewing, Katherine. 1994. "Dreams from a Saint: Anthropological Atheism and the Temptation to Believe." *American Anthropologist* 96 (3): 571–83.

Fader, Ayala. 2009. *Mitzvah Girls: Bringing Up the Next Generation of Hasidic Jews in Brooklyn*. Princeton, NJ: Princeton University Press.

Faubion, James. 2001a. *The Shadows and Lights of Waco: Millennialism Today*. Princeton, NJ: Princeton University Press.

———. 2001b. "Toward an Anthropology of Ethics: Foucault and the Pedagogies of Autopoiesis." *Representations* 74 (1): 83–104.

———. 2011. *An Anthropology of Ethics*. Cambridge: Cambridge University Press.
Favret-Saada, Jeanne. 1981. *Deadly Words: Witchcraft in the Bocage*. Cambridge: Cambridge University Press.
Finke, Roger, and Rodney Stark. 2005. *The Churching of America, 1776–2005: Winners and Losers in Our Religious Economy*. New Brunswick, NJ: Rutgers University Press.
Fogel, Robert William. 2000. *The Fourth Great Awakening and the Future of Egalitarianism*. Chicago: University of Chicago.
Foucault, Michel. 1971. *The Order of Things: An Archaeology of the Human Sciences*. New York: Pantheon Books.
———. 1977. *Discipline and Punish: The Birth of the Prison*. New York: Pantheon Books.
———. 1990. *The History of Sexuality*. Vol. 2. *The Use of Pleasure*. New York: Vintage Books.
Freud, Sigmund. 2010. *The Interpretation of Dreams*. New York: Basic Books.
Garriott, William, and Kevin Lewis O'Neill. 2008. "Who Is a Christian? Toward a Dialogic Approach in the Anthropology of Christianity." *Anthropological Theory* 8 (4): 381–98.
Geertz, Clifford. 1973. *The Interpretation of Cultures: Selected Essays*. New York: Basic Books.
Gell, Alfred. 1992. *The Anthropology of Time: Cultural Constructions of Temporal Maps and Images*. Oxford: Berg.
———. 1998. *Art and Agency: An Anthropological Theory*. Oxford: Clarendon Press.
Goffman, Erving. 1981. *Forms of Talk*. Philadelphia: University of Pennsylvania Press.
Goldman, Mario. 2007. "How to Learn in an Afro-Brazilian Spirit Possession Religion: Ontology and Multiplicity in Candomblé." In *Learning Religion: Anthropological Approaches*, edited by David Berliner and Ramon Sarró, 103–19. New York: Berghahn Books.
Goldstone, Brian. "The Miraculous Life." *Johannesburg Workshop in Theory and Criticism* 4:81–96.
Graeber, David. 2001. *Toward an Anthropological Theory of Value: The False Coin of Our Own Dreams*. New York: Palgrave.
Guyer, Jane. 2007. "Prophecy and the Near Future: Thoughts on Macroeconomic, Evangelical, and Punctuated Time." *American Ethnologist* 34 (3): 409–21.
Hallward, Peter. 2006. *Out of This World: Deleuze and the Philosophy of Creation*. London: Verso.
Hamilton, Jennifer, and Aimee Placas. 2011. "Anthropology Becoming . . . ? The 2010 Sociocultural Anthropology Year in Review." *American Anthropologist* 113 (2): 246–61.
Handman, Courtney. 2014. "Becoming the Body of Christ: Sacrificing the Speaking Subject in the Making of the Colonial Lutheran Church in New Guinea." *Current Anthropology* 55 (S10): S205–15.

———. 2015. *Critical Christianity: Translation and Denominational Conflict in Papua New Guinea*. The Anthropology of Christianity. Berkeley: University of California Press.

Hann, Chris. 2007. "The Anthropology of Christianity Per Se." *European Journal of Sociology* 48 (3): 383–410.

Hann, Chris, and Hermann Goltz. 2010. *Eastern Christians in Anthropological Perspective*. Berkeley: University of California Press.

Harding, Susan Friend. 2000. *The Book of Jerry Falwell: Fundamentalist Language and Politics*. Princeton, NJ: Princeton University Press.

Hardt, Michael. 1999. "Affective Labor." *Boundary 2* 26 (2): 89–100.

Harman, Graham. 2011. *The Quadruple Object*. Winchester, UK: Zero Books.

Haynes, Naomi. 2012. "Pentecostalism and the Morality of Money: Prosperity, Inequality, and Religious Sociality on the Zambian Copperbelt." *Journal of the Royal Anthropological Institute* 18 (1): 123–39.

———. 2013. "On the Potential and Problems of Pentecostal Exchange." *American Anthropologist* 115 (1): 85–95.

———. 2015. "'Zambia Shall Be Saved!': Prosperity Gospel Politics in a Self-Proclaimed Nation." *Nova Religio* 19 (1): 5–24.

———. Forthcoming. *Moving by the Spirit: Pentecostal Social Life on the Zambian Copperbelt*. Berkeley, University of California Press.

Henare, Amiria, Martin Holbraad, and Sari Wastell, eds. 2007. *Thinking through Things: Theorising Artefacts Ethnographically*. London: Routledge.

Heywood, Paolo. 2012. "Anthropology and What There Is: Reflections on 'Ontology.'" *Cambridge Anthropology* 30 (1): 143–51.

Higgins, Thomas. 2012. "Kenn Gulliksen, John Wimber, and the Founding of the Vineyard Movement." *Pneuma* 34 (2): 208–28

Hirschkind, Charles. 2006. *The Ethical Soundscape: Cassette Sermons and Islamic Counterpublics*. New York: Columbia University Press.

Hodges, Matt. 2008. "Rethinking Time's Arrow: Bergson, Deleuze and the Anthropology of Time." *Anthropological Theory* 8 (4): 399–429.

Holbraad, Martin. 2007. "The Power of Powder: Multiplicity and Motion in the Divinatory Cosmology of Cuban Ifa (or Mana, Again)." In *Thinking through Things: Theorising Artefacts Ethnographically*, edited by Amiria Henare, Martin Holbraad, and Sari Wastell, 189–225. London: Routledge.

———. 2012. *Truth in Motion: The Recursive Anthropology of Cuban Divination*. Chicago: Chicago University Press.

Holston, James. 1999. "Alternative Modernities: Statecraft and Religious Imagination in the Valley of the Dawn." *American Ethnologist* 26 (3): 605–31.

Holvast, René. 2009. *Spiritual Mapping in the United States and Argentina, 1989–2005*. Leiden: Brill.

Howell, Brian. 2003. "Practical Belief and the Localization of Christianity: Pentecostal and Denominational Christianity in Global/Local Perspective." *Religion* 33 (3): 233–48.

Irvine, Judith T., and Susan Gal. 2000. "Language Ideology and Linguistic Differentiation." In *Regimes of Language: Ideologies, Polities, and Identities*, edited by Paul V. Kroskrity. Oxford: James Currey.
Jackson, Bill. 1999. *The Quest for the Radical Middle: A History of the Vineyard*. Cape Town: Vineyard International.
Jaspers, Karl. 1953. *The Origin and Goal of History*. New Haven, CT: Yale University Press.
Jenkins, Philip. 2002. *The Next Christendom: The Coming of Global Christianity*. Oxford: Oxford University Press.
Jenkins, Timothy. 2012. "The Anthropology of Christianity: Situation and Critique." *Ethnos* 77 (4): 459–76.
———. 2014. "'Religious Experience' and the Contribution of Theology in Tanya Luhrmann's *When God Talks Back*." *HAU* 3 (3): 369–73.
Johnson, Paul Christopher. 2011. "An Atlantic Genealogy of 'Spirit Possession.'" *Comparative Studies in Society and History* 53 (2): 393–425.
Johnson-Laird, P. N. 2002. "Peirce, Logic Diagrams, and the Elementary Operations of Reasoning." *Thinking and Reasoning* 8 (1): 69–95.
Jones, Robert P. 2016. *The End of White Christian America*. New York: Simon and Schuster.
Jorgensen, Dan. 2005. "Third Wave Evangelism and the Politics of the Global in Papua New Guinea: Spiritual Warfare and the Recreation of Place in Telefolmin." *Oceania* 75 (4): 444–61.
Justaert, Kristien. 2012. *Theology after Deleuze*. London: Continuum.
Kaell, Hillary. 2014. "Born-Again Seeking: Explaining the Gentile Majority in Messianic Judaism." *Religion* 45 (1): 42–65.
Kapferer, Bruce. 1997. *Feast of the Sorcerer: Practices of Consciousness and Power*. Chicago: Chicago University Press.
———. 2004. "Ritual Dynamics and Virtual Practice: Beyond Representation and Meaning." *Social Analysis* 48 (2): 35–54.
———. 2007. "Virtuality." In *Theorizing Rituals: Issues, Topics, Approaches, Concepts*, edited by Jens Kreinath, Jan Snoek, and Michael Stausberg, 671–84. Leiden: Brill.
———. 2013. "Montage and Time: Deleuze, Cinema, and a Buddhist Sorcery Rite." In *Transcultural Montage*, edited by Christian Suhr and Rane Willerslev, 20–39. New York: Berghahn.
Kauffman, Stuart. 1993. *The Origins of Order: Self-Organization and Selection in Evolution*. Oxford: Oxford University Press.
Keane, Webb. 1997. "Religious Language." *Annual Review of Anthropology* 26:47–71.
———. 2007. *Christian Moderns: Freedom and Fetish in the Mission Encounter*. Berkeley: University of California Press.
———. 2009. "On Multiple Ontologies and the Temporality of Things." *Material World* (blog), July 7, 2009. www.materialworldblog.com/2009/07/on-multiple-ontologies-and-the-temporality-of-things/.

———. 2013. "Ontologies, Anthropologists, and Ethical Life: Comment on G.E.R. Lloyd, *Being, Humanity, and Understanding.*" *HAU* 3 (1): 186–91.
———. 2016. *Ethical Life: Its Natural and Social Histories.* Princeton, NJ: Princeton University Press.
Keller, Catherine. 2003. *Face of the Deep: A Theology of Becoming.* London: Routledge.
Kent, John. 2002. *Wesley and Wesleyans: Religion in Eighteenth Century Britain.* New York: Cambridge University Press.
Khan, Naveeda. 2012. *Muslim Becoming: Aspiration and Skepticism in Pakistan.* Chapel Hill, NC: Duke University Press.
King, Rebekka. 2012. "The New Heretics: Popular Theology, Progressive Christianity, and Protestant Language Ideologies." PhD diss., University of Toronto.
Kohn, Eduardo. 2012. *How Forests Think: Toward an Anthropology beyond the Human.* Berkeley: University of California Press.
Kraft, Charles. 2005. *SWM/SIS at Forty: A Participant/Observer's View of Our History.* Pasadena, CA: William Carey Library.
Kroskrity, Paul V. 2000. "Regimenting Languages: Language Ideological Perspectives." In *Regimes of Language: Ideologies, Polities, and Identities*, edited by Paul V. Kroskrity, 1–34. Santa Fe, NM: School of American Research Press; Oxford: James Currey.
Lacan, Jacques. 1978. *The Four Fundamental Concepts of Psychoanalysis.* New York: W.W. Norton.
Ladd, George Eldon. 1959. *The Gospel of the Kingdom: Scriptural Studies in the Kingdom of God.* Grand Rapids, MI: Eerdmans.
———. 1974. *The Presence of the Future: The Eschatology of Biblical Realism.* Grand Rapids, MI: Eerdmans.
Laidlaw, James. 1995. *Riches and Renunciation: Religion, Economy, and Society among the Jains.* New York: Oxford University Press.
———. 2002. "For an Anthropology of Ethics and Freedom." *Journal of the Royal Anthropological Institute* 8 (2): 311–32.
———. 2014. *The Subject of Virtue: An Anthropology of Ethics and Freedom.* Cambridge: Cambridge University Press.
Laidlaw, James, and Paolo Haywood. 2013. "One More Turn and You're There." *Anthropology of This Century* 7 (May). http://aotcpress.com/articles/turn/.
Lambek, Michael. 2003a. "Introduction: Irony and Illness—Recognition and Refusal." *Social Analysis* 47 (2): 1–19.
———. 2003b. *The Weight of the Past: Living with History in Mahajanga, Madagascar.* Basingstoke: Palgrave Macmillan.
Lampe, Fritz. 2010. "The Anthropology of Christianity: Context, Contestation, Rupture and Continuity." *Reviews in Anthropology* 39 (1): 66–88.
Laplanche, Jean, and J.-B. Pontalis. 1988. *The Language of Psycho-Analysis.* London: Karnac.

Latour, Bruno. 1987. *Science in Action: How to Follow Scientists and Engineers through Society*. Cambridge, MA: Harvard University Press.
——— . 1993. *We Have Never Been Modern*. Cambridge, MA: Harvard University Press.
——— . 2010. *On the Modern Cult of the Factish Gods*. Durham, NC: Duke University Press.
Leach, Edmund. 1996. *Lévi-Strauss*. 4th ed. London: Fontana.
Lempert, Michael. 2015. "Discourse and Religion." In *The Handbook of Discourse Analysis*, edited by Deborah Tannen, Heidi E. Hamilton, and Deborah Schiffrin, 2nd ed., 902–19. Malden, MA: Wiley Blackwell.
Lester, Rebecca. 2005. *Jesus in Our Wombs: Embodying Modernity in a Mexican Convent*. Berkeley: University of California Press.
Lévi-Strauss, Claude. 1964. *Mythologies I: Le cru et le cuit*. Paris: Plon.
——— . 1970. *The Raw and the Cooked*. New York: Harper and Row.
——— . 1987. *Introduction to the work of Marcel Mauss*. London: Routledge and Kegan Paul.
Lewis, Thomas A. 2015. *Why Philosophy Matters for the Study of Religion—and Vice Versa*. New York: Oxford University Press.
Leys, Ruth. 2011. "The Turn to Affect: A Critique." *Critical Inquiry* 37 (3): 434–72.
Lindquist, Galina, and Simon Coleman. 2008. "Introduction: Against Belief?" *Social Analysis* 52 (1): 1–18.
Lofton, Kathryn. 2011. *Oprah: The Gospel of an Icon*. Berkeley: University of California Press.
Loveland, Anne, and Otis B. Wheeler. 2003. *From Meetinghouse to Megachurch: A Material and Cultural History*. Columbia: University of Missouri Press.
Luhrmann, T.M. 2004. "Metakinesis: How God Becomes Intimate in Contemporary U.S. Christianity." *American Anthropologist* 106 (3): 518–28.
——— . 2012a. "A Hyperreal God and Modern Belief: Toward an Anthropological Theory of Mind." *Current Anthropology* 53 (4): 371–95.
——— . 2012b. *When God Talks Back: Understanding the American Evangelical Relationship with God*. New York: Alfred A. Knopf.
Mahmood, Saba. 2005. *Politics of Piety: The Islamic Revival and the Feminist Subject*. Princeton, NJ: Princeton University Press.
Markus, George, and Erkan Saka. 2006. "Assemblage." *Theory, Culture, and Society* 23 (2–3): 101–6.
Marsden, George. 1987. *Reforming Fundamentalism: Fuller Seminary and the New Evangelicalism*. Grand Rapids, MI: W.B. Eerdmans.
Marshall, Ruth. 2009. *Political Spiritualities: The Pentecostal Revolution in Nigeria*. Chicago: University of Chicago Press.
——— . 2010. "The Sovereignty of Miracles: Pentecostal Political Theology in Nigeria."*Constellations* 17 (2): 197–223.
Martin, David. 2002. *Pentecostalism: The World Their Parish*. Oxford: Blackwell.
Massumi, Brian. 1992. *A User's Guide to Capitalism and Schizophrenia: Deviations from Deleuze and Guattari*. Cambridge, MA: MIT Press.

———. 2002. *Parables for the Virtual: Movement, Affect, Sensation.* Durham, NC: Duke University Press.
Masuzawa, Tomoko. 2005. *The Invention of World Religions, or, How European Universalism Was Preserved in the Language of Pluralism.* Chicago: University of Chicago Press.
Mauss, Marcel. 2016. *The Gift.* Chicago: HAU Books.
Mayblin, Maya. 2010. *Gender, Catholicism, and Morality in Brazil: Virtuous Husbands, Powerful Wives.* New York: Palgrave Macmillan.
Mazzarella, William. 2009. "Affect: What Is It Good For?" In *Enchantments of Modernity: Empire, Nation, Globalization,* edited by. Saurabh Dube, 291–309. London: Routledge.
McAlister, Elizabeth. 2012. "From Slave Revolt to a Blood Pact with Satan: The Evangelical Rewriting of Haitian History." *Studies in Religion/Sciences Religieuses* 41 (2): 187–215.
———. 2013. "Humanitarian Adhocracy, Transnational New Apostolic Missions, and Evangelical Anti-dependency in a Haitian Refugee Camp." *Nova Religio* 16 (4): 11–34.
McLoughlin, William G. 1978. *Revivals, Awakenings, and Reform: An Essay on Religion and Social Change in America, 1607–1977.* Chicago: University of Chicago Press.
McManus, Michael Orion. 2009. "Teaching Transformation: Technology, Sound, and Embodied Worship Practices in a Kingdom Fellowship." BA thesis, Reed College.
Meillassoux, Quentin. 2008. *After Finitude: An Essay on the Necessity of Contingency.* London: Continuum.
Merritt, Jonathan. 2015. "Evangelicals' Claims of Conservative Supremacy Are Overstated—and Misread: America's Religious Landscape." Religious News Service, May 13. http://jonathanmerritt.religionnews.com/2015/05/13/evangelicals-claims-of-conservative-supremacy-are-overstated-and-misread-americas-religious-landscape/#sthash.MgdehEAD.dpuf.
Meyer, Brigit. 1998. "'Make a Complete Break with the Past.' Memory and Post-colonial Modernity in Ghanaian Pentecostalist Discourse." *Journal of Religion in Africa* 28 (3): 316–49.
———. 2010. "Aesthetics of Persuasion: Global Christianity and Pentecostalism's Sensational Forms." *South Atlantic Quarterly* 109 (4): 741–63.
———. 2015. *Sensational Movies: Video, Vision, and Christianity in Ghana.* Oakland: University of California Press.
Miller, Daniel. 2005. "Routinizing Charisma: The Vineyard Christian Fellowship in the Post-Wimber Era." In *Church, Identity, and Change: Theology and Denominational Structures in Unsettled Times,* edited by David A. Roozen and James R. Nieman, 141–62. Grand Rapids, MI: Eerdmans.
Miller, Donald. 1997. *Reinventing American Protestantism: Christianity in the New Millennium.* Berkeley: University of California Press.
Miyazaki, Hirokazu. 2004. *The Method of Hope: Anthropology, Philosophy, and Fijian Knowledge.* Stanford, CA: Stanford University Press.

Mosko, Mark. 2010. "Partible Penitents: Dividual Personhood and Christian Practice in Melanesia and the West." *Journal of the Royal Anthropological Institute* 16 (2): 215–40.

Muehlebach, Andrea. 2012. *The Moral Neoliberal: Welfare and Citizenship in Italy.* Chicago: University of Chicago Press.

Murphy, Keith, and Jason Throop, eds. 2010. *Toward an Anthropology of the Will.* Stanford, CA: Stanford University Press.

Nathan, Rich, and Ken Wilson. 1995. *Empowered Evangelicals: Bringing Together the Best of the Evangelical and Charismatic Worlds.* Ann Arbor, MI: Vine Books.

Navaro-Yashin, Yael. 2012. *The Make-Believe Space: Affective Geography in a Postwar Polity.* Durham, NC: Duke University Press.

Needham, Rodney. 1972. *Belief, Language, and Experience.* Oxford: Blackwell.

Nongbri, Brent. 2013. *Before Religion: A History of a Modern Concept.* New Haven, CT: Yale University Press.

Norget, K., Valentina Napolitano, and Maya Mayblin, eds. Forthcoming. *The Anthropology of Catholicism: A Reader.* Berkeley: University of California Press.

O'Neill, Kevin Lewis. 2010. *City of God: Christian Citizenship in Postwar Guatemala.* Berkeley: University of California Press.

———. 2013. "Beyond Broken: Affective Spaces and the Study of American Religion." *Journal of the American Academy of Religion* 81 (4): 1093–116.

———. 2015. *Secure the Soul: Christian Piety and Gang Prevention in Guatemala.* Oakland: University of California Press.

O'Neill, Kevin Lewis, and Tomas Matza, eds. 2014. "Politically Unwilling." Special issue, *Public Culture* 120:1–127.

Pandian, Anand. 2012. "The Time of Anthropology: Notes from a Field of Contemporary Experience." *Cultural Anthropology* 27 (4): 547–71.

Partridge, Tristan. 2014. "Diagrams in Anthropology: Lines and Interactions." *Life Off the Grid* (blog), March 5. http://lifeoffthegrid.net/ethnograms/diagrams-in-anthropology/.

Parry, Jonathan. 1986. "The Gift, the Indian Gift and the 'Indian Gift.'" *Man* 21 (3): 453–73.

Pedersen, Morten Axel. 2007. "Multiplicity Minus Myth: Theorizing Darhad Perspectivism." *Inner Asia* 9 (2): 311–28.

———. 2011. *Not Quite Shamans: Spirit Worlds and Political Lives in Northern Mongolia.* Ithaca, NY: Cornell University Press.

Pelkmans, Mathijs. 2015. "Mediating Miracle Truth: Permanent Struggle and Fragile Conviction in Kyrgyzstan." In *The Anthropology of Global Pentecostalism and Evangelicalism,* edited by Simon Coleman and Rosalind I. J. Hackett. New York: NYU Press.

Perrin, Robin Dale. 1989. "Signs and Wonders: The Growth of the Vineyard Christian Fellowship." PhD diss., Washington State University.

Peters, John Durham. 1999. *Speaking into the Air: A History of the Idea of Communication.* Chicago: University of Chicago Press.

Pfiel, Gretchen. 2011. "Imperfect Vessels: Emotion and Rituals of Anti-ritual in American Pentecostal and Charismatic Devotional Life." In *Practicing the Faith: The Ritual Life of Pentecostal-Charismatic Christians*, edited by Martin Lindhardt, 277–305. New York: Berghahn Books.

Poloma, Margaret. 2003. *Main Street Mystics: The Toronto Blessing and Reviving Pentecostalism*. Walnut Creek, CA: AltaMira Press.

Povinelli, Elizabeth. 2012. "The Will to Be Otherwise/The Effort of Endurance." *South Atlantic Quarterly* 111 (3): 453–75.

Quine, W. V. 1948. "On What There Is." *Review of Metaphysics* 2 (5): 21–38.

Rakow, Kata. 2013. "Therapeutic Culture and Religion in America." *Religion Compass* 7 (11): 485–97.

Ramey, Joshua. 2012. *The Hermetic Deleuze: Philosophy and Spiritual Ordeal*. Durham, NC: Duke University Press.

Raschke, Carl A. 2008. *GloboChrist: The Great Commission Takes a Postmodern Turn*. Grand Rapids, MI: Baker Academic.

Rauschenbusch, Walter. 1917. *A Theology for the Social Gospel*. New York: Macmillan.

Reed, Adam. 2004. "Expanding 'Henry': Fiction Reading and Its Artifacts in a British Literary Society." *American Ethnologist* 31 (1): 111–22.

Reinhardt, Bruno. 2014. "Soaking in Tapes: The Haptic Voice of Global Pentecostal Pedagogy in Ghana." *Journal of the Royal Anthropological Institute* 20 (2): 315–36.

———. 2015. "A Christian Plane of Immanence? Contrapuntal Reflections on Deleuze and Pentecostal Spirituality." *HAU* 5 (1): 405–36.

———. 2016. "'Don't Make It a Doctrine': Material Religion, Transcendence, Critique." *Anthropological Theory* 16 (1): 75–97.

Richards, Analiese, and Daromir Rudnyckyj. 2009. "Economies of Affect." *Journal of the Royal Anthropological Institute* 15 (1): 57–77.

Robbins, Joel. 2001a. "God Is Nothing but Talk: Modernity, Language and Prayer in a Papua New Guinea Society." *American Anthropologist* 103 (4): 901–12.

———. 2001b. "Ritual Communication and Linguistic Ideology: A Reading and Partial Reformulation of Rappaport's Theory of Ritual." *Current Anthropology* 42 (5): 589–612.

———. 2001c. "Secrecy and the Sense of an Ending: Narrative, Time, and Everyday Millenarianism in Papua New Guinea and in Christian Fundamentalism." *Comparative Studies in Society and History* 43 (3): 525–51.

———. 2002. "My Wife Can't Break Off Part of Her Belief and Give It to Me: Apocalyptic Interrogations of Christian Individualism among the Urapmin of Papua New Guinea." *Paideuma* 48:189–206.

———. 2003a. "On the Paradoxes of Global Pentecostalism and the Perils of Continuity Thinking." *Religion* 33 (3): 221–31.

———. 2003b. "What Is a Christian? Notes toward an Anthropology of Christianity." *Religion* 33 (3): 191–99.

———. 2004a. *Becoming Sinners: Christianity and Moral Torment in a Papua New Guinea Society.* Berkeley: University of California Press.

———. 2004b. "The Globalization of Pentecostal and Charismatic Christianity." *Annual Review of Anthropology* 33:117–43.

———. 2007a. "Continuity Thinking and the Problem of Christian Culture: Belief, Time, and the Anthropology of Christianity." *Current Anthropology* 48 (1): 5–38.

———. 2007b. "You Can't Talk behind the Holy Spirit's Back: Christianity and Changing Language Ideologies in a Papua New Guinea Society." In *Consequences of Contact: Language Ideologies and Sociocultural Transformations in Pacific Societies,* edited by M. Makihara and B. Schieffelin, 125–30. Oxford: Oxford University Press.

———. 2009. "Is the Trans- in Transnational the Trans- in Transcendent? On Alterity and the Sacred in the Age of Globalization." In *Transnational Transcendence: Essays on Religion and Globalization,* edited by Thomas J. Csordas, 55–72. Berkeley: University of California Press.

———. 2012a. "On Enchanting Science and Disenchanting Nature: Spiritual Warfare in North America and Papua New Guinea." In *Nature, Science, and Religion: Intersections Shaping Society and the Environment,* edited by C.M. Tucker. Santa Fe, NM: School for Advanced Research Press.

———. 2012b. "Transcendence and the Anthropology of Christianity: Language, Change, and Individualism." *Suomen Antropologi* 37 (2): 5–23.

Robbins, Joel, and Matthew Engelke. 2010. Introduction to "Global Christianity, Global Critique," edited by Matthew Engelke and Joel Robbins. Special issue, *South Atlantic Quarterly* 109 (4): 623–31.

Robins, R.G. 2004. *A.J. Tomlinson: Plainfolk Modernist.* Oxford: Oxford University Press.

Rudnyckyi, Daromir. 2010. *Spiritual Economies: Islam, Globalization, and the Afterlife of Development.* Ithaca, NY: Cornell University Press.

———. 2011. "Circulating Tears and Managing hearts: Governing through Affect in an Indonesian Steel Factory." *Anthropological Theory* 11 (1): 63–87.

Ruel, Malcolm. 1997. *Belief, Ritual and the Securing of Life: Reflexive Essays on a Bantu Religion.* Leiden: Brill.

Rutherford, Danilyn. 2013. "Affect: Provocation." Cultural Anthropology, February 3. https://culanth.org/fieldsights/60-affect-provocation.

Sahlins, Marshall. 1972. *Stone Age Economics.* Chicago: Aldine-Atherton.

———. 1994. "The Sadness of Sweetness: The Native Anthropology of Western Cosmology." *Current Anthropology* 37 (3): 395–428.

Saler, Benson. 1987. "Religio and the Definition of Religion." *Cultural Anthropology* 2 (3): 395–99.

Sargeant, Kimon Howland. 2000. *Seeker Churches: Promoting Traditional Religion in a Nontraditional Way.* New Brunswick, NJ: Rutgers University Press.

Schaefer, Donovan O. 2015. *Religious Affects: Animality, Evolution, and Power.* Durham, NC: Duke University Press.

Scherz, China. 2013. "Let Us Make God Our Banker': Ethics, Temporality, and Agency in a Ugandan Charity Home." *American Ethnologist* 40 (4): 624–36.

Schilbrack, Kevin. 2014. *Philosophy and the Study of Religions: A Manifesto.* Chichester, UK: Wiley Blackwell.

Schram, Ryan. 2010. "Finding Money: Business and Charity in Auhelawa, Papua New Guinea." *Ethnos* 75 (4): 447–70.

Scott, Michael W. 2005. "'I Was Like Abraham': Notes on the Anthropology of Christianity from the Solomon Islands." *Ethnos* 70 (1): 101–25.

———. 2007. *The Severed Snake: Matrilineages, Making Place, and a Melanesian Christianity in Southeast Solomon Islands.* Durham, NC: Carolina Academic Press.

———. 2013. "The Anthropology of Ontology (Religious Science?)." *Journal of the Royal Anthropological Institute* 19 (4): 859–72.

Sherman, J. H. 2009. "No Werewolves in Theology? Transcendence, Immanence, and Becoming Divine in Gilles Deleuze." *Modern Theology* 25 (1): 1–20.

Shibley, Mark. 1996. *Resurgent Evangelicalism in the United States: Mapping Cultural Change Since 1970.* Columbia: University of South Carolina Press.

Shoaps, Robin. 2002. "Pray Earnestly': The Textual Construction of Personal Involvement in Pentecostal Prayer and Song." *Journal of Linguistic Anthropology* 12 (1): 34–71.

Shults, F. LeRon. 2014. *Iconoclastic Theology: Gilles Deleuze and the Secretion of Atheism.* Edinburgh: Edinburgh University Press.

Simon, Gregory. 2009. "The Soul Freed of Cares? Islamic Prayer, Subjectivity, and the Contradictions of Moral Selfhood in Minangkabau, Indonesia." *American Ethnologist* 36 (2): 258–75.

Simondon, Gilbert. 1992. "The Genesis of the Individual." In *Incorporations,* edited by Jonathan Crary and Sanford Kwinter, 297–319. New York: Zone Books.

Simons, Ronald. 1996. *Boo! Culture, Experience, and the Startle Reflex.* New York: Oxford University Press.

Simpson, Christopher Ben. 2012. *Deleuze and Theology.* London: New York: Bloomsbury T and T Clark.

Smith, James K.A. 2010. *Thinking in Tongues: Pentecostal Contributions to Christian Philosophy.* Grand Rapids, MI: Eerdmans.

Smith, Jonathan Z. 1998. "Religion, Religions, Religious." In *Critical Terms for Religious Studies,* edited by Mark C. Taylor, 269–84. Chicago: University of Chicago Press.

Spencer, Jonathan. 2007. *Anthropology, Politics and the State: Democracy and Violence in South Asia.* Cambridge: Cambridge University Press.

Spiro, Melford. 1966. "Religion: Problems of Definition and Explanation." In *Anthropological Approaches to the Study of Religion,* edited by Michael Banton, 85–126. London: Tavistock.

Stasch, Rupert. 2006. "Structuralism in Anthropology." In *Encyclopedia of Language and Linguistics* 2:167–70.

Stewart, Kathryn. 2007. *Ordinary Affects*. Durham, NC: Duke University Press.

Strhan, Anna. 2015. *Aliens and Strangers? The Struggle for Coherence in the Everyday Lives of Evangelicals*. Oxford: Oxford University Press.

Stromberg, Peter G. 1993. *Language and Self-Transformation: A Study of the Christian Conversion Narrative*. Cambridge: Cambridge University Press.

Sun, Anna Xiao Dong. 2013. *Confucianism as a World Religion: Contested Histories and Contemporary Realities*. Princeton, NJ: Princeton University Press.

Taves, Ann. 2009. *Religious Experience Reconsidered: A Building Block Approach to the Study of Religion and Other Special Things*. Princeton, NJ: Princeton University Press.

Taylor, Charles. 2007. *A Secular Age*. Cambridge, MA: Belknap Press of Harvard University Press.

Thornton, Brendan Jamal. 2016. *Negotiating Respect: Pentecostalism, Masculinity, and the Politics of Spiritual Authority in the Dominican Republic*. Orlando: University of Florida Press.

Tomlinson, Matt. 2009. *In God's image: The Metaculture of Fijian Christianity*. Berkeley: University of California Press.

———. 2014a. "Bringing Kierkegaard into Anthropology: Repetition, Absurdity, and Curses in Fiji." *American Ethnologist* 41 (1): 163–75.

———. 2014b. *Ritual Textuality: Pattern and Motion in Performance*. New York: Oxford University Press.

Tompkins, Silvan. 1995. *Exploring Affect: The Selected Writings of Silvan S. Tomkins*. Cambridge: Cambridge University Press.

Turner, Edith. 2003. "The Reality of Spirits." In *Shamanism: A Reader*, edited by G. Harvey, 141–52. London: Routledge.

Tweed, Thomas A. 2006. *Crossing and Dwelling: A Theory of Religion*. Cambridge, MA: Harvard University Press.

Tylor, Edward Burnett. 1874. *Primitive Culture*. Vol. 1. Boston: Estes and Lauriat.

Urban, Greg. 1989. "The 'I' of Discourse." In *Semiotics, Self, and Society*, edited by Benjamin Lee and Greg Urban, 27–51. Berlin: Mouton de Gruyter.

Vilaça, Aparecida. 2011. "Dividuality in Amazonia: God, the Devil, and the Constitution of Personhood in Wari' Christianity." *Journal of the Royal Anthropological Institute* 17 (2): 243–62.

———. 2016. *Praying and Preying: Christianity in Indigenous Amazonia*. Berkeley: University of California Press.

Viveiros de Castro, Eduardo. 2007. "The Forest of Mirrors: A Few Notes on the Ontology of Amazonian Spirits." *Inner Asia* 9 (2): 153–72.

———. 2014. *Cannibal Metaphysics: For a Post-structural Anthropology*. Minneapolis, MN: Univocal.

Wagner, Roy. 1986. *Symbols That Stand for Themselves.* Chicago: University of Chicago Press.
Wasserman, Emma. 2008. *The Death of the Soul in Romans 7: Sin, Death, and the Law in Light of Hellenistic Moral Psychology.* Tübingen: Mohr Siebeck.
Weber, Max. 1968. *Economy and Society: An Outline of Interpretive Sociology.* New York: Bedminster.
Weber, Timothy. 1979. *Living in the Shadow of the Second Coming: American Premillennialism, 1875–1925.* New York: Oxford University Press.
Webster, Joseph. 2013a. *The Anthropology of Protestantism: Faith and Crisis among Scottish Fishermen.* New York: Palgrave Macmillan.
———. 2013b. "The Immanence of Transcendence: God and the Devil on the Aberdeenshire Coast." *Ethnos* 78 (3): 380–402.
Wendall Jones, Martyn. 2016. "Inside the Popular, Controversial Bethel Church." *Christianity Today,* April 24.
Werbner, Richard. 2011. *Holy Hustler, Schism, and Prophecy: Apostolic Reformation in Botswana.* Berkeley: University of California Press.
West, Harry G. 2007. *Ethnographic Sorcery.* Chicago: University of Chicago Press.
Whitehouse, Harvey. 1995. *Inside the Cult: Religious Innovation and Transmission in Papua New Guinea.* Oxford: Oxford University Press.
———. 2004. *Modes of Religiosity: A Cognitive Theory of Religious Transmission.* Walnut Creek, CA: AltaMira Press.
Wiegele, Katharine. 2005. *Investing in Miracles: El Shaddai and the Transformation of Popular Catholicism in the Philippines.* Honolulu: University of Hawaii Press.
Willard, Dallas. 1998. *The Divine Conspiracy: Rediscovering Our Hidden Life in God.* San Francisco: HarperSanFrancisco.
Willerslev, Rane. 2007. *Soul Hunters: Hunting, Animism and Personhood among the Siberian Yukaghirs.* Berkeley: University of California Press.
———. 2011. "Frazer Strikes Back from the Armchair: A New Search for the Animist Soul." *Journal of the Royal Anthropolotical Institute* 17 (3): 504–26.
Williams, James. 2011. *Gilles Deleuze's Philosophy of Time: A Critical Introduction and Guide.* Edinburgh: Edinburgh University Press.
Wimber, John, and Kevin Springer. 1986. *Power Evangelism.* San Francisco: Harper and Row.
Woolard, Kathryn. 1985. "Language Variation and Cultural Hegemony: Toward an Integration of Sociolinguistic and Social Theory." *American Ethnologist* 12 (4): 738–48.
Woolard, Kathryn, and Bambi Schieffelin. 1994. "Language Ideology." *Annual Review of Anthropology* 23:55–82.
Zdebik, Jakub. 2012. *Deleuze and the Diagram: Aesthetic Threads in Visual Organization.* London: Continuum.
Zigon, Jarrett. 2010a. *"HIV Is God's Blessing": Rehabilitating Morality in Neoliberal Russia.* Berkeley: University of California Press.

———. 2010b. "Moral and Ethical Assemblages: A Response to Fassin and Stoczkowski." *Anthropological Theory* 10 (1–2): 3–15.

———. 2015. "What Is a Situation? An Assemblic Ethnography of the Drug War." *Cultural Anthropology* 30 (3): 501–24.

Zourabichvili, François. 2012. *Deleuze, a Philosophy of the Event: Together with the Vocabulary of Deleuze*. Edinburgh: Edinburgh University Press.

Index

Affect, xvii, 36, 67–68, 73, 80, 84, 91, 101, 119, 120, 122, 123, 134, 140, 156, 160, 162, 164–165, 171, 186, 188, 194, 198, 199, 204, 210, 224–225; anthropological discussions of, 221–222; prophecy and affect, 162; surprise as affect 71, 85–97; worship and, 28, 31–32. *See also* intensity; surprise; tears

Agamben, Giorgio, 46

Already/not-yet, 7, 37–38, 71; initial evidence doctrine and, 43; Ladd, George Eldon formulation of, 41–42; messianic time and, 46; other temporalities and, 45–47; politics and, 80, 193; World War 2 metaphor and, 44–45. *See also* kingdom theology; temporality

Anthropology, xviii, xvii, xvii, 9, 19, 20, 50, 79, 144, 191, 192, 206; and Gilles Deleuze, 222–223; of affect, 221–222; of ethics, 63, 83, 126, 215, 220, 221, 234; of ontology, 222; of religion, 6; of will, 222; speculative anthropology, 201, 233. *See also* anthropology of Christianity

Anthropology of Christianity, xvii, 102, 190, 219–220, 226; subjectivity and, 220; temporality and, 219–220

Autopoiesis, 18–19, 208, 212–213, 234

Axial age, 215

Badiou, Alain, 229

Barber, David Colucciello, 229

Belief xviii, 148, 204; miracles and 169–171, 229

Benjamin, Walter, 87

Bethel Church, 175, 179

Bible and Bible reading: as speech act, 87; as collective guide to conduct, 89; as personally directed communication, 87–91; diagrammatic nature of, 188–190; fiduciary duty and, 187; general legislation and, 187; presence and, 90; schedules, 86; translations, 86–87. *See also* literalism; textual/juridical diagram

Bureaucracy (Weberian), 204

Centripetal and centrifugal forces 56, 61–62, 67–68, 160, 227. *See also* lines of flight; territorialization

Charisma (Weberian), 204

Charismatic diagram. *See* Pentecostal/Charismatic diagram

Charismatic Christianity, 12–16, 20–21

Christianity: "actually existing" Christianity, 8–9; as an invention, 212–213; fiduciary relationship of churches and, 57–58; 'global' Christianity, 12; problems and, 9–11; promise of transformation and modernity in, 18; underlying sets of

Christianity: *(continued)* regularities within, 19; will as problem within 71–73. See also anthropology of Christianity; charismatic Christianity; churches; denominations; emergent church; fundamentalism; mainline Protestantism; Messianic Judaism; New Apostolic Reformation; Pentecostalism; Vineyard

Churches: co-constituting relations with constituent members, 63; house churches, 168–169; services 54–56; stewardship of tithing, 185; variation of individuals within 26–28, 63–64. See also pastors; Vineyard

Church growth movement, 3, 16, 27, 52, 59

Code switching, 155, 157. See also language ideology

Coleman, Simon, 21, 167, 232

Commodity form, 27–28, 53, 56, 59, 177–178

Corporations, 57

Cullmann, Oscar, 44–45

Degrees of freedom, 21, 62, 187, 202, 212–213

Deleuze, Gilles xviii, 20, 69, 163–164, 199, 222–224, 224–225, 228–229, 232, 234, 235; and anthropology, 222–223; Guattari, Felix and, 223, 229, 232, 235; religious and theological studies and, 228–229

Deliverance. See demonization

Demonization: as rite of passage in Vineyard, 153; causes of, 155, 156–158; charismatic activity as necessary prerequisite for attack, 158, 163; deliverance from as different from exorcism, 151; deliverance from as part of continuum with other forms of prayer, 157; difference between deliverance from and possession, 151; discerning, 2–3, 157–158; disruptive nature to church services, 55, 153; firsthand account of deliverance from, 149–151; free will and, 152, 155–156; frequency of, 152–153, 154; gender and deliverance, 153, 154, 232; indicators of 152, 157; intensification of beliefs in, 177; misfortune as indicator of attack by, 154–155; parallel explanations for demonic phenomena, 155, 158–159; prophylactic measures against, 157–158; psychiatric treatment and, 158; trauma and, 157–158. See also healing

Denominations, 14, 17, 24, 43–44, 48, 50–51, 63, 65, 77, 159, 168, 220–221

Diagram: as partial solution to problem, 70; assemblages and, 79–81; catalyzing other actualizations; 159–160, 163, changes of constituting forces within, 75; collapse of, 167–171; Deleuze, Gilles as originator of concept, 20, 69; difference from other similar concepts, 69; different historical examples of, 70, 228; ethics and, 79–81; healing and, 145–146; imbrication of diagram with other diagrams, 81, 160; independence from materials expressed through, 69; indifference to boundaries, 135–136, 146, 159; iterability of, 70; Kantian schemas and, 228; mutation to different diagrams, 76; panopticon as example of, 70; plasticity within, 73; play of relative constituting forces, 68–70; political expressions of, 80–81; recounting diagrammatic events as another instance of the diagram, 133–134; sense of temporal sequence within, 74; simultaneity of expression of forces within, 74; thresholds and, 120; virtual aspects of and, 74–75; zones of indistinction, 159, 160, 232. See also Deleuze, Gilles; "Diagram r"; Pentecostal/ Charismatic diagram; possibility space; problem; textual/juridical diagram; virtual

"Diagram 1", 203
Discernment, 2–3, 99–100, 112–113, 157–158
Dispensationalism, 39–40
Douglas, Mary, 235
Duns Scotus, John, 224

Emergent Church, 106–107, 110, 168, 232
Engelke, Matthew, 57, 227
Eschatology. *See* already/not-yet; dispensationalism
Ethics and ethical formation: anthropology of, 234; as expression of Pentecostal/Charismatic diagram, 80, 164; composite ethical subjects, 80; difficulty of ethical Christian behavior, 184; fiduciary duty as 58, 187; individual's relationship with churches and, 62–63; modeling life on Jesus as, 96; moral code, 45, 187–188; personal fulfillment and, 33; spiritual formation as, 84; tithing as ethical practice, 185–186. *See also* Foucault, Michel
Experiential religion, 6

Fiduciary duty: churches and, 57–58; ethics as, 58, 187; mediators and, 187; tithing and, 184–185. *See also* commodity form; corporation; ethics and ethical formation; textual/juridical diagram
Fonts, 52–53, 226–227
Foucault, Michel, 70, 83, 187, 222. *See also* ethics and ethical formation
Freud, Sigmund, 36, 122, 228, 231
Fuller School of World Missions, xvi, 102; importation of Global South Pentecostal spirituality by 15–16. *See also* church growth movement; Wagner, C. Peter; Wimber, John
Fuller Theological Seminary, xvi, 3, 39. *See also* Fuller School of World Missions
Fundamentalism, 39–40, 42, 86, 180. *See also* literalism

Geertz, Clifford, 71, 229
Gender: attitude in Vineyard towards homosexuality, 193, 194; deliverance and, 153, 154, 232; leaving churches and, 172; membership in Vineyard and, 230; pastors, and 24; prophecy as form of abuse, 130–131
Giftings: charismatic Christianity and, 15; early Church and, 12–14; distribution of relative strength of gifts, 131, 142, 175; pedagogy and, 102–103; Pentecostalism and, 14; "prophetic scripture" as, 88; skills and personality traits seen as, 26, 118. *See also* demonization; glossolalia; healing; miracles; prophecy and prophesying
Gifts as exchange: 181–183, 185, 189
Glossolalia, 104, 136–140, 147; absence of knowledge about among Vineyard believers, 136–137; as acquired ability, 137–138; as gift from God, 139; exterior nature of, 139–140, 144; initial evidence doctrine and, 13–14, 136; intended overhearers and, 139; interpretation of, 139; lack of semantic content, 139–140; trance state and, 137; xenoglossy as, 14, 138–139.
Grid/Group theory, 235

Hallward, Peter, 229
Handman, Courtney, 220–221
Harding, Susan, 40
Healing: as form of deliverance from demons, 144; conventional medicine influenced by God, 141; differing frameworks for, 145; firsthand description of, 142–143, 181–182; improvisatory nature of, 145; language use during, 141–144, 145; physical proximity to person receiving, 141–142; raising the dead and, 140–141; subject verbally addressed during healing sessions, 143–144; Vineyard narratives about, 140–141
Heaven, 33

Holy Spirit: distribution of gifts, 26–27; "First Fruits" of Kingdom theology, 42; lack of control over, 37; unfixed nature of, 5. *See also* gifting; glossolalia; healing; miracles; prophecy and prophesying; worship

Immanence, 6, 7, 10, 20, 62, 65–66, 169, 188, 190, 203, 204, 207–208, 210, 214, 215, 229, 233
Intensities, 12, 13, 49, 66–69, 73, 79, 81–82, 97, 119, 120, 134, 140, 146, 160, 167, 199, 201, 204, 222; definition of 224–225

Johnson, Bill, 175
Jonah, 74

Keane, Webb, 140, 205–206, 234
Kingdom Theology, 38; church structure and, 44; Cullman, Oscar and, 44–45; Ladd, George Eldon and, 40–43; mainline Protestantism and, 38; Wimber, John and, 43. *See also* already/not-yet; Ladd, George Eldon; Wimber, John

Ladd, George Eldon, 39–44
Language Ideology, 123; ambivalence in, 140; chiasmus in, 126; ex-centric elements of, 162; materiality and, 205; problem of presence and, 205; prophetic speech and, 125–134; religious reform and, 140; Vineyard view of Pentecostal language ideology, 124. *See also* glossolalia; materiality; sincerity
Leach, Edmund, 236
Lévi-Strauss, Claude, 236
Line of Flight, 164
Literalism, 40, 180
Losing faith, 171–173
Luhrmann, Tanya, 219, 220, 230, 232

Mainline Protestantism, 38, 40, 42, 180
Materiality, 205–206, 208–209
McGavran, Donald, 27, 52

Messianic Judaism, 106–107, 109
Methodological atheism, 76–78, 214, 229
Miller, Donald, 219
Miracles: as contagion, 161; as events, 67; as evangelical sign, 54, 161–162; certitude regarding, 169–171; coincidence and, 108; dental fillings transmuted into gold as, 177; "drunk in the spirit" as, 173, 175; exchange-gift as miracle, 189; "glory feathers" and "glory dust" as, 175, 177; grave soaking, 175; holy laughter, 173, 175; inability to look behind, 78–79; kinship with New Testament Miracles, 34; political expression viewed as, 193, 196; production of new forms of, 189; prophetic message as, 91–101; slain in the spirit, 34, 168. *See also* demonization; gifting; glossolalia; healing; prophecy; surprise
Modes of religion, 5, 6, 12, 13, 14–15, 18–19, 20, 65, 154, 202–205, 2–8–213; Spinoza, Baruch and, 224. *See also* Pentecostal/Charismatic diagram; problem of presence; religion; textual/juridical diagram
Money: exchange, gifting of, 181–183; thrift concerning, 184–185. *See also* fiduciary duty; materiality; tithing
Moral Code, 187–188. *See also* ethics and ethical formation; Foucault, Michel; textual/juridical diagram

Neoliberalism, 49–50
New Apostolic Reformation, 174–175, 177–178. *See also* Wagner, C. Peter
Nominalism, xvii; in academic definitions of Christianity, 7–9; in academic definitions of religion, 202

O'Neill, Kevin, 232

Part Culture, 21, 167, 232
Pastors: abuse of prophecy and, 130–131; concerns about quality of Church presentation and, 53–59;

frequency of deliverances performed by, 152–153; house church and, 168–169; income of, 24; lack of institutional Vineyard support, 51–52; self-authorization of in classical Pentecostalism, 14; speech patterns during sermons, 124; tithing and, 25

Paul, St., 13, 37, 46, 72–73, 74

Peirce, Charles Sanders, 69

Pentecostal/Charismatic diagram, 20–21, 71–72, 74, 76, 78–79, 81, 82, 83, 96, 101, 110, 119—120, 136, 146, 159–160, 163–164, 166–167, 170, 179, 188, 189, 191, 193, 196, 199–200, 201, 232; competing truth procedures within 78–79. *See also* diagram; textual-juridical diagram

Pentecostalism, 13–15: certitude regarding miracles, 170; demons in, 151–152; initial evidence doctrine, 13–14, 43, 136; race and class in evangelical perception of, 15; surprise as part of Pentecostal worship, 96; tensions with evangelicalism, 15, 42

Petitionary prayer, 74–75, 83–85; dry seasons in, 85; healing and, 141; sincerity and authenticity in, 124. *See also* healing; language ideology; sincerity

Plasticity, 3–7, 47, 73, 206, 208, 209, 221

Politics, 190; anthropological study of theological conservative politics, 190–191; attitudes towards homosexuality and, 193, 194; conservative Vineyard politics, 192, 196; generation differences in attitude towards, 192; politics as expression of Pentecostal/Charismatic diagram, 193, 196; progressive Vineyard politics, 107, 108, 193–196; variation in Vineyard political positions, xv, 191–192

Possibility space, 10, 61–62, 67, 187, 209–213, 215. *See also* diagram; virtual

Potential. *See* virtual

Power evangelism, 180. *See also* miracles

Problem of presence, 6, 11, 71, 202–204; as plenitude 214–215. *See also* language ideology; Pentecostal/Charismatic diagram, religion

Problems, 70; genetic role in Christianity, 9–11; as obscured by solutions, 11; interlocking structure of problems, 207–208. *See also* diagram, problem of presence, virtual

Prophecy and prophesying: abuse of prophecy, 130–131; as production of truth, 161; Bible text as personally directed prophecy, 87–91; debates about, 107–110; disruptive nature to church services, 54–55; exteriority and, 95; failure of, 162–163; first hand description of, 113–117, 148–151; inability to personally receive, 108–110; inviting someone to receive, 128–130; language ideology and, 125–134; life events as evidence of prophecy, 117; limitations on prophecy, 112, 122, 148; pedagogy, 113–117; presented as intuition, 169; prophecy as communication with the divine, 91–101; prophesying concerning birth or marriage, 112; protocol for delivering prophecy to a large audience, 130–131; recounting prophecy as another moment of that prophetic event, 133–134; reluctance to share prophecy, 128–129, 134; testing prophecy, 163; typification of, 100, 120; visions of written words on face as means of conveying prophetic knowledge, 1–3

Prophets, 131, 146–147, 174, 177, 178

Proposition 8 (California), 193

Protestant language ideology. *See* language ideology

Raising the dead, 141–142, 166

Ramey, Joshua, 229

Rauschenbusch, Walter, 38

Redding, California, 175
Reed, Adam, 221, 230
Reinhardt, Bruno, 233
Religion: as alloplastic strata, 235; as engine of controlling change, 214, 215–217; as evangelical category, 25; axial age religion, 215; cognitive science accounts of, 224, 236; critique of the category of, 19–20, 200–202; Geertz, Clifford and, 71, 229; historicist definitions of, 202; materiality and, 205–209; porous borders of category of, 202; relation to art, 208–209; relation to nationalism, 209; Tylor, Edward definition of, 204
Religious language ideology. *See* language ideology
Richard Nixon Presidential Library, 147

Secularism, 169
Simondon, Gilbert, 216
Sincerity, 109–110, 123–124, 126, 166; in glossolalia, 138. *See also* language ideology
Slain in the spirit, 34, 168
Smith, James K.A., 96
Spinoza, Baruch, 224
Spiritual Mapping, 174–175
Spiritual Warfare, 135, 148, 174. *See also* demonization
Stewardship, 62. *See also* fiduciary duty; textual juridical diagram
Stout, Phil, 50
Strhan, Anna, 221
Sugarland, Texas, 50
Surprise, 37, 58, 61, 71, 95–97, 100–101, 119–121, 122, 123, 145–146, 159, 160, 163, 168, 177–179, 188–189, 195, 196, 199–200, 211, 234,

Tears, 2, 30–31, 84–85, 109, 114, 119, 140, 163, 194
Temporality: Christian literature and, 178; commodity-logic and, 27; diagrammatic thinking and, 74–75; disjunctive synthesis of, 46–47; events and, 68; healing and, 145–146; instantaneous change and, 34; jokes about temporality and promptness, 22–23; non-linear conceptions, 67; physiological reactions and, 35; rupture and, 219–220; simultaneity and, 74; volunteerism and, 25–27; worship and 32–37, 45–47. *See also* already/not-yet
Territorialization, 81
Textual/juridical diagram, 187–190, 191, 200
Tithing, 184–185; as ethical practice, 185–186
Tongues. *See* glossolalia
Topography, 66, 70, 187, 188, 189
Topology, 66–67, 70, 81, 187, 188, 189, 202, 234, 235
Toronto blessing, 173–174, 176–177
Transcendence, 5–6, 58, 187, 190, 211–212, 214, 233
Transduction, 216
Tweed, Thomas, 234
Tylor, Edward, 2041
Typification, 100, 120–122. *See also* language ideology; Pentecostal/charismatic diagram; prophecy

Vineyard: as instance of Pentecostal and charismatic Christianity xv–xvii, 15–16, 25; conferences, 48; consistency as a value in, 56; decentralization of, 51; denominationalism and, 51; egalitarianism in, 25–26, 61; fonts, 52, 236–227; founding, xvi, 3, 16; governance, 50–52, 227; graphic design, 52–53; international affiliate Vineyards, 227; national headquarters, 50; neo-liberalism and, 49–50; novelty and, 5; jokes about "Vineyard time", 23–24; regional variation, 65; sense of belonging to, 24, 48; social justice and, 107, 108, 178–179; social science accounts of, 219; tensions within, 16; transfer growth movement, 180; variation in size, xv; variation in politics, xv ,191–192; variation in demographics, xv; variation within and between Vineyards, 61; Vineyard USA, 50; volunteerism in, 23–25, 56. *See also* charismatic Christianity; churches; miracles; pastors; Stout, Phil; Waggoner, Bert; Wimber, John

Virtual, 74–76; broken symmetry and, 189. 191, 228; definition of, 223–224; occlusion of by the actual 75, 77

Visions. *See* prophecy

Waggoner, Bert, 50
Wagner, C. Peter, 39, 52, 173, 174, 178
Waria Valley, 220
Welcome ministry/team, 22–23
Whitehouse, Harvey, 224
Will, willfulness and unwilling: Pauline heritage of concepts, 71–73
Willard, Dallas, 126, 129
Willerslev, Rane, 233
Wimber, John: anticipating personally raising the dead, 141; archive, xvi; church growth consultant, 16; critique of church growth movement, 59; denominationalism and, 51; "doing the stuff", 113; explanation of causes for demonic attack, 155; founding role in development of the Vineyard, xvi; healing and, 140; pedagogy of miracles and, 102; reputation, 3; spiritual warfare and, 174; seeing words on faces as prophecy 1–2; Toronto blessing and, 174; Yorba Linda church and, 139

Worship: adoption of vineyard worship by other churches, 180; affect, 31–32, 36–37; as expression of Pentecostal/charismatic diagram, 81–82; musical structure of, 19–30; narratives about, 34–35; participation in, 30; physiological response to, 35; setting up for, 29; shifts in subjectivity during, 32; small groups and, 104, 147; worship teams and professional musician, 225–226

Yorba Linda, 139

THE ANTHROPOLOGY OF CHRISTIANITY

Edited by Joel Robbins

1. *Christian Moderns: Freedom and Fetish in the Mission Encounter,* by Webb Keane
2. *A Problem of Presence: Beyond Scripture in an African Church,* by Matthew Engelke
3. *Reason to Believe: Cultural Agency in Latin American Evangelicalism,* by David Smilde
4. *Chanting Down the New Jerusalem: Calypso, Christianity, and Capitalism in the Caribbean,* by Francio Guadeloupe
5. *In God's Image: The Metaculture of Fijian Christianity,* by Matt Tomlinson
6. *Converting Words: Maya in the Age of the Cross,* by William F. Hanks
7. *City of God: Christian Citizenship in Postwar Guatemala,* by Kevin O'Neill
8. *Death in a Church of Life: Moral Passion during Botswana's Time of AIDS,* by Frederick Klaits
9. *Eastern Christians in Anthropological Perspective,* edited by Chris Hann and Hermann Goltz
10. *Studying Global Pentecostalism: Theories and Methods,* by Allan Anderson, Michael Bergunder, Andre Droogers, and Cornelis van der Laan
11. *Holy Hustlers, Schism, and Prophecy: Apostolic Reformation in Botswana,* by Richard Werbner
12. *Moral Ambition: Mobilization and Social Outreach in Evangelical Megachurches,* by Omri Elisha
13. *Spirits of Protestantism: Medicine, Healing, and Liberal Christianity,* by Pamela E. Klassen
14. *The Saint in the Banyan Tree: Christianity and Caste Society in India,* by David Mosse
15. *God's Agents: Biblical Publicity in Contemporary England,* by Matthew Engelke
16. *Critical Christianity: Translation and Denominational Conflict in Papua New Guinea,* by Courtney Handman
17. *Sensational Movies: Video, Vision, and Christianity in Ghana,* by Birgit Meyer

18. *Christianity, Islam, and* Orisa *Religion: Three Traditions in Comparison and Interaction,* by J. D. Y. Peel

19. *Praying and Preying: Christianity in Indigenous Amazonia,* by Aparecida Vilaça

20. *To Be Cared For: The Power of Conversion and Foreignness of Belonging in an Indian Slum,* by Nathaniel Roberts

21. *A Diagram for Fire: Miracles and Variation in an American Charismatic Movement,* by Jon Bialecki

22. *Moving by the Spirit: Pentecostal Social Life on the Zambian Copperbelt,* by Naomi Haynes

www.ingramcontent.com/pod-product-compliance
Lightning Source LLC
Chambersburg PA
CBHW030530230426
43665CB00010B/834